Drs. Stevic-Rust and Maximin have done a great service in writing this book as it fills an enormous need for non-psychiatric mental health professionals. It will also be very useful for primary care physicians. At the beginning of this new millennium it is sad to say that many psychiatrists, perhaps under economic pressures, see patients with only minimal focus on medical issues. Hopefully this book will help correct this inattention.

—Richard C. Preisman, M.D., Chairman, Department of Psychiatry, Franciscan Skemp Healthcare, Mayo Health System

This book provides a comprehensive scholarly treatment of depression in the medically ill in a clear, straightforward style. The authors have integrated a huge and diverse literature into a very readable book. They raise important questions that stimulate thought and active differential diagnosis and treatment planning. This book should be required reading and a well-used reference manual for anyone attempting to treat depression. Although this book is written for professionals, many patients are highly motivated and informed, and are actively involved in their medical care. They too will appreciate the authors' sensitivity and clarity. With this empowering book, no longer will it be accepted that illness and depression inevitably go hand in hand.

—Anne Eshelman, Ph.D., ABPP, Senior Staff Psychologist, Henry Ford Hospital, Detroit

Depression and medical illnesses are prevalent and potentially devastating conditions with ramifications that extend to all aspects of one's life. This text provides a highly readable summary of research findings as well as clinical recommendations for the diagnosis and treatment of depression specifically in the medical population. This excellent resource belongs in the library of anyone involved with the fields of medicine, psychology, and psychiatry.

—Lori W. Kenyon, Ph.D., psychologist and co-author of *Heart Therapy: Regaining Your Cardiac Health*

Treating Depression in the Medically Ill

A Clinician's Guide

Lori Stevic-Rust, Ph.D.
Anita Maximin, Psy.D.
contributions by Michael B. Ganz, M.D.

New Harbinger Publications, Inc.

Publisher's Note

This publication is designed to provide accurate and authoritative information in regard to the subject matter covered. It is sold with the understanding that the publisher is not engaged in rendering psychological, financial, legal, or other professional services. If expert assistance or counseling is needed, the services of a competent professional should be sought.

Distributed in the U.S.A. by Publishers Group West; in Canada by Raincoast Books; in Great Britain by Airlift Book Company, Ltd.; in South Africa by Real Books, Ltd.; in Australia by Boobook; and in New Zealand by Tandem Press.

New Harbinger Publications, Inc.
5674 Shattuck Avenue
Oakland, CA 94609

Cover design by Poulson/Gluck Design
Edited by Andrew Liotta
Text design by Michele Waters

Library of Congress Catalog Card Number: 99-74380
ISBN 1-57244-177-2 Paperback

Printed in the United States of America

New Harbinger Publications' Web site address: www.newharbinger.com

02 01 00

10 9 8 7 6 5 4 3 2 1

First printing

This book is dedicated to a group of professionals who first taught me about treating patients, by challenging me to think critically and inspiring me through their genuine commitment to caring for patients. Specifically, Dr. Anne Eshelman for serving a s a mentor in every sense of the word and Dr. Mark Ketterer for graciously offering his knowledge and expertise. I would also like to acknowledge Dr. Antoun Manganas who had the ability to impart medical knowledge with a warmth and sense of humor that made learning fun. Finally, with deepest respect and admiration, I would like to recognize Dr. Richard Preisman. His integrity, expertise, and dedication to patients continues to inspire me a decade later.

Lori Stevic-Rust, Ph.D.

I would like to dedicate this book to all of the patients who have suffered with chronic medical illnesses and were willing to share their struggles. May you continue to be strong in spirit.

Anita Maximin, Psy.D.

Contents

Acknowledgment

The writing of a book requires the time and talent of many. We would like to recognize many people for their contributions to this project. A treatment manual such as this would not be possible without the significant contributions of researchers who have devoted their careers to studying depression and medical illness.

We would like to thank Christine Mitchell for assistance in finding resources and materials. Her skill, expertise, and ability to tolerate last minute requests made our lives much easier.

Thanks again to the wonderful staff at New Harbinger. This is our third book with them and we continue to be impressed by their professional and courteous work ethic. Thanks to Kristin Beck for her continued support both personally and professionally. Thanks to Amy Shoup and Lauren Dockett for their warm support with all aspects of the project. We would like to extend a special thanks to Andrew Liotta for his meticulous and skilled editing of this project.

Special thanks to our families—Jay, Sarah, and Katelyn Rust; and Rudi, Vijay, and Ravi Kobetic—for their patience and understanding with deadlines and the juggling of other responsibilities.

Introduction

Day was departing, and the darkening air
Called all Earth's creatures to their evening quiet
While I alone was preparing as though for war
To struggle with my journey . . .

—*Dante's Inferno* (Canto II, 1-4)

"What do you do when your worst fears come true?" This was a question posed by a medical patient who was told he had end-stage renal disease and would need dialysis to stay alive. This poignant question calls to mind how often we hear people say that if they had to live on a machine, or were unable to walk, or could no longer eat or engage in activities that they enjoyed, they would rather be dead. This sentiment is usually expressed by individuals when they are healthy. When people are *actually* confronted with the choice between death and living with these kinds of restrictions, their feelings are often quite a bit more complicated.

When physically healthy people become ill, a transition must occur. This transition often involves rethinking their self-image, altering their current lifestyle, mourning losses that may follow from the illness, and confronting their own mortality. During this period of time the patient may begin to feel anxious, demoralized, scared, and depressed; thoughts may become pessimistic and at times suicidal. The challenge for clinicians is to identify unhealthy transitioning that could potentially result in major depression. Untreated depression complicates medical conditions, treatment, and increases mortality. As you will see throughout this book the importance of recognizing and treating depression can not be overstated.

Our goal in writing this book is to provide a manual for the recognition and treatment of depression among the medically ill. The impetus for writing it came from our experience as health psychologists working and providing training in the medical setting. We have continued to be impressed by the lack of an integrated and comprehensive approach in the recognition and treatment of depression in this population, despite the fact that the prevalence rate for depression in the medically ill inpatients is approximately 25 to 33 percent and closer to 50 percent for those between 60 and 70 years of age (Kathol et al. 1990). Evaluation of depression constitutes the single greatest referral question posed to mental health clinicians who work in the medical arena. Most textbooks that address treatment of depression as a comorbid condition among the medically ill typically dedicate a small percentage of the discussion to psychological treatment strategies, and even then these techniques are often presented in a cursory way.

After a discussion of the link between depression and illness, part II will address the differential diagnosis of depression. In these chapters, we will provide a framework for taking the symptom of depression among medically ill patients and examining the different mental disorders that can share similar clinical presentations. These diagnostic categories will reflect the changes that are found in the DSM-IV, particularly with regard to the elimination of the Organic Mental Disorder section and the addition of the new category entitled Mood Disorders Due to a General Medical Condition. We will also cover metabolic disorders and how to identify them by examination of lab values and clinical presentations. We will then describe the following disorders as they relate to depression: grief, adjustment reaction with depressed mood, apathetic delirium, personality styles that can imitate depression (such as schizoid or avoidant), medication- and substance-induced depression.

Part III will focus on the treatment of depression in the medically ill. "The Patient's Introduction to Therapy" will offer strategies to engage the patient in treatment as well as educating the patient as to the complexity of the interaction between depression and the medical illness. The physical symptoms of depression such as sleep and appetite problems, fatigue, and low sex drive are often the most problematic for patients. We offer strategies to manage these symptoms, which often overlap with symptoms of many medical illnesses. We present techniques for improving coping skills, including problem-solving skills, communication skills, and coping with loss. Helping the patient address issues of the meaning of the illness and spirituality as means of coping is also discussed. Since social support has been shown to improve symptoms of depression and buffer the impact of medical illness, a chapter on social support including family adjustment is included. We then discuss suicide and ambivalence, and what can be done to lower the risks of a patient harming him- or herself. The adjunct use of medications for depression and when it is appropriate to use them is addressed in the pharmacology chapter. Finally, a chapter on the consultation process integrates all of the information presented in the book by describing a step-by-step format for consulting in a hospital setting as well as in an outpatient setting. A case example is provided as a sample of an evaluation and treatment of depression in a medically ill patient.

We hope this book serves a useful guide for clinicians working with medically ill patients, whether you are a mental health professional, physician, or other health care professional working with the medically ill. By adequately recognizing and treating depression in the medically ill, the patient's adherence to medical regimens, recovery from illness, and the overall quality of life and function will be improved.

Part I

Overview of Depression in the Medically Ill

Chapter 1

Depression and Medical Illness

The term "depression" has become an everyday word to describe a state of feeling "blue." People often use this word to describe a negative feeling about events ranging from a relationship breakup to their favorite team losing an important game. A person can feel depressed when grieving a significant loss, but this is different from clinical depression. Depression, as part of the grief process, tends to diminish over time and does not significantly impair daily functioning for a substantial period of time. In clinical depression, the negative feelings become so overwhelming that daily functioning is impaired. Signs of clinical depression can include sleep and appetite disturbances, fatigue, an inability to concentrate, memory problems, a decreased sex drive, excessive feelings of guilt, helplessness, and hopelessness, and sometimes thoughts of suicide. Though the results can be devastating, depression is a highly treatable disorder when it is accurately detected and treated. It becomes even more important to treat depression when a person is medically ill, because when depression is left untreated, it can complicate a patient's medical condition and interfere with medical treatments, which ultimately increases the likelihood of mortality.

A primary challenge that clinicians face when assessing, treating, or consulting about depression is that everyone has his or her own beliefs, expectations, and preconceived notions about the disorder. In part, this stems from the fact that the word is used so commonly, both in everyday language and in the clinical arena. People don't ask for clarification when they hear the term "depression" the way they would if you were discussing schizophrenia or hypothyroidism.

As a result, depression can be a fuzzy concept with connotations and consequences that can vary from person to person. For some the word "depression" implies a weak moral character, the cure being that the depressed person must "simply get it together." Consequently, patients may feel uncomfortable discussing their feelings for fear that they will be viewed as weak or that the condition is not worth bothering the physician about, since it is not something that can be medically treated (Katon 1987). This situation is further exacerbated by the fact that physicians and other health care providers often see depression as an expected and understandable psychological reaction to a medical illness or to a stressful life event. They therefore inadequately treat the symptoms of a serious depression, which, in turn, can complicate a medical condition (Popkin 1988).

Theories of Depression

Before one can discuss the diagnosis and treatment of a disorder, attention must be given to the theories of what causes and exacerbates it. There are many different theories and explanations for what causes depression. Depression among the medically ill is even more complex when we factor in the medical condition as a cause and contributing factor. The following section briefly summarizes three primary theories of depression. Realize that the causes, risk factors, and contributing factors can vary from person to person and depressive episode to depressive episode. Therefore, understanding and incorporating each of the theories is important if a comprehensive treatment is to occur.

Biological Theories

Nerve cells or neurons communicate to one another through chemicals, called *neurotransmitters*. The place at which the neurotransmitters are released is called the *synapse*. The synapse is a small space that exists between two nerve cells, which are very close but do not touch. At the synapse, a transmitting neuron, known as the *presynaptic* neuron, emits a small amount of the neurotransmitter to the *postsynaptic* or receiving neuron. A typical neuron receives thousands of messages from other neurons, each at a different synapse; some of these messages are inhibiting while others are stimulating. When the balance of stimulating messages that one neuron receives passes a threshold, the neuron "fires": this in turn stimulates the neurons to which it will transmit its message.

The messages that are exchanged between the neurons constitutes the information processing of the brain. The information consists of everything that we feel and understand: it is our memories, a sense of our bodies, our impulses, our thoughts, and our moods; in essence, our humanness (Heston 1992).

Neurotransmitters can be influenced by drugs in several different ways. First, many neurotransmitters are stored in the *synaptic vesicles* located within a nerve cell near the synapse. Some drugs shortcut the normal communication process by releasing neurotransmitters from the vesicles and thereby stimulating the receiving neurons. Neurotransmitters and receptor cells fit together like a lock and key based on their shape and electro-chemical affinities. Typically, only one neurotransmitter can fit the receiving cell's receptors and stimulate it. However, many drugs work by mimicking the physical properties of a neurotransmitter well enough to stimulate the receptor. Others occupy receptors without stimulating them, thereby blocking the neurotransmitter. Finally, once a neurotransmitter is released it cannot normally remain in the synaptic cleft, because its signal must be turned off. Some drugs slow or prevent the destruction of neurotransmitters within the synaptic cleft, while others prevent reabsorption; both actions result in greater stimulation of the receiving neuron.

Biological theories of depression hypothesize that when certain neurotransmitters, such as norepinephrine and serotonin, reach too low a concentration in certain areas of the brain, depression can result. Tricyclic antidepressants (nortriptyline, naprotiline, desipramine, imipramine, norpramine trazadone, trimipramine, protriptyline, amitriptyline, and doxepin) block the reabsorption of norepinephrine and serotonin, thereby leaving them more available for the receptors. Monoamine oxidase is an enzyme that is normally present in all tissues including the brain. This enzyme breaks down the serotonin and norepinephrine. The monoamine oxidase inhibitors are a group of drugs that prevent monoamine oxidase from destroying the neurotransmitters and thereby increasing their concentration. Many of the older classes of drugs work by increasing the action of serotonin, norepinephrine, and dopamine. However, a new class of drugs is more selective for one of the neruotransmitters, serotonin; this class is called selective serotonin reuptake inhibitors (sertraline, fluoxetine, paroxetine, citalopram). These drugs work by blocking the reuptake of serotonin and thereby allowing this neurotransmitter to remain in the synaptic cleft longer and ultimately increasing its concentration.

Biological theories also point out the association between depression and certain medications and physical disorders. Briefly, these include prescription medications (reserpine, oral contraceptives, antihypertensives), drugs of abuse (cocaine, alcohol, stimulants, and barbiturates), neurological disorders, metabolic-endocrine disorders, vitamin deficiencies, heart disease, as well as kidney and pulmonary diseases. These will be covered in detail later in the book.

Finally, some evidence to support the biological theories comes from studies that examine family histories of depression. Major depressive disorders are 1.5 to 3 times more common among first degree biological relatives of persons with major depression as compared to the general population (DSM-IV). These findings are related to the growing area of research that focuses on genetic links and pathways of many other medical conditions.

Intrapersonal Theories

Intrapersonal theories emphasize depression as a problem *within* the person. These include psychodynamic, cognitive, and "learned helplessness" models.

The primary component of the *pyschodynamic model* "is that a sense of loss" is the main cause for depression. Freud (1917) theorized that some individuals, as a result of too little or too much gratification during the oral stage of development, have become overly dependent on others as a source of their self-esteem. Therefore, when the object of the dependency is lost through death or rejection, the individual becomes enraged but is unable to directly express this anger and subsequently turns it inward on the self. It is this inward anger that becomes guilt, self-blame, and self-hatred that, according to Freud, characterizes depressed people. Turning anger inward is often a strategy for individuals when there is no identifiable target for the anger. Where should medically ill patients vent their anger for the illness? At God?

The doctors? The environment? Maybe. But more often than not the tendency is to blame themselves or to turn the anger inside where it may be safer. Oftentimes this results in depression. This strategy of turning the anger inward often seems safer and less complicated because if they blame God or significant others, they may still need to depend on them in the future for guidance and protection.

The *cognitive theory* of depression was primarily developed by Aaron Beck in 1963. In his model, depression is the consequence of negative and unrealistic thoughts. The negative belief system may have been established very early in life and may serve as a template for the interpretation of events and people throughout life. Negative thinking can result in negative events, which in turn reinforces the negative belief about the world. Beck (1976) identified processes that lead to the distortion of reality and subsequently the development of pathological cognitive schema that lead to depression. These processes include selective inattention, arbitrary inference, magnification and minimization, and personalization. Through these distortions a patient faced with the traumatic and painful experiences of being medically ill can compound the effects of these events through negative thoughts, which eventually lead to depression.

A related theory is Seligman's (1974) *learned helplessness* model of depression. Seligman's original work came from observations made in the laboratory with yoked dogs. He noted that animals exposed to "inescapable shock" demonstrated an apparent debilitation in their abilities to respond in subsequent situations where the shock was avoidable. Instead of learning adaptive responses to avoid the pain they adopted a passive acceptance, which he labeled "learned helplessness." His theory suggests that when an organism is exposed to traumatic conditions in which the consequences of responding are either equal to or independent of the consequences of not responding, the organism develops an attitude of learned helplessness as it perceives the outcome is not within voluntary control. He argues that the symptoms of depression and those of learned helplessness are quite similar, suggesting that they may result from similar processes. This model suggests that when individuals are subjected to negative events (such as medical illness), that they perceive as outside of their control, they become hopeless, passive, and depressed.

Interpersonal Theories

Interpersonal models emphasize that depression exists in the social context and that poor communication and inadequate social skills are important contributing factors. Depression can easily develop among people who are inadequately rewarded or appreciated by others or who perceive lack of recognition as a result of poor communication. *Systems theory* focuses on breaking problem-perpetuating chains, which allows dysfunctional behavior, from whatever source, to be maintained through present day interactive sequences. The *behavior theorists* tend to view problem-maintaining behaviors as resulting from faulty learning experiences. Strategic therapy, also referred to as "directive therapy," relies on indirect and subtle techniques to alter the patient's behavior. Conceptually, the depressed individual is viewed as not living alone but rather in a larger system that needs to be altered in order for the depression to improve.

Integrating Theories

It is important realize that no single theory of depression has been shown to account for all cases of depression. Recognizing the mind-body connection will lead to a better conceptualization of depression and subsequent improvements in treatment. Each of the above theories provides great contributions to understanding the different components of this phenomena of depression: there appears to be chemical alterations in the brain that influence depression; a family history may predispose one to depression; distortions in cognition and negative behavioral patterns can lead to depression; and the influence of our environment (poor social support and intense stress) can also contribute to depression. Each of these different components appear to interact and influence each other. Intense stress and trauma can lead to alterations in brain chemistry and thereby produce symptoms of hopelessness, low self-esteem, negative thinking, and alterations in sleep patterns (Matsakis 1994). Physical illness and its treatment can alter brain chemistry, can create stress, and interfere with healthy thinking, which in turn may lead to unhealthy behaviors and increase stress, which alters physiology, and the cycle goes on. Remaining wedded to only one theory can lead to an oversimplified view of depression and thereby limit treatment. Therefore, as a clinician, it is important to incorporate each of these different theories when reviewing the clinical presentation of the patient in order to develop a framework for treatment.

Depression and Illness

Approximately 10 percent of the population, 17.6 million adult Americans, suffer from a depressive disorder during the course of any given year. Major depression is an all too common psychiatric illness that affects twice as many women as men. The prevalence rate for a major depressive disorder varies from 10 to 25 percent for women and from 5 to 12 percent for men, with approximately a 6 percent overall rate for dysthymic disorder. Individuals with a chronic dysthymic disorder have an almost 90 percent risk for developing a major depressive episode. Further, approximately 15 percent of individuals with depression die by suicide.

Depression may begin at any age with an average onset in the mid-twenties. The general chances for recurrence of depression include a 50 percent chance for a second episode to occur after the first and an 80 to 90 percent risk for a third episode after a second episode has occurred (DSM-IV). The course is variable, with some people experiencing isolated episodes and others having more frequent episodes of depression. Chronic medical conditions or other severe psychosocial stressors such as death, divorce, and other major life changes can trigger these depressive episodes.

When medical illness is coupled with depression the effects can be profound. In the medically ill population, rates of depression can range from 20 to 50 percent depending on diagnostic criteria and the specific medical illness (Katon et al. 1987). For example, the prevalence of depressive illness among patients with Huntington's disease is 50 percent; Alzheimer's disease, 40 percent; myocardial infarction, 30 percent; left central stroke, 40 percent; and end-stage renal disease patients undergoing hemodialysis, 20 to 50 percent (Cassem 1995; Hansten and Horn 1994). The incidence of suicide among dialysis patients is 400 times higher than the general population when withdrawal from treatment and noncompliance with the complete medical regimen are included as causes of death (Shukla et al. 1987). Further, some researchers have suggested that depression may affect blood glucose levels through changes in the neuroendocrine function (Eaton et al. 1992). It has also been identified as a significant risk factor and complication of heart disease. Recent studies have shown that even moderate depression raised the rate of heart disease caused by obstructed arteries by 60 percent and increased the rate of heart attacks by 50 percent (Frasure-Smith et al. 1993).

Depression has a further indirect influence, interfering with a patient's compliance with medical regimens and facilitating a "learned helplessness" coping strategy. In addition, depression frequently fails to resolve spontaneously and, left untreated, can lead to suicide. Approximately 60 percent of suicides are directly linked to depression.

Depression can be debilitating, resulting in chronic impairment, decreased work and social functioning, and a lowered quality of life (Ford et al. 1977). Impairment in social, vocational and family functions and relapse rates of 5 percent are frequently found in those who suffer a single episode of depression. Further, depressive disorders can significantly complicate the overall treatment of general medical conditions, since depressed patients tend to experience more pain, physical illness, and decreased physical and social functioning (Stoudemire 1995). When subjects with one or more chronic medical illnesses were compared to subjects with no medical illness (adjusted for age and sex) those with medical illnesses had a 41 percent higher adjusted prevalence rate for recent psychiatric disorders and a 28 percent higher lifetime rate for disorders than those with no medical illness (Tassett et al. 1985). Moreover, patients with depressive symptoms have a reduced ability to concentrate, enjoy pleasurable activities, and cope with adverse events (Verbosky et al. 1993). Depressed medical patients compared to non-depressed patients are less likely to use active cognitive-behavioral or problem-solving coping strategies and are more likely to take an avoidance approach (Rodin and Vashart 1987). Avoidance and ineffective coping often hinder compliance, increase morbidity and mortality, and reduce overall quality of life among medical patients. In addition, rates of suicide are significantly higher among chronic, incurable, and painful medical conditions such as spinal cord injury, Huntington's disease, end-stage renal disease, and acquired immunodeficiency syndrome. Primary care physicians recognize only about 62 percent of the cases of depression (Simon and Katzelnick 1997), and when depression is recognized it is often treated as a symptom of the physical disorder rather than as a separate psychiatric disorder. Although the frequency and intensity of depression does *not* necessarily increase with age (Myers et al. 1984), failure to recognize and aggressively treat it places the older adult at greater risk. Older adults typically experience more medical illnesses, therefore untreated depression makes them more vulnerable to the complications of a preexisting condition or the development of other illnesses.

Depression should not be viewed simply as a normal or appropriate response to a medical illness, but rather as a serious *complication* of the medical illness (Bukberg et al. 1984). All too frequently, depression is left untreated or is not treated aggressively enough, because clinicians fall into the belief that if it is an "appropriate response" it is not a serious one. If we can shift our attitudes and think of depression as a complication to the medical illness rather than an "understandable" response, we improve our ability to effectively evaluate and treat both the depression and the medical illness.

In addition to the medical and personal consequences of depression, there are also economic considerations. Mood disorders account for 45 percent of all private psychiatric admissions. Depression alone costs our society an estimated 44 billion dollars a year in direct and indirect costs, including treatment-related costs and lost or reduced productivity (Gerber et al. 1989). These high costs are due, in part, to underdiagnoses and inadequate treatment (Gregory et al. 1992). This figure does not include the effect that depression has on medical illness by way of extending medical and surgical care. Several outcome studies examining the effect of an additional psychiatric diagnosis have found that depression was a significant variable that contributed to an increase in a patient's length of stay and in the use of other health care resources (Sacks et al. 1994). Patients with mental illnesses, including depression, consume two to four times as much medical care when compared to patients without mental illnesses (Callahan et al. 1994).

Studies performed in general medical hospital patients whose depression was recognized and adequately treated spent an average of 31.8 fewer days in the hospital (Shukla et al. 1987). There is also the expense paid by users of long-term medical services: patients with end-stage renal disease receiving hemodialysis are a prime example. The cost of dialytic treatment (not including frequent hospitalizations) for a single ESRD patient receiving hemodialysis is approximately $45,000 per year. When depression complicates the treatment of such patients, the financial impact can be severe.

Problems with Diagnosing Depression

Although estimates suggest that between 70 and 90 percent of people with depression will seek assistance from their primary care physician (Blacker and Clare 1987), 50 percent of the cases will be misdiagnosed and under-treated. A multitude of factors interfere with the detection and aggressive treatment of depression among the medically ill.

There are several causal relationships that can exist between depression and medical illness: the depression can be an early symptom of a medical illness sometimes manifesting itself before any other outward signs of that illness; depression can be a physiological *result of* an illness; depression can be a psychological *reaction to* a medical illness; and in some patients, depression can be a separate disorder that is unrelated to the coexisting medical conditions. Even if the depression is not connected to the illness it can still complicate the management of the patient's medical conditions.

The "masked" presentation of depression among the medically ill can make accurate diagnosis difficult. The symptoms of depression often overlap with symptoms of other illnesses and conditions. Some symptoms of depression such as changes in sleep patterns and appetite, fatigue, pain, and gastrointestinal disturbances can also be related to coexisting medical illnesses. Confusion, poor concentration and attention, short-term memory loss and irritability can all be symptoms of depression and medical conditions such as dementia or delirium or can be induced by medication. Feelings of hopelessness, anger, and guilt are all symptoms of depression but also may be related to a patient's natural personality style, or can be situationally induced by the current medical condition.

Consider the following challenges to a good diagnosis of depression: If a patient is physically ill and feeling fatigued, is that depression? Are grief and depression different phenomenons? When electrolytes are not balanced and can trigger depressed mood, is that depression? When an older medically ill patient shows symptoms of fatigue, memory loss, and lack of interest in activities, is the fatigue related to the underlying medical condition or to depression or is it just old age? Is a patient's memory loss related to medication, medical illness, a coexisting but independent depression, or dementia? Is the lack of interest in activities related to depression or is it avoidance due to changes in visual acuity, hearing loss, or physical limitations related to age or illness? Depression can be caused by many different sets of circumstances, can manifest itself in many different forms, and can be subjectively experienced in a variety of ways. It is not surprising then that depression is frequently misdiagnosed and therefore inadequately treated. Nowhere is it more important to accurately diagnosis, treat, and communicate information about depression than among the medically ill.

Because depressive symptoms can have many sources such as a medical illness, medications, substance abuse, or as an adjustment to the effects of an illness, it is essential to first get an accurate diagnosis so that treatment approach can most effectively serve the patient. An accurate diagnosis or classification of the depression will guide your clinical decisions about the course of treatment and assist you in communicating with other professional staff. The following chapters address the diagnosis of depression. We have used the classification system of the current *Diagnostic and Statistical Manual* (DSM-IV) to differentiate the various ways in which depression manifests itself. As you can see, there is significant overlap in the symptoms of depression and medical illness, so the distinctions lie more in the underlying cause of the symptoms, the severity of the symptoms, and the duration. For example, the classification of "depression due to a general medical condition" assumes that a medical condition is causing the depression. That is not to say that a patient may not also be simultaneously experiencing an adjustment reaction to the limitations imposed by the illness itself.

The diagnosis of major depressive episode is the most severe in terms of its consequence on medical illness and health and thus is the focus of this book. The differential diagnosis of major depression and other forms of depression (such as dysthymia and adjustment reaction, depressed feature) is made in part by the severity of the impairment, the loss of functioning, and the duration of the symptoms. The next section attempts to describe these categories to aid in your understanding of the many complex ways depressive symptoms can manifest.

Part II

Assessment of Depression in the Medically Ill

Chapter 2

Depressive Disorders

Medical patients who experience depression can present in either a clinical manner consistent with major depression seen among the non-medically ill, or they can present with some unique variation that typically may not be thought of as related to depression. Below is a list of cognitive, emotional, and behavioral manifestations of depression often seen in the medical setting. Keep in mind that the symptoms in the list may be related to major depression, bereavement, adjustment disorder with depressed mood, mood changes associated with dementia, mood disorder secondary to a medical condition, substance-induced depression, bipolar disorder, depressed mood of a post-traumatic stress disorder, or depression related to a personality style.

The purpose of examining one comprehensive list of symptoms is to highlight how symptoms of depression in the medically ill can be all-encompassing for a person and therefore can significantly interfere with the medical condition. Impairment in functioning can be in areas of occupation, social network, and emotional well-being, but it can also readily be seen in the patient's inability to participate in the medical regimens. Once these symptoms and behaviors are recognized as potential indicators of depression, the next step is to assign a differential diagnosis so that appropriate treatment may follow.

Clinical Manifestation of Depression Among The Medically Ill:

- Feelings of hopelessness
- Pessimistic attitude
- Persistent feelings of sadness
- Depressed mood

- Loss of interest in activities including sex, visits from friends and family members
- Decreased energy or feelings of slow movement and thought
- Insomnia with complaints of early morning wakening
- Hypersomnia with decreased desire for interactions with others
- Difficulty concentrating or remembering things, including instructions from the medical staff
- Indecisiveness
- Preoccupation with physical symptoms
- Feelings of worthlessness
- Ambivalence about living with illness
- Self-blame for causing the illness or viewing the illness as a punishment for something in the past
- Tearfulness
- Poor compliance with medication, keeping appointments, or following dietary or other restrictions
- Slow and deliberate speech, with frequent pauses
- Decreased inflection of speech (monotone voice)
- Rubbing of skin or clothing
- Decreased efficiency when attempting tasks
- Poor appetite or recent weight loss
- Restless or irritable
- Feelings of helplessness, that one's action will not make a difference
- Poor self-image
- Exaggerated sense of personal weaknesses
- Demoralization
- Obsessive ruminations, often over trivial matters
- Exaggerated sense of frustration even over minor irritations
- Increased sensation of pain
- Gastrointestinal complaints
- Even small tasks feel overwhelming
- Intrusive thoughts
- Overwhelming feelings of anger

- Physical and emotional withdrawal
- Direct or indirect interference with medical treatment (for instance, hemodialysis patients cutting their time short on the machine, cardiac patients continuing to smoke)
- Pattern of delay when seeking treatment for medical condition
- Suspiciousness as evidenced by doubting and questioning medical staff usually related to fear

Classification of Depression

In an attempt to more accurately classify mood disorders and subsequently improve treatment strategies, several different nosological models were developed. Although the clinical terminology that was generated from some of these models has been deleted or replaced by other concepts, some of the terms are still used by clinicians to conceptualize and describe mood disorders. The earliest model with perhaps the most lasting effects was Kraepelin's (1913) endogenous-reactive model. The word "endogenous" comes from the Greek roots meaning coming or growing from within. Kraepelin defined endogenous depression as being caused by internal derangement or degeneration. In contrast, reactive or exogenous depression is caused by an external event.

Another classification system that warrants some discussion because of its potential utility with medical patients is the distinction between primary and secondary mood disorders. This taxonomy was initially proposed by Robins and his colleagues in 1972. According to their definition, a primary mood disorder is one that arises independent of other events and is seen in individuals with no prior history of a mood disorder. Alternatively, secondary depression refers to a condition that arises in the context of a medical illness or preexisting psychiatric disorder. The strength of this system is that the criteria are relatively unambiguous and therefore avoids the conceptual confusion seen in other systems. However, criticism of this system stems from its lack of predictive power when compared to other systems.

With a clear recognition that it is difficult to differentiate symptoms of fatigue, loss of appetite, sadness, and demoralization related to the medical illness itself or a mood disorder, Popkin and colleagues (1987) proposed a different classification system. He suggested that depression seen in medically ill patients be classified along three variables: nature of the medical illness, the integrity of the brain, and the cognitive status of the patient.

The current operational system used in the United States to assign psychiatric diagnoses is the *Diagnostic and Statistical Manual of Mental Disorders* (DSM-IV).

In the DSM-IV system, mood disorders can be divided into four classifications: depressive disorders, bipolar disorders, mood disorders secondary to medical condition, and substance-induced mood disorder. However, a depressed mood can also be diagnosed in the adjustment disorders section, the personality disorder section, as mood changes that are consistent with dementia and delirium, concomitant with post-traumatic stress disorder, and as part of bereavement.

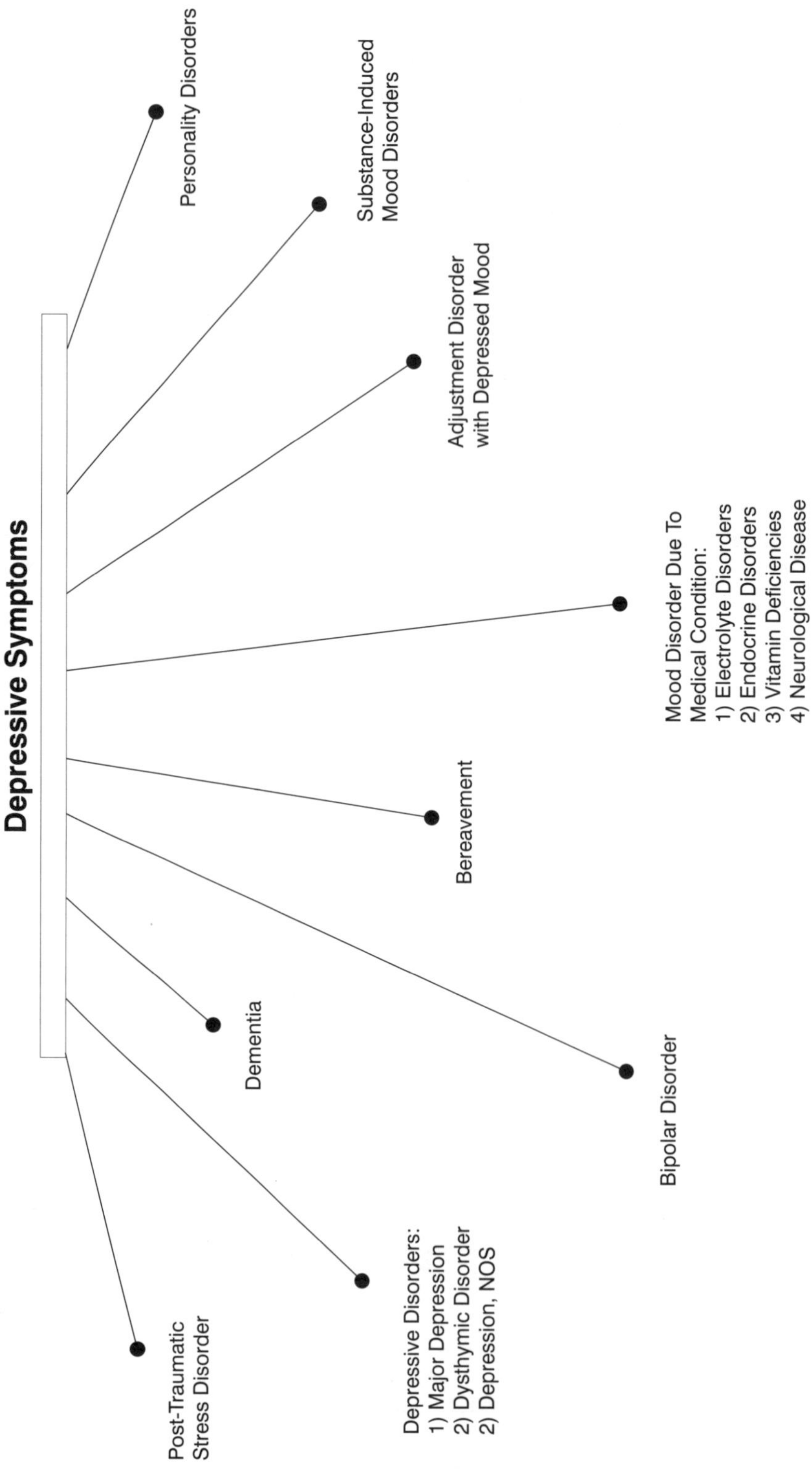
Depressive Symptoms
Personality Disorders
Substance-Induced
Mood Disorders
Adjustment Disorder
with Depressed Mood
Mood Disorder Due To
Medical Condition:
1) Electrolyte Disorders
2) Endocrine Disorders
3) Vitamin Deficiencies
4) Neurological Disease
Bereavement
Bipolar Disorder
Dementia
Depressive Disorders:
1) Major Depression
2) Dysthymic Disorder
2) Depression, NOS
Post-Traumatic
Stress Disorder

The following criteria are taken from the DSM-IV. They provide a good reference for evaluating depression among the general population. The following sections will provide additional information to be considered when attempting to make a differential diagnosis among medically ill patients. A differential diagnosis refers to the process of distinguishing one disorder or disease from another (for example, distinguishing a depressive episode from hyponatremia).

Depressive Disorders

The depressive disorders include major depression, dysthymia, and depression not otherwise specified.

Major Depressive Disorder

A major depressive disorder is characterized by one or more depressive episodes. Therefore, you can have a major depressive disorder, single episode or major depressive disorder, recurrent. In order to make a clinical diagnosis of major depression, five or more of the following symptoms have to have been present during the same two-week period and represent a change from previous functioning; at least one of the symptoms must be (1) depressed mood or (2) loss of interest or pleasure.

Criterion A1: Depressed Mood

"Mood" is the word often used to describe an emotional tone, the prevailing feeling over an extended period of time. Mood typically remains relatively consistent over time. A "normal" mood is reactive; that is, it can be influenced and affected by things that happen in our lives. The mood reacts negatively to unhappy events and positively to happy ones. An "abnormal" mood is one that lacks this reactive component and remains unusually elevated or depressed regardless of the context or circumstances. Another distinction between a normal and abnormal mood is the proportion of the response. For example, if someone were to win the lottery, we would expect an extremely euphoric and happy mood to follow. However, if someone won $5 in a bet, we would expect a happy mood, but certainly not with the same intensity as the former example. With an abnormal mood or a mood disorder the mood response to circumstances may be distorted: an individual with a depressed mood may even view positive events as negative. The mood therefore would be inappropriate.

In contrast, our affect can change from moment to moment. Affect can be described along certain clinical parameters, such as range, lability, intensity, and appropriateness. For example, a patient may demonstrate a full or wide range of affect from tearful to happy during an interview or may show restricted affect such as depressed with no variation throughout the clinical interview. Lability is used to describe the affect of patients who fluctuate rapidly from one emotional state to another, often in a way that is unrelated or marginally related to the topic. This can frequently be observed with patients who suffer from some type of insult to the brain, either structural or metabolic. Intensity is often used to describe the level of the emotional expression. This can be used to describe the level of rage observed with a borderline patient, the volume of the histrionic patient, or the flat and blunted affect of a patient with Parkinson's disease. The appropriateness of the affect refers to the level of consistency between the content of the discussion and the emotion being expressed. For example, laughing or appearing euphoric when describing a traumatic or sad event would be described as inappropriate. In contrast, crying while reporting a sad event would be described as appropriate.

Although we have clinical descriptors to guide our assessment of mood and affect, these concepts are still subjective. From a phenomenological perspective mood reflects not only emotions, but also our view of the world, the future, others, and our overall sense of well-being. Therefore, when evaluating the mood of a medical patient, the context of the mood, duration, and matching observations are important. For example, medical patients are frequently described by staff as "looking" depressed based on observations of tearfulness, not smiling, and the patient's being somewhat quiet or withdrawn. An important distinction to be exploring at this point is the effect of pain, medications, coping, and personality style. Tearfulness as a symptom is often seen with depression, but can also have other etiologies, such as emotional lability related to left-hemisphere lesions (Robinson et al. 1987). Further, a mild depressed mood with rather shallow affect can often be the early sign of an acute confusional state like delirium (Lishman 1987). Some patients may become depressed and withdrawn with the early recognition of their cognitive deficits. It is important to remember that a depressed mood alone does not constitute depression. When evaluating a depressed mood among the medically ill, reactivity is important. That is, does the mood improve with changes in the medical condition or respond to support from others. A mood that is non-reactive to positive events, all-pervasive, and persistent is most likely related to major depression (Cavanough 1991).

Criterion A2: Diminished Interest or Pleasure in Activities (Apathy and Anhedonia)

Apathy refers to the loss of interest or desire for previously pleasurable activities, while anhedenoia is the inability to experience pleasure. It is important to keep in mind that the medically ill may be experiencing pain, physical limitations in mobility, and a decrease in energy to actually enjoy or participate in activities. The distinction to be made here is between a *lack of desire* for the activity and an *inability to engage* in the activity. Cavanough (1991) suggests that the most reliable indicator of anhedonia among the medically ill is the loss of interest in or pleasure from family and friends. In contrast, patients suffering from an adjustment disorder with a depressed mood may be quite pleased and demonstrate an improvement in their mood when visiting with friends and family. It is also important to note that many patients may not readily admit to feelings of anhedonia but may demonstrate behavioral manifestations (such as loss of interest in self-care with resulting poor hygiene or malnutrition) and become physically withdrawn (Cavanough 1991).

This physical withdrawal can lead to limited social support. This lack, or perceived lack, of social support is both a contributing and a resultant factor of depression. That is, individuals who have limited social support have a higher prevalence rate of depression, and those who are depressed tend to further isolate themselves. Research has very clearly shown that social support and depression predict survival in patients with coronary artery disease (Frasure-Smith et al. 1993; Barefoot 1997; Ruberman et al. 1984; Berkman 1995). Behaviorally, low social support and depression have been associated with health damaging behaviors such as smoking and noncompliance and subsequently can influence morbidity and mortality. Oxman and Hull (1997) found that the perceived adequacy of social support among heart surgery patients at one month post-surgery predicted depression scores five months later.

Criterion A3: Significant Weight Loss

Forty-one percent of medically ill patients report anorexia and 58 percent lose weight (Cavanough 1983). Although the vegetative symptoms of depression are among the hardest to distinguish among the medically ill, it is important to consider whether the patient is simply not *interested* in eating or is *unable* to eat. Is the loss of appetite and related weight loss secondary to the illness and medical treatment, inability to cook, financial limitations, or because the patient simply doesn't care and behaviorally makes little effort to attempt to eat despite knowledge and understanding that it is necessary?

In a study examining major depression before and after a myocardial infarction (MI), Lesperance and his colleagues (1996) found that, when examining depressive symptomatology, sleep and appetite disturbances were found for all patients. However, when sleep and appetite disturbances were statistically eliminated from the analysis, 88.6 percent of the depressed patients maintained the diagnosis of depression. Further, the risk of mortality was greater for those with depression after sleep and appetite disturbances were excluded. Therefore, the authors argue that when these vegetative symptoms make the difference in diagnosing depression post-MI, more aggressive medical evaluation may be warranted as these patients may not be depressed.

Criterion A4: Insomnia or Hypersomnia

Given that 54 percent of medically ill patients report sleep disturbances (Cavanough 1983), it is important to separate interrupted sleep related to the medical setting (such as being interrupted for vital signs or a loud roommate) from a vegetative symptom of depression. Moreover, numerous medical conditions that affect the respiratory, cardiovascular, gastrointestinal, and neurological systems can interfere with sleep. Specifically, patients with coronary artery disease may experience sleep difficulties related to alterations in normal breathing patterns and blood oxygenation (Regenstein 1992). Further, patients with angina may experience frequent episodes of awakening particularly during the REM phase of sleep, due to fluctuation in cardiac rates. Patients with end-stage renal disease frequently complain of difficulty initiating and maintaining sleep. Although the exact etiology has not been clearly identified, increased prevalence of sleep apneas or periods of sleep associated with cessation of breathing have been implicated.

To further complicate the picture, many medications and other over the counter agents such as alcohol, caffeine, and nicotine can interfere with sleep. For example, caffeine can decrease the quality of sleep and can increase early morning drowsiness as it has lasting effects for up to twenty hours (Regenstein 1987). Alcohol is frequently used by people to induce sleep due to the sedating effects. However, alcohol has been associated with abrupt awakenings throughout the night resulting in a fragmented quality of sleep (Vitielio et al. 1990). Smokers are more likely to experience sleep difficulties related to nicotine effects. Specifically, duration of sleep is decreased with the increased use of nicotine, and sleep patterns normalize after nicotine withdrawal is completed (Soldatos et al. 1989). In addition, medication such as alpha-methlydopa, propanolol, theophyline, oral contraceptives, thyroid hormones, catecholamine blocking agents, b-adrengergic agonists, and antidepressants that have a stimulant effect (such as fluoxetine, bupropion, and protriptyline) can interfere with sleep.

Perhaps our own personal experiences or simple common sense reminds us that a good night's sleep will yield better energy, healthier attitudes, and increased concentration in the daytime hours. Further, an extensive empirical data base has demonstrated a relationship between sleep disturbances and depression. Therefore, changes in sleep patterns has been maintained throughout the revisions of the DSM system as an important vegetative symptom of depression. As has been briefly outlined above, however, prevalence of insomnia and hypersomnia among medical patients is quite high, which frequently confounds the differential for depression among this population.

The following are issues to consider when evaluating sleep as it relates to depression in the medically ill:

- Is the symptom of sleep disturbance significantly disproportionate to the medical condition? In other words, does the sleep disturbance continue or become worse despite an overall improvement of the medical condition?
- Has the person been evaluated for a primary sleep disturbance?
- Examine the patient's description and interpretation of the symptom. Depressed patients are more likely to complain about lying down to sleep and being troubled by their thoughts racing or experiencing intrusive thoughts or worry.
- When utilizing psychometric instruments, choose those that are limited in the somatic items or have eliminated them completely. For example, Beck is currently developing a questionnaire that will eliminate the somatic items and only retain cognitive items as a way of reducing the number of false positives among the medically ill. This instrument is scheduled to be released sometime in 1999.
- The age of the patient should be considered when evaluating sleep, as sleep patterns typically undergo changes in later years unrelated to medical illness or depression (Prinz et al. 1990). Thus, if the patient is younger with other indicators for depression, findings of sleep disturbances may be more diagnostic than when found among older medically ill patients.

Despite the fact that changes in sleep patterns may not be the best or most sensitive indicator of major depression among the medically ill due to the confounding effects listed above, the prognostic significance of insomnia in predicting suicide make it important. Both hypersomnia and insomnia (Fawcett et al. 1990) have been shown to be related to suicidal tendencies in patients with major depression. The mechanism underlying this association is still controversial, with some researchers hypothesizing a relationship between abnormalities in serotonin neurotransmission (Sabo et al. 1991). Therefore, among those who are depressed and medically ill, it is important to consider sleep disturbances and suicidal ideation as potential risk factors for suicidal tendencies.

Criterion A5: Psychomotor Retardation or Agitation

Psychomotor retardation in even a mild form has been identified in approximately 81 percent of the medically ill patients (Schwab et al. 1967). Numerous medical conditions, treatments, and medications can cause agitation or slowed movements such as delirium, dementia, Parkinsons's disease, hyponatremia, hyperphosphatemia, hyperthyroidism, hyperkalemia, anoxia, as well as other neurological disorders. Further, changes in movement can also be a result of extended bed rest. Therefore, the utility of using this criterion to diagnosis depression among the medically ill is questionable.

Criterion A6: Fatigue or Loss of Energy

Fatigue is a non-specific symptom whose meaning varies from person to person. Further, it is a common complaint among medically ill patients. Cavanough (1983) reported that 77 percent of medical inpatients reported feelings of fatigue or loss of energy. Specifically, the prevalence rate for fatigue among HIV patients who are in the asymptomatic stage is 2 to 27 percent and 30 to 54 percent among the symptomatic HIV and AIDS patients. In a study of post-MI patients, feeling fatigued was three times more common among depressed patients in the hospital than those who were not depressed. Moreover, fatigue was not found to be associated with disease severity (Lesperance et al. 1996). Therefore, lack of energy and fatigue may be important indicators of depression particularly in this population.

Fatigue can be caused by many medical conditions including active cancer, neurological injury, acute viral infection, cardiopulmonary disease, hypothyroidism, Addison's disease, rheumatological disease, infection, and myopathy. In addition, medications and substances such as antihistamines, sedatives, narcotics, lithium, alcohol, and others can contribute to fatigue.

Numerous metabolic conditions can present with symptoms of poor energy, weakness, or apathy. For example, disruption in thyroid functioning can often produce symptoms of apathy, fatigue, and related poor energy or desire. Hyponatremia or low sodium levels can present with weakness, depression, and apathy. More extensive discussion of metabolic disorders will be presented in chapter 5.

From a psychological perspective, feelings of fatigue can undermine a patient's motivation and compliance with their medical care. It can also interfere with their ability to make the necessary lifestyle changes that are often important in preventing and managing medical illnesses. In order to evaluate whether fatigue is a symptom of depression or a result of the medical illness and related treatment, consider the following:

- By history, did the fatigue coincide with the onset of a depressed mood or anhedonia?
- Is the presentation of the fatigue and its severity proportionate to the medical illness?
- Is the patient's description of the fatigue suggestive of lack of interest or desire for activities, which is consistent with anhedonia, or related to pain, weakness, or limitations in strength?
- It is important to consider the age of the patient, as fatigue as an indicator for depression is less sensitive among older adults (Gallagher 1986). Although fatigue is not a symptom of aging in and of itself, it is often related to age-related medical conditions. Fatigue in an older adult, however, who does not have multiple medical complications and who was premorbidly physically healthy is a pathonomic sign.

Criterion A7: Feelings of Worthlessness or Inappropriate Guilt

The distinction to be made here is between feeling badly about oneself and feeling guilty about the medical illness and related situations (Cavanough 1983). Depressed patients are more likely to make comments about feeling that the illness is their punishment for being bad.

A related construct is that of hopelessness, which is defined as negative expectancies about oneself and the future. In Arthur Schmale's studies of hopelessness and the development of cancer, he refers to hopelessness as "feelings of doom, the end, finished"; "nothing can be done"; and "since the individual assumes primary responsibility for the loss, there is no expectation that anyone else can provide a solution" (Schmale and Iker 1996, p. 718). Seligman (1991) showed that the way in which an individual explains losses, disappointments, and failures greatly influences mental as well as physical health. The notion of learned helplessness is characterized by a view that problems are permanent, extend throughout life, and are a reflection of one's shortcomings. This is a particularly important concept when evaluating medical patients. The differential here is whether or not the person feels hopeless about specific aspects of the medical condition and resulting losses for the future or does he or she project an all-pervasive sense of failure and lack of hope for all aspects of life, past and present.

Hopelessness appears to exert its influence on health through a variety of channels. It seems to affect neurological, endocrine, and immunological processes. It also influences health-related behaviors, with hopeless patients giving less attention to self-care and demonstrating poor compliance with medical regimens. This careless behavior and the related lack of belief that their compliant behavior will influence the future increases morbidity and mortality. In other words, the hopeless cognitive beliefs make it difficult for the patient to appraise the medical situation and undermines any efforts to cope. Further, patients who feel hopeless lack self-confidence to solve problems and are unable to ask others for help because they believe it is futile.

Anda and colleagues (1993) found that hopelessness significantly predicted fatal and non-fatal ischemic heart disease. This study was conducted on a cohort of 2800 initially healthy men and women from the National Health Examination Follow-up Survey. Interestingly, the one question that measured hopelessness was more strongly related to mortality, cancer incidence, and MI than the entire four-item depression scale. These results strongly support a growing body of research that identifies feelings of hopelessness as a strong predictor of increased morbidity and mortality among medically ill patients *independent* of depression. Specifically, although hopelessness is often an essential feature of depression, studies have shown that suicidal intent consistently is more strongly associated with hopelessness than with depression (Greene 1989).

Morbid preoccupation with worthlessness coupled with suicidal ideation and psychomotor retardation or significant impairments in functioning may indicate bereavement that may or may not be complicated by depression. This is discussed in more detail in the section on bereavement.

Criterion A8: Inability to Think or Concentrate; Indecisiveness

When medical patients complain of difficulty concentrating or thinking, the differential becomes whether medication or the underlying illness is clouding the sensorium or if an underlying cognitive deficit exists. Polypharmacy is a common occurrence among older adults and those with multiple medical illnesses and can induce or complicate depression (Salzman 1992). As many as 28 percent of all hospitalized patients have a score of 23 or lower on the Mini-Mental State Exam (Cavanough 1983), which indicates a mild to moderate range of impairment.

Criterion A9: Recurrent Thoughts of Death

In a population where pain and suffering are frequent occurrences, fear of dying and wishing for death to end suffering are often recurrent thoughts. The question for the clinician then becomes at what point do thoughts of death indicate suicidal ideation as a symptom of depression as opposed to a "normal" response to the illness. In the DSM-IV, it is noted that patient's who simply fear dying do not meet this criteria. Cavanough suggests that this criterion should be expanded to exclude those patients who are "wishing to be dead to end physical suffering" (Cavanough 1995, p. 997). Further, he notes that thoughts of death and recurrent suicide plans should be temporally related to affective and cognitive symptoms of depression in order for a diagnosis of depression to be made. This addition appears to be particularly useful as a guide for distinguishing those patients who are physically in pain or may be faced with significant changes in their lifestyle due to the illness and think about ways to end their suffering from those patients who are suicidal related to primary depression. In the absence of other cognitive and emotional symptoms of depression, a diagnosis of depression with suicidal ideation should not be made in this population. In addition, wanting to be dead may be a logical and reasonable request of critically ill patients whose suffering is significant. However, decisions regarding death through termination of life-sustaining procedures, such as dialysis for patients with ESRD, should not be made in the presence of a primary depression.

Criterion B

The symptoms do not meet criteria for mixed episode.

Criterion C

The symptoms cause clinically significant distress or impairment in social, occupational, or other important areas of functioning that are not due to the illness or treatment.

As a criteria this does not appear to be specific enough to guide the clinician in evaluating the medical patient. For example, the vague caveat of "not due to illness or treatment" does not give direction for how these symptoms may clinically impact the medical patient's functioning. Further, a patient's medical illness may contribute to a patient's inability to work, but the depression may also limit the patient's ability to seek out alternative employment. A suggestion made by Cavanough is to remove the descriptor of "not due to illness or treatment" and replace it with "patient not participating in medical care despite ability to do so, is not progressing despite improvement in medical care, and/or is functioning at a level lower than the medical condition warrants" (Cavanough 1995, p. 52). This description more clearly allows the clinician to examine the extent to which the symptoms of depression are interfering directly with the medical illness and related regimens. Subsequently, a more definitive diagnosis based on the extent of impaired functioning can separate major depression from other subclinical types of depression such as dysthymia and adjustment disorder with depressed mood.

Criterion D

The symptoms are not attributable to physiological effects of a substance (drugs of abuse, medications) or a general medical condition (such as hypothyroidism). These will be discussed in detail in chapter 3.

Criterion E

The symptoms are not better accounted for by bereavement. That is, after the loss of a loved one, the symptoms persist for longer than two months or are characterized by marked functional impairment, morbid preoccupation with worthlessness, suicidal ideation, psychotic symptoms, or psychomotor retardation. It is important to keep in mind that depression can complicate bereavement and therefore can coexist with bereavement. These issues will be covered in more detail in the bereavement section.

Dysthymic Disorder

Dysthymic disorder is characterized by a depressed mood for at least two years with symptoms of either appetite changes, sleep disturbances, low energy, poor self-esteem, difficulty making decisions, and feelings of hopelessness. Given the significant overlap between symptoms of major depression and dythymia, the distinction can usually be made by gathering a complete history.

The primary distinction between dysthymia and major depression is the onset, duration, persistence, and severity of the symptoms. The onset of a dysthymic disorder is usually early in childhood, adolescence, or early adulthood with an insidious presentation that typically becomes a chronic way of existence. Most patients who suffer from a dysthymic disorder are unlikely to report symptoms as they are often viewed and felt to be so much a part of their lives. That is, they can't remember or don't believe their is another way of existing. These patients will typically be critical of themselves and often suffer from poor self-esteem. Studies suggest that the most common symptoms found among individuals who suffer from dysthymia are feelings of inadequacy, irritability, intense periods of anger and poor productivity and effectiveness. In contrast to patients with major depression, patients with a dysthymic disorder often experience fewer vegetative symptoms than those who suffer from major depression. Moreover, the chronic feelings of inadequacy and the intense anger among patients with dysthymia can frequently interfere with interpersonal relationships leading to further alienation and an increase in depressed symptoms.

Among medically ill patients it is especially important to recognize a dysthymic disorder given that some studies indicate a 90 percent likelihood of developing a major depression (Akiskal 1983), particularly during periods of intense stress such as chronic illness.

Depressive Disorder Not Otherwise Specified

Depressive disorders in this category do not meet full criteria for any of the other depressive disorders and are currently under investigation for inclusion as separate categories, but have to date insufficient data to warrant inclusion. These include premenstrual dysphoric disorder, minor depression, recurrent brief depressive disorders, and depressive episodes that cannot be differentiated.

Chapter 3

Mood Disorder Due to a General Medical Condition

The presence of depression may be one of the first symptoms of an underlying medical condition. In a study examining rates of undiagnosed physical illness in a psychiatric clinic population, Koranyi (1979) found that 46 percent of the sample had major medical problems that were not detected by the referring physician. In 18 percent of the patients studied, medical conditions were the only cause of the psychiatric symptoms and 69 percent of the medical conditions contributed in some way to the psychiatric symptomatology. In some illnesses, such as hypothyroidism, hyperthyroidism, Cushing's disease, Addison's disease, and Huntington's disease, symptoms of major depression present well before other physical findings (Fava et al. 1987; Folstein et al. 1983). Therefore, it is important to investigate medical causes of depression when assessing a patient even if the referral is from a physician.

According to the DSM-IV this condition is diagnosed when there is a prominent and persistent disturbance in mood, which predominates in the clinical picture and is characterized by either or both of the following:

- depressed mood or markedly diminished interest or pleasure in all, or almost all, activities
- elevated, expansive, or irritable mood

There must also be evidence from the history, physical examination, or laboratory findings that the disturbance is the direct physiological consequence of a general medical condition. The symptoms must cause clinically significant distress or impairment in social, occupational, or other important areas of functioning. Other areas of functioning for the medically ill may include compliance with the medical regimen (following diet, taking medication, and showing up for appointments), and active participation in rehabilitation or daily hygiene. Finally, a mood disorder can not be diagnosed during the course of a delirium.

Although establishing a direct physiological correlate for the mood changes can be difficult, the DSM-IV provides some guidelines:

- Consideration should be given to the temporal relationship between onset, exacerbation, or remission of the medical condition and that of the mood disorder.
- Examination should be made of atypical features for a primary mood disorder (such as age of onset, course, or absence of family history) that may be more suggestive of an etiology related to the medical condition.
- Evidence should be sought in the literature that supports a direct association between the particular medical condition of the patient and the mood disturbance.

The importance of accurate recognition and aggressive treatment, particularly for patients suffering from depression due to the medical condition, is highlighted by the significant risk for suicide. Suicide attempts and completions are typically quite high. Although rates of suicide across medical conditions vary, chronic, incurable, and painful conditions carry the highest risk for suicide. For example, the incidence of suicide in dialysis patients is 400 times higher than that of the general population when withdrawal from treatment and noncompliance with the medial regimen (e.g., diet, medication) are included (Abram et al. 1971).

The medical literature is replete with examples of depressive illness along with other psychiatric symptoms accompanying alterations in the biochemical milieu, endocrine abnormalities, and vitamin deficiencies. Such disturbances in the normal physiology of the patient can be subtle, yet produce profound mental abnormalities. Unfortunately, while recognized in the literature as a critical aspect of the evaluation of the patient with cognitive and mood disturbances, these physiological disorders are often overlooked in the evaluation of the patient. The complex effects from alterations in the human physiology can lead to changes in consciousness, confusion, and depressive symptoms. It has been proposed that these symptoms afflict as many as 50 percent of our hospitalized critically ill patients, and at a minimum, 25 percent of our chronically ill outpatients. Moreover, there are medical conditions that commonly provoke mental illness without any obvious laboratory imbalance. In these circumstances the depression may rest on a disturbed physiologic mechanism in the central nervous system that is not yet understood.

Historically, treatment modalities for depression in the ill patient have focused on defining the *one* metabolic dysfunction, or the *specific* hormonal imbalance that would account for depressive illness being diagnosed. However, through rapid advancements in diagnosis and, in part, molecular medicine, we are now even more aware that small hormonal or electrolyte changes in the individual can precipitate depression in those more vulnerable to this response. Some patients with specific illnesses (for instance, diabetes mellitus) may be more at risk for the development of depression. Less recognized is that even the most modest metabolic derangement may interfere with the person's ability to cope and subsequently increase the likelihood for depression to develop. It therefore is imperative for the medical care provider to detect, diagnose, and then successfully treat the aforementioned disorders before masking the symptoms with psychiatric medications. The purpose of this chapter is not to discuss all possible medical conditions that can cause depression, but to briefly concentrate on the more common ones. These disorders often confuse the health care provider and produce significant morbidity in our hospitalized patients and reduce their quality of life.

Electrolyte Disorders

Fluid and electrolyte disturbances usually occur as complications of an underlying illness, and the disorders to be considered in this section must therefore be viewed not as isolated entities, but in the context of the specific illness and total clinical presentation of the patient. Electrolyte disorders—imbalances in sodium, potassium, and calcium—are found in almost 50 percent of our patients with chronic illnesses (Devita and Michelis 1993; Narins 1982). The central nervous system is exquisitely sensitive to the slightest changes in the solutions that bathe it (Strange 1992). In other words, subtle changes in electrolytes can lead to significant mental disturbances. Of these changes, the simplest alterations and often the most lethal occur when there are changes in volume in the patient.

As general background to the following discussion it should be recalled that the water content of the body (approximately 60 percent of total body weight) is distributed between the intracellular and the extracellular compartments (Narins 1982). Approximately two-thirds of the water is within the cells, and water moves freely across the cell membrane and into the interstitial space and serum. Therefore, changes in the tonicity of one compartment will lead to a transfer of fluid until a new steady state is achieved. However, the ions (electrically charged particles) that are most responsible for alterations in cognitive and affective states are distributed in an asymmetric pattern. That is, most of the ions in the extracellular fluid consist of sodium, chloride, and bicarbonate, while potassium and organic ions make up the bulk of the intracellular ions.

Sodium (Na)

Symptoms of Hypernatremia (high sodium)

- disoriented
- emotional lability
- poor attention
- hallucinations

Symptoms of Hyponatremia (low sodium)

- irritability

- confusion
- intense anxiety
- weakness
- apathy
- depression

The most common disturbance that we see in both outpatient and inpatient settings is volume depletion. These states most often lead to an increase in serum sodium (hypernatremia) (Kamel and Bear 1993; Robertson and Trimble 1983). The simplest form of dehydration is when there is only loss of water without loss of electrolytes (such as sodium). The minimal amount of fluid intake to maintain balance is approximately 1 liter per day. Naturally, thirst serves to maintain water intake. However, when medical patients are too weak, dehydration often occurs. This fluid loss will only be aggravated if the patient has a fever, as increased body temperature can double the daily loss of fluid. The elderly are at the highest risk for suffering neurological complications, as they become progressively volume depleted due to loss of thirst sensation that occurs with normal aging. The absence of an effective circulating volume can lead to shock, increases in heart rate, and decrease in urine output. In less severe cases, the subtle changes in volume may be manifested in disorientation and other cognitive deficits and may be among the first presenting symptoms.

If the loss in volume is predominantly water, the result may be a rise in serum sodium, chloride, and bicarbonate among other serum electrolytes. The normal sodium in humans ranges from 135 to 145 meq/L. Depending on the rate of volume loss (rapid water loss will lead to more rapid and often more severe neurological sequelae than a gradual change) progressive volume depletion will produce mental changes as the sodium rises beyond 150 meq/L (Robertson 1983). The patient may clinically present with a delirium. Specifically, they may appear somewhat withdrawn and apathetic with acute confusion and other cognitive deficits. Further increases (sodium greater than 160 meq/L) can lead to seizures, stupor, coma, and even death. It is essential at this level that aggressive treatment is implemented before permanent neurological damage occurs.

There is another form of dehydration that is often seen clinically and this is the loss of water and sodium together. This is often manifested in gastrointestinal losses (diarrhea), skin losses (burns), and abnormal kidney function. The most common causes are summarized below in table I (Kamel and Bear 1993). It is important to remember that the serum sodium is not only determined by fluid and electrolyte loss but fluid intake. Changes in serum sodium may occur only if there is a greater loss of water than sodium or vice versa. Skin losses are the result of excessive sweating or burns. Sweat is hypotonic (sodium is only 50 meq/L) and therefore these patients may exhibit an increase in serum sodium. Burns, on the other hand, can lead to a profound loss of fluids from weeping wounds or from increased evaporation from the damage skin epithelium. Finally, renal losses are seen in states wherein patients with preexisting renal disease are "sodium-wasters" and are unable to retain sodium and water equally.

Table I. Causes of Volume Depletion

Loss of water without electrolytes

Simple dehydration

Combined depletion of water and sodium

Skin losses

- Sweating
- Burns

Gastrointestinal losses

- Vomiting
- Bowel drainage
- Diarrhea
- Colostomy
- Ileostomy

Renal Losses

- Chronic renal failure
- Postobstructive nephropathy
- Osmotic diuresis
- Diuretics

It is essential that diagnosis must first come from the history. Patients should be questioned closely about their intake of fluids and their losses (diarrhea, sweating, frequent urination). The physical examination is critical and extremely useful in these patients. Reduction in skin turgor and orthostatic hypotension (when the patient sits up, he or she becomes light-headed as their blood pressure drops) need to be examined. These aspects of the physical exam reflect a decrease in effective circulating volume. On further examination one may note a dry tongue, rapid resting pulse, and dry skin. Laboratory values may reveal an artificially high hematocrit and changes in renal function. Aiding in the diagnosis is the measurement of the patient's serum creatinine. Creatinine is a measurement that reflects kidney function. If elevated it can support the diagnosis of volume depletion. Creatinine can also be used by itself to make a diagnosis of volume depletion. Increases in serum creatinine may reflect intrinsic kidney disease in patients who are euvolemic (have a normal body volume).

Once the diagnosis is made of volume depletion, replacement needs to be instituted. If the patient is profoundly depleted, then rapid correction with fluid is needed. Once that is achieved, a more leisurely approach to volume and hence correction of serum sodium can be undertaken. If sodium is near normal then giving isotonic fluids is appropriate; however, this should be done slowly. If sodium is corrected too quickly (from high back to normal), this can damage the myelin sheath that protects nerves and lead to permanent neurological damage. It is essential to the evaluation of the patient that correction of the serum sodium be undertaken if it is abnormal in order to prevent and correct mental status changes (Robertson 1983).

The converse of hypernatremia is that of hyponatremia (low sodium). A variety of disturbances can lead to an abnormal and sustained reduction in serum sodium. The more common causes are outlined in table II. The signs and symptoms of hyponatremia are referred to as water intoxication; there is too much water that leads to the dilution of the patient's serum sodium. When the serum sodium falls below 120 meq/L the patient may exhibit irritability, confusion, and depression. Below 110 meq/L the patient can become lethargic, comatose, or suffer from seizures. Additional decreases will quite often lead to death if not readily corrected (Kamel and Bear 1993).

In summary, correction of both hyper- or hyponatremia is important for the prevention of further neurological damage. It is essential to realize that in both conditions, the elderly often do not rapidly return to their previous mental status baseline even after correction of the electrolyte abnormality. They may continue to experience confusion, depression, and even stupor. Some patients, particularly the elderly, can become frustrated and depressed with the noted deficits. In sum, these electrolyte disorders highlight the extreme sensitivity of changes in normal physiology in the elderly individual who are already at greater risk for depression.

Table II. Common Causes of Decreased Serum Sodium

Functional disorders leading to defective excretion of water

- Inappropriate secretion of the antidiuretic hormone
- Addison's disease (adrenal insufficiency)
- Depletion of sodium and extracellular fluid volume

Renal disease with defective excretion of water

- Acute renal failure with significant decrease in urine output
- Chronic renal failure

Idiopathic hyponatremia

- Congestive heart failure
- Cirrhosis of the liver

Excessive water intake in the presence of normal renal function

- Psychogenic polydipsia

Potassium (K)

Symptoms of Hyperkalemia (high potassium)

- muscle weakness
- inability to walk (often misdiagnosed as conversion disorder)
- depression

- amotivational
- dull in mental presentation

Symptoms of Hypokalemia (low potassium)

- depression
- apathy
- weakness
- disturbances in sleep
- apprehension
- irritability
- paranoid ideation
- impairment of memory

In addition to changes in sodium, alterations in potassium can affect the patient's mental status. Although not as common as changes in sodium, changes in potassium are found in approximately 15 to 26 percent of all hospitalized patients. The normal serum potassium ranges from 3.5 to 5.1 meq/L. Deficiencies in potassium can be seen in chronic diarrhea (in ulcerative colitis), gastrointestinal malabsorption syndromes, starvation, and excessive use of laxatives. Oftentimes the condition can be seen among patients with eating disorders. However the most common cause of hypokalemia occurs with diuretic use (see table III). Diuretics induce potassium excretion in the kidney, and if intake of potassium is not maintained patients may become profoundly hypokalemic (Narins 1982; DeFronzo 1992; Knochel 1984).

Table III. Common Causes of Potassium Deficiency

Renal

- Aldosteronism
- Cushing's syndrome
- Exogenous steroid administration
- Diuretics
- Renal tubular disease

Extrarenal

- Vomiting
- Gastric drainage
- Diarrhea

Studied best in the elderly hospitalized population, the hypokalemic patient will exhibit depression, apathy, weakness, and disturbance in their sleep pattern (DeFronzo 1992). Young patients may first show signs of apprehension and irritability. The clinical manifestations of potassium deficiency may be in one or more organ systems. Quite often changes in bowel function (paralytic ileus), constipation, and anorexia are seen. Perhaps the most serious changes are those in the neuromuscular system, as evidenced by profound muscle weakness (DeFronzo 1992). In profound hypokalemia (potassium less than 2.5 meq/L) paralysis may occur. The severity of the neuromuscular disturbance tends to be proportional to the speed with which the potassium level has declined.

Under many circumstances potassium deficiency can be corrected by oral replacement of potassium salts. This route should be tried first, before giving the patient intravenous administration, to prevent rapid changes in potassium. While both the electrocardiogram and gastrointestinal disturbances are readily treated with a replacement of the serum potassium, a return to the normal behavior pattern quite often lags days behind.

The converse of hypokalemia is hyperkalemia, a potentially lethal medical condition. Most often the result of a defect in kidney excretion, the clinical manifestations of potassium intoxication are primarily occur in the heart and the neuromuscular system. These changes are seen when the serum potassium is over 7.0 meq/L. Flaccidity, apathy, weakness, and depressive signs are often evident in patients with significant hyperkalemia. However, cardiac arrest may occur before any of these symptoms are evident. Therefore the most important guide for appraising the threat of hyperkalemia is the electrocardiogram. Treatment involves a very rapid return to near normal serum level of potassium. As with hypokalemia, many of the depressive symptoms may lag behind even when potassium has returned to normal.

Calcium (Ca)

Symptoms of Hypercalcemia (high calcium)

- depression
- lethargy
- dulling of the senses
- irritability
- explosive outbursts
- hallucinations
- paranoia

Symptoms of Hypocalcemia (low calcium)

- depression
- anxiety
- irritability
- intellectual impairment
- hypomania

Finally, the third most common electrolyte abnormality that can profoundly affect mental status is changes in serum calcium (normal levels are 8.5 to 10.5 meq/L but that is dependent on the individual laboratory measuring calcium and the patient's serum albumin). Changes in serum calcium have long been recognized to be a common disorder responsible for profound mental disturbances. Mental status changes have been identified in 50 percent of patients with hypocalcemia (Smith 1972).

Calcium is an ion that is found in greater amounts in the serum than within the cell. Calcium is predominately regulated by the parathyroid hormone (PTh), which is secreted by the parathyroid gland. In addition, calcium in the body is also regulated by vitamin D metabolism. Decreases in calcium (hypocalcemia) can produce tetany—intermittent muscle spasms that are severe and progressive. Profound lowering of calcium is an emergent medical condition that develops suddenly and requires prompt medical care.

Table IV. Common Causes of Hypocalcemia

- Hypoparathyroidism
- Vitamin D deficiency
- Renal insufficiency
- Acute pancreatitis
- Hypomagnesium

More common and of greater morbidity and mortality is that of hypercalcemia. The most common causes for hypercalcemia are summarized in table V.

Table V. Common Causes of Hypercalcemia

- Malignancies
- Hyperparthyroidism
- Milk-alkali syndrome
- Sarcoidosis
- Drugs
- Renal failure
- Vitamin D intoxication

The typical neurological presentation of the patient with increased serum calcium is one of extreme lethargy, dulling of the patient's senses, and progressive weakness. If the rise in calcium is slow and insidious there is a gradual decrease in the patient's ability to work, which can be coupled with symptoms of depression. Many of these patients will have constitutional complaints (muscle weakness, bone pain) that contribute to their depression and irritability. Sometimes explosive outbursts are followed by periods of sullen behavior. Reports of hallucinations and paranoia have been described among patients with calcium levels over 13 meq/L. On occasion a mistaken diagnosis of presenile dementia is made as the patient has developed mild to moderate intellectual impairment (Bilezkian 1989). With significant increases in calcium (levels greater than 18 meq/L) stupor and coma may also result. A further contributing factor to symptoms of depression is that patients who are hypercalcemic are often volume depleted. The persistently high levels of calcium contribute to diuresis and free water loss. Therefore, many of these patients will be hypernatremic, too.

Confirmation of this disorder is obtained by finding elevated serum calcium. Once defined, an intensive examination for the underlying cause (for example, malignancy) needs to be started. However, in the acute setting, patients are often infused with saline coupled with a loop diuretic (furosemide), which induces calcium loss in the urine; the saline replaces the lost fluid (Bilezkian 1989). Most patients will have a significant decrease in their serum calcium with this therapy. Additional therapy may be directed to further lowering the calcium with other pharmaceutical agents, but the main thrust will be to find the underlying etiology and direct therapy to treating that disorder.

Endocrine Disorders

It has been recognized for hundreds of years that an imbalance of endocrine function may not only result in changes in the normal physiologic response of the patient, but also produce a wide array of psychiatric illnesses. These disorders most commonly involve the thyroid, adrenals, parathyroid, pituitary, and the pancreas. It would be impossible to cover in detail in this brief section the many different abnormalities that one may see in clinical practice. Parathyroid disorders and their major psychiatric presentation were covered wherein we discussed changes in serum calcium: high calcium is the hallmark of hyperparathyroidism and low calcium the marker for hypoparathyroidism (Abboud 1986). Therefore the most common disorders of hypo- and hyperthyroid, Cushing's syndrome, Addison's disease, and diabetes mellitus will be briefly addressed below.

Thyroid Disorders

Symptoms of Hypothyroidism (low TSH, T4, and T3 levels)

- slowing of cognition
- clouded sensorium
- fatigue
- anhedonia
- apathy

- paranoid ideation
- delusions
- hallucinations

Symptoms of Hyperthyroidism (high TSH, T4, and T3 levels)

- anxiety
- irritability
- weight loss
- trouble sustaining attention
- poor concentration
- histrionic presentation
- delirium

Dysfunction of the thyroid makes up some of the most common endocrine disorders seen. The thyroid is responsible for normal metabolic and electrolyte metabolism, and disorders of the thyroid run the gamut from failure (profound hypothyroidism) to overactivity (hyperthyroidism). Patients exhibiting hypothyroidism (myxedema) are often misdiagnosed with anxiety and depressive disorders. Overlooked early on in the disease, mental changes and complaints are often evident by the time the patient presents to the health care provider (McDougal 1991; Hamburger 1987). As with most thyroid disorders, hypothyroidism is more common in the female patient (by a factor of 8 to 1) and often becomes evident when the patient is in their middle age. These patients will present with a dry, rough, and often baggy skin and have complaints of hair loss, constipation, and a generalized feeling of sluggishness. Reflexes are slowed and the male may complain of impotence while the female may have changes in her menses.

The generalized slowing of cognitive symptoms may resemble a depressive mood state. The patient will complain of clouded sensorium, fatigue, and a loss in interest and ability to perform routine tasks (McDougal 1991; Hamburger 1987). The patient becomes apathetic and, with progression of the disease, may become even slower and unable to perform the most menial of tasks. Organic psychoses has been reported in many of the patients, some will have paranoid ideation, while others will be delusional with auditory hallucinations and impairment of cognitive function. Depressive psychosis may also be present accompanied by other cognitive deficits with often severe and bizarre delusions and hallucinations. Developing insidiously, dementia will supercede as the patient becomes progressively more hypothyroid. If left untreated these patients can suffer respiratory difficulties and die.

Diagnosis can only be made with the use of radioimmunoassays that will measure the thyroid stimulating hormone (TSH) and thyroid hormones (T3 and T4). These levels need to be measured before treatment is instituted (McDougal 1991; Hamburger 1987). Once hyperthyroidism is suspected from the clinical presentation and symptoms, measurement of the thyroid hormones is necessary; implementation of therapy will readily reverse the progressive myxedema. Replacement therapy will restore vitality and mental processes to their usual efficiency. It is important, however, that replacement therapy occur slowly, as too much thyroid replacement can lead to cardiac arrhythmias and other complaints normally seen in hyperthyroidism. This is one disorder that should always be in the back of every clinician's mind when a middle-aged female patient comes into the office with a myriad of complaints related to physical and mental fatigue, constipation, and general lethargy.

Hyperthyroidism also afflicts females more than males, but is most common in people in their twenties and thirties and is often misdiagnosed as anxiety disorders. The most common cause is a diffuse overactive gland, although adenomas are possible. It has been proposed that emotional disturbances are quite often the immediate antecedent to the diagnosis of this disorder (McDougal 1991; Hamburger 1987). Psychological disturbances in some degree are seen universally in patients with thyroid overactivity. Restlessness, irritability, heightened tension, feelings of intolerance, and difficulty sustaining attention and concentration are the most common symptoms. Often these patients are misdiagnosed with personality disorders due to their histrionic behavior. Prior to the advent of modern antithyroid medicine, heightened emotional tension with extreme anxiety were frequently encountered. Although a "thyroid crisis" with acute organic reactions such as delirium, psychosis, and mania can occur among febrile patients and is reported in as many as 20 percent of the cases, the majority of patients have a previous history of mental illness.

As with hypothyroidism the measurement of thyroid stimulating hormone and T3 and T4 are essential for making the diagnosis. The patient may also exhibit a fine tremor, tachycardia, weight loss, and palpitations. These patients will also have sweating sensitivity to heat and will appear profoundly agitated. It is important to distinguish this very treatable medical disorder from anxiety disorders. Those with anxiety and agitated depressive disorders will have the same physical symptoms described above, but with extreme agitation, irritability, and frustration. Therefore, it is important that thyroid levels be examined prior to making a diagnosis of depression with agitation, dementia, or a primary anxiety disorder.

Depressive symptoms will improve in about 50 percent of the patients with thyroid replacement. The other 50 percent may require thyroid replacement as well as antidepressant medications to treat the depression (Smith 1972).

Cushing's Syndrome

Overproduction of corticosteroids is commonly referred to as Cushing's syndrome and can be the result of the production of ACTH from the pituitary (85 percent), or an adrenal adenoma. Regardless of the cause the adrenal gland will produce corticosteroids that produce physical and metabolic changes in the patient. More common in middle-aged females the disorder will manifest itself by buffalo hump, moon face, truncal obesity, and marked changes in skin pigmentation (Suda 1988; Williams and Dluhy 1989). Further examination will reveal mild to moderate hypertension, impotence, and amenorrhea (Munck 1984; Rao 1989; Schlaghecke 1992).

Psychiatric disturbances are found in 23 to 48 percent of all hospitalized patients with Cushing's. Depression is the major psychiatric illness (75 percent) with paranoid features also quite common. It has been noted that many patients who exhibited depressive symptoms had a family history of depression. Prior to advances in medicine that allow for early detection and treatment, severe cases of psychosis were reported. It is rare today to see patients with Cushing's have florid delusional symptoms bordering on generalized stupor (Atkinson 1991). However, for some patients the adjustment to gross physical changes and disfigurement coupled with hormone imbalances can contribute to symptoms of depression. Treatment of this disorder almost universally leads to an alleviation of the cognitive and emotional symptoms, however, depression may remain even after hormone levels return to normal. In part this may be due to the fact that improvement in body changes also lag behind the return to normal hormone levels. In addition, many patients report feelings of poor self-esteem and related body image disturbances as a result of the "trauma" of disfigurement.

Addison's Disease

Atrophy of the adrenal gland leads to a reduction in corticosteroids and hypoadrenalism, commonly termed Addison's disease (Williams and Dluhy 1996; Wulfratt 1988). This disorder afflicts men more than women and is also found commonly in middle age. Typically the onset of Addison's is gradual regardless of the etiology. The patient will complain of fatigue, loss of appetite, intolerance to cold temperatures, changes in voice timber, and impotence or amenorrhea. Unlike Cushing's, a delay in the diagnosis can be life threatening: severe abdominal pain accompanies significant and severe hypotension, and the chance of infection becomes very high. These patients lose sodium and retain potassium and therefore may have the concomitant medical problem of severe electrolyte imbalance that can also contribute to their change in mental condition.

Without exception patients with moderate to advanced Addison's exhibit some psychiatric symptoms. These patients will suffer from depression, emotional withdrawal, apathy, poor attention and concentration, and emotional lability with wide fluctuations in mood. Chronic physical exhaustion, profound hypotension, and weakness can contribute to the psychiatric presentation. Many times Addisonian crises, which are periods when the patients is profoundly hypotensive and weak, are accompanied by delirium with a more apathetic and apprehension presentation. In making the diagnosis, the clinician must exclude chronic debilitating disease, such as chronic rhematoid arthritis and chronic infections. However, this is a disorder where measurement of the patients blood chemistries (low sodium, high potassium), coupled to a physical examination (low blood pressure and abdominal pain), should raise the index of suspicion for the disease. Once proper corticosteroids are given, the patient will experience a rapid return to their previous mental status.

Diabetes Mellitus

Diabetes mellitus is a chronic systemic disease characterized by disorders in metabolism of insulin, fat, protein, and carbohydrates. Early signs and symptoms of the disease are related to these metabolic defects. As the disease progresses, symptoms are typically related to complications resulting from vascular defects such as nephropathy (lesions in the kidneys), retinopathy (degenerative non-inflammatory disease of the retina in the eye), and neuropathy (disease of the nervous system). Complications of the disease can also include increased susceptibility to infections, high-risk pregnancies, and accelerated atherosclerosis (buildup of the fatty deposits in the lining of the arteries interfering with the flow of blood) causing coronary artery disease.

Only in recent years has the high incidence of psychiatric illness in diabetic patients been recognized. Lustman and colleagues (1986) studied 113 adult diabetics and found that 71 percent had a lifetime prevalence of psychiatric illnesses with the most common being depression and anxiety. Poorer control of glucose secondary to noncompliance with medication, diet, exercise regimens, and blood-sugar monitoring was associated with depression and anxiety disorders. There also appears to be a high incidence of depression and eating disorders found among young female diabetics (Marcus and Wing 1990).

Although the role that psychosocial factors (including depression, anxiety, and stress) plays in the onset of diabetes remains controversial, a clear relationship appears to exist with metabolic control (Helz and Templeton 1990). These psychosocial factors seem to affect metabolic control directly through neuroendocrine effects and indirectly through compliance (Helz and Templeton 1990).

Psychological sources for depression among the diabetic patient are often readily apparent. Consider that diabetic patients must endure numerous painful conditions or neuropathies of their extremities. Further, they are at an increased risk for potential loss of limbs with advanced stages of the disease due to limitation in blood supply to these areas. They also live with severe limitations on their diet, not only what to eat, but when to eat it. Insulin-dependent diabetics must learn to give themselves injections or take oral insulin at regular intervals. They are often faced with numerous medical complications associated with the diabetes, including increased risk for kidney disease, heart disease, and loss of vision. There is also a relatively high incidence of sexual dysfunction among both men and women with diabetes, including low desire and arousal for women and impotence for men.

In addition, changes in blood sugar (glucose) can also contribute to symptoms of depression. As a clinician, it is important that these fluctuations are taken into account when evaluating for depression.

Hyperglycemia (abnormally high sugar in the blood) in the early stages can be misdiagnosed as hypochondiasis due to symptoms of polyphagia (morbid or pathological overeating), polydipsia (insatiable thirst), weight loss, and fatigue. Depressive symptoms have also been observed.

Hyperglycemia (high glucose)

- weight loss
- excessive thirst
- pathological eating
- depression
- fatigue
- confusion

Hypoglycemia (abnormally low sugar in the blood) symptoms can mirror that of panic disorders. They include tachycardia, irritability, anxiety, palpitations, sweating, and weakness.

Hypoglycemia (low glucose)

- irritability
- lability of mood
- anxiety
- weakness
- palpitations
- sweating
- tachycardia

Vitamin Deficiencies

Although less common in the Western world, vitamin deficiencies have been recognized as causing both cognitive and emotional changes. The clinical presentation typically consists of impairments in short-term memory, apathy, and on occasion psychotic episodes. Older patients are most susceptible to these deficiencies due to the fact that many live on a fixed income, which can result in poor diet. Also, elderly patients with cognitive or physical deficits frequently are unable to prepare or recognize balanced diets.

There have been cases of deficiencies in all vitamins leading to some mental status change. However, confirmation of specific vitamin deficiency has been difficult as multiple deficiencies will quite often be found together. Moreover, specific clinical implication of vitamins A, C, and D has not been made, and therefore the focus will be on vitamin B and folic acid deficiencies.

Vitamin B Complex Deficiencies

Functional and pathologic changes in the central nervous system have been clearly documented in patients with deficiencies in vitamin B. Vitamin B plays an essential role in the brain's metabolic processes. The vitamin B complex consists of thiamin, nicotinic acid, riboflavin, panthothenic acid, and pyridoxine. Thiamin is an essential co-enzyme important in pyrvuate metabolism and carbohydrate metabolism, while nicotinic acid (nicotinamide) functions as the component of two important co-enzymes (DPN and TPN) which are functional groups in intracellular oxidation-reduction enzyme systems necessary for tissue respiration, glycolysis, and fat synthesis. Riboflavin acts similarly to nicotinic acid, while panthothenic acid is involved in the formation of acetylcholine. Finally, pyridoxine is converted into a co-enzyme fundamental to the central nervous system's metabolic processes.

Thiamin Deficiency

Symptoms of Thiamin Deficiency

- fatigue
- weakness
- emotional lability
- depression
- cognitive deficits associated with Wernicke's encephalopathy

Termed "beriberi," thiamin deficiency is a disorder that is classically characterized as neuropathy with circulatory collapse secondary to cardiac failure. Other clinical features are muscle tightening and fatigue. Wrist or foot drop and peripheral neuropathies are frequently encountered in the adult population. This is most likely due to the degeneration of peripheral and cerebrospinal nerves.

The most dramatic in thiamin deficiency is that of Wernicke's encephalopathy. This represents the acute neuropsychiatric reaction to severe thiamin deficiency. In Wernicke's encephalopathy, histologic changes are found in the brain in specific areas (tegmentum of the medulla) that may account for ataxia of gait, global confusion, and nystagmus. While thought initially to be related only to alcoholics, it is found in all patients with thiamin deficiency (patients with malignancy of the stomach and pancreas, severe diarrhea). Often abrupt in presentation, Wernicke's presents with confusion and a staggering gait along with diploplia (double vision). Often associated with Wernicke's is Korsakoff's psychosis. This syndrome is an amnesic syndrome with polyneuritis. Attempts to link thiamin to Korsakoff's have been unsuccessful but a clinical link with Wernicke's has been established. Features of both disorders are seen together and the cerebral pathology is identical, differing only in the acuteness and chronicity of the pathologic process: Wernicke's representing the acute organic reaction, while Korsakoff's psychosis represents the residual and quite often permanent defect. These are two disorders that are merely different facets of the same pathological process.

Treatment consists of a rapid administration of thiamin, because a delay in treatment may result in permanent cerebral damage. The biochemical lesions are rapidly reversed but structural defects require long recovery periods. All alcoholics with changes in their mental status should be treated initially as if they were thiamin deficient. It is essential that these vitamins be given prior to eating as the increase of glucose may precipitate an organic psychotic process.

Niacin Deficiency

Symptoms of Nicotinic Acid Deficiency

- weakness
- depression
- irritability
- skin lesions

The clinical term for niacin deficiency is "pellagra." Associated with maize diets (corn is low in niacin), the disease has disappeared from the United States except in alcoholics. The early signs are quite often nonspecific and include anorexia, weakness, and irritability, along with depression. Many patients complain of the feeling of incapacity. Depression associated with pellagra is often severe and subsequently increases the risk for suicide. As the deficiency progresses further, medical problems such as soreness of the tongue with progressive inflammation and ulceration of all mucous membranes of the body become pronounced, contributing to the patient's level of depression. As the deficiency progresses, the nonspecific psychic and emotional changes are replaced with a florid delirium. The delirium may be accompanied by a hyperactive, manic presentation or an apathetic, lethargic, or stuporous style. In the late stages of the disease, confabulation and memory deficits are present. Treatment involves the simple replacement of niacin with foods rich in the vitamin (liver, peanuts) or if the patient is unable to eat (sore tongue) then supplements are given intravenously. All alcoholics upon admission to any hospital should be treated as if they may have some form of this deficiency and be given niacin acutely.

Pyridoxine (B_6) Deficiency

Symptoms of Pyridoxine (Vitamin B_6) Deficiency

- depression
- irritability
- anxiety
- confusion
- lethargy

Pyridoxine (vitamin B_6) deficiency has been associated with depression, irritability, and affective disorders (Carney 1990). It is hypothesized that the mechanism for this relationship involves changes in central serotonin levels. That is, deficiencies in pyridoxine can result in lower levels of serotonin, which have been shown to be associated with major depression and suicidality (Meltzer et al. 1987). Further evidence for this association can be found in the literature documenting the efficacy of selective serotonin reuptake inhibitor medications in treating depression (Filteau et al. 1993). Pyridoxine has been recommended in the treatment of depression associated with hormone imbalances including postpartum depression and depressive side effects related to oral contraceptives (Adams et al. 1973).

In a study of HIV-1 seropositive men, a significant decline in psychological distress was found when pyridoxine was normalized (Shor-Posner et al. 1994). Similarly among a group of bereaved homosexual men, pyridoxine deficiency was found to be significantly associated with increases in depressed mood, confusion, and fatigue. Fatigued mood level was also found to be related to pyridoxine deficiencies, which is particularly relevant for HIV-infected patients as fatigue may be inaccurately assumed to be related to progression of the underlying medical condition as opposed to a vitamin deficiency. Furthermore, therapeutically it is important to note that fatigued mood can be readily treated by psychotherapeutic or pharmacotherapeutic means (Baldewicz et al. 1998).

From a treatment perspective, it is imperative that adequate pyridoxine activity status be maintained. The required daily allowance for pyridoxine is 2.0 mg a day for men. Deficiency states are typically treated with 50 mg to 200 mg oral daily doses. Pyridoxine supplementation is frequently prescribed in combination with tryptophan to increase the brain serotonin levels and subsequently provide greater potential for treating depression, fatigue, confusion, insomnia, and pain. However, caution is warranted as there have been no clinical trials to date to provide a recommended regimen of supplementation of pyridoxine alone or in combination with tryptophan. Potential concerns associated with toxic levels of these supplements include inducing a peripheral neuropathy and cognitive-motor impairments or seizures.

Changes in diet that limit tryptophan, a branched chain amino acid that provides the dietary substrate for serotonin synthesis, can exacerbate depressive symptoms in patients with major depression (Young et al. 1985). Moreover, dietary limitation of tryptophan, which is found in common proteins, can produce mild depressive symptoms. Regardless of the amount of dietary substrate present, the total amount of serotonin that can be synthesized depends on adequate amounts of pyridoxine to catalyze serotonin. Therefore, a reduced synthesis of serotonin in the brain can be related to pyridoxine deficiency.

Vitamin B_{12} Deficiency

Symptoms of Vitamin B_{12} Deficiency

- suspiciousness
- paranoia
- depression
- irritability
- short-term memory deficits
- confusion
- apathy

Insufficient absorption of vitamin B_{12} is responsible for not only macrocytic anemia (commonly known as pernicious anemia), but subacute degeneration of the spinal cord, optic nerves, cerebral white matter, and peripheral nerves. Approximately 80 percent of all patients with B_{12} deficiency will develop some neurological symptoms (Borch 1986). The changes in the nerves are manifested as burning and tingling of the feet and hand. This progressive parathesias accompanies general weakness and an unsteadiness of gait that is worse in the dark. Following these symptoms come spasticity and loss of bladder function and diminution of vibratory and position senses (Beck 1991; Babior 1990). Surveys of the psychiatric population have revealed that there may be an connection between vitamin B_{12} deficiency and organic mental illness. The psychological symptoms that accompany the early aspects of this disease are irritability, apathy, suspiciousness, confusion, memory deficits, and depression.

These patients are often misdiagnosed with a dementia. As with other vitamin and electrolyte disorders, the elderly are more susceptible to exhibiting mental illnesses that may accompany vitamin B_{12} deficiency. It is important to realize that the psychological symptoms may be the first and only neurological symptoms present. Therefore, further evaluation, blood work, and correction of the deficiency is essential before the diagnosis of dementia or depression can be made (Kapadia and Donaldson 1985; Waters 1993).

While found throughout the Third World, here in the U.S. this disorder is seen mainly in the severely malnourished, alcoholic patient or those few individuals that have had significant gastrointestinal surgery. Patients in the early stages of B_{12} deficiency may present with mood swings and vague neurological complaints (Herbert 1988; Hsing 1993). This disorder is readily treated with parental vitamin B_{12} complex. Many neurological and visual disorders will correct with proper vitamin replacement.

Folate Deficiency

Symptoms of Folate Deficiency

- depression
- short-term memory deficits
- confusion
- poor attention and concentration
- easily distracted
- irritable
- confabulation

Folic acid (folate) deficiency quite often has a similar presentation to B_{12} deficiency. It is, however, much less common than B_{12} deficiency and is distinctly uncommon in the United States (Chanarin 1987). Both will present with pernicious anemia, irritability, and early signs of depression and dementia. The majority of patients with folic acid deficiency are nutritionally deprived: alcohol and barbiturates may depress folate levels, too. The most common mental disorder related to folic acid deficiency is depression. As many as 50 percent of patients with folate deficiency manifest depression, while only 25 percent of vitamin B_{12} deficiency patients become depressed. This is easily corrected with the administration of folic acid.

We have only briefly reviewed the more common metabolic, endocrine disorders, and vitamin deficiencies. With an increasing aging population and more chronic illness these disorders will worsen the already very delicate psychological balance of the infirm aged individual. These are all treatable disorders. Finally, it should be realized that other possible disorders, such as magnesium or zinc deficiencies and hypervitaminosis (such as vitamin A), may present with changes in mental status. While these are even less common, the vigilant health care provider, once he or she has fully evaluated the patient and has eliminated the more commonly described disorders, should be aggressive in looking at other laboratory parameters.

Neurological Disorders

The following sections will provide a brief overview of common neurological disorders that can present with depressive symptoms.

Cerebrovascular Disease (Stroke)

Estimates of the prevalence of depression immediately following a stroke range from 30 percent to 50 percent (Robinson et al. 1983, 1984, 1987; Sinyor et al. 1986). In a two-year longitudinal study, Robinson et al. (1984, 1987) reported that 26 percent of patients had symptoms of major depression, and another 20 percent had dysthymia or a minor depression. At the six-month follow-up, 34 percent of the 103 patients met criteria for major depression and 26 percent exhibited symptoms of minor depression. Other studies (Eastwood et al. 1989; Ebrahim et al. 1987) report similar findings. Longitudinal studies suggest that the risk of post-stroke depression continues for at least one to two years (Lipsey et al. 1984). Depression in the recovery phase was also found to be associated with increased mortality in a ten-year follow-up study by Morris and colleagues (1993).

Clinical features of post-stroke depression include the following:

- A higher frequency and severity of depression occurs in left hemisphere versus right hemisphere strokes, with the highest frequency observed in patients with left anterior lesions.
- Patients with strokes close to the left frontal area experience more severe depression.
- A higher frequency of depression has been noted in subcortical and brain stem lesions.
- Lacunar infarcts, often secondary to hypertension, can lead to depression.
- Social, cognitive, and functional impairment are more highly correlated in depressed patients (Robinson et al. 1983, 1987).
- Patients suffering from aprosodia, the loss of the affective component of speech, can present as though they are suffering from depression.
- Lack of motivation in physical therapy is helpful in diagnosing depression.
- Premorbid depression or a family history of depression are risk factors for developing post-stroke depression (Starkstein et al. 1989).

Parkinson's Disease

Parkinson's disease is a disorder characterized by stiffness and slowness of voluntary movement, stooped posture, rigidity of facial expression, and tremor. Onset is typically in middle age, with the course of the illness occurring over a long period.

The most commonly found mental change in patients with Parkinson's disease is depression (Mayeux 1990). Estimates of the prevalence of depression in this population range from 25 percent to 70 percent (Cummings 1992). Mayeux (1990) and Starkstein and colleagues (1990) found that half of Parkinson's disease patients with depressive symptoms met criteria for major depression and the rest had symptoms characteristic of minor depression. Risk factors include prior history and decreased functional ability from gait changes, akinesia, and rigidity (Cummings 1992). Parkinson's disease patients with depression exhibit increased anxiety, shorter REM latency, and decreased thoughts of worthlessness compared to other depressive disorders (Cummings 1992). Depression in this group can be attributed to an adjustment reaction to progressive decline in physical function to a neurochemical etiology. Depletion of dopamine, norepinephrine, and serotonin is found in patients with Parkinson's disease (Mayeux et al. 1986; Starkstein et al. 1990). In a study of 105 patients, Starkstein and colleagues (1990) found a bimodal distribution of depression, with one group developing depression early in the disease and the other group developing symptoms late in the course of the illness. It was further observed that the early onset group had right-sided symptoms secondary to left hemisphere pathology and higher L-dopa dosages. Depressive symptoms in the late course group were more associated with impairment in functioning.

Huntington's Chorea

Huntington's disease, a genetically transmitted degenerative disorder, is marked by degeneration of the basal ganglia and cerebral cortex. Symptoms of the illness include depression and behavioral changes early in the course and choreiform movements and dementia later. Onset usually occurs in middle life and the duration varies from 17 to 30 years (Martin and Gusella 1986). Prevalence rates of depression for this rare disorder may be over 50 percent for major affective disorder (Maricle 1993). The suicide rate among Huntington's disease patients is 2 to 23 times greater than age-matched groups without the disease (Schoenfeld et al. 1984). A study by Caine and Shoulson (1983) reported that 24 out of 30 patients had behavioral problems linked with dysthymia or major depression.

Multiple Sclerosis

Multiple sclerosis (MS), a demyelinating degenerative disease, is characterized by lesions that cause ataxic gait, dysarthria, sensory loss in limbs, urinary incontinence, intentional tremor, and paraparesis. Onset is between ages 20 and 40 with the illness seen in women more than in men. Depression is commonly seen in patients with MS, with the likelihood of developing a major depression following the diagnosis ranging from 27 to 54 percent (Joffe et al. 1987; Minden and Schiffer 1990). Minden and colleagues (1987) described the depression as moderate to severe and marked by irritability, emotional lability, worry, and discouragement, as opposed to withdrawal, self-criticism, and anhedonia. The strongest predictors of a depressive episode were found to be a prior history of depression and an acute exacerbation of MS symptoms requiring treatment with prednisone or adrenocorticotropic hormone (ACTH). The authors further noted that the severity of depressive symptoms was not strongly associated with the extent of the disability, duration of illness, clinical status, fatigability, sex, age, or socioeconomic status. Patients with MS experience more depressive symptoms than do patients with similar disabling diseases, such as amyotrophic lateral sclerosis (Rabins 1986).

Seizure Disorders

Seizures are caused by excessive and disorderly electrical discharge of neurons. Generalized seizures are marked by involvement of both cerebral hemispheres. Partial seizures are characterized by focal involvement in a limited area of the brain. Complex partial seizures are associated with loss of consciousness and most often originate in the temporal lobe area. Depression is observed in patients with seizure disorder with rates estimated at 55 percent compared to 30 percent for matched medical and neurological outpatients (Mendez et al. 1986). The incidence of suicide in patients with seizure disorders ranges from 5 to 25 times that of the general population (Barraclough 1981; Mendez et al. 1986; Robertson and Trimble 1983). Depression is thought to be associated with left hemisphere and limbic area involvement. Other clinical features include less anxiety and preoccupation with worthlessness, more irritability, dysthymia, and emotional lability (Mendez 1986).

Other Medical Conditions

End-Stage Renal Disease

End-stage renal disease (ESRD) is a condition that is marked by a cessation in kidney function. Metabolically, this is represented by elevated blood urea nitrogen (BUN) levels and creatinine (Cr) levels. This condition is known as uremia—a poisoning of the system as the kidneys are no longer able to clear the body of toxins. When uremia has developed slowly, cognitive and emotional changes can be the initial presenting condition. This may be marked by depression, slow comprehension, poor memory, lethargy, and poor concentration with great difficulty sustaining attention for complex mental tasks (Lishman 1987). With the progressive uremic condition, patients may complain of anxious restlessness, emotional withdrawal, worsening depressed mood, and delirious presentation with acute hallucinations and profound apprehension and fear.

Symptoms of Uremia (high BUN and CR)

- depression
- poor comprehension
- emotional lability
- irritability
- short-term memory deficits
- restlessness

- anxiety
- severe apprehension
- fear
- withdrawal

Patients who suffer from ESRD and ultimately require hemodialysis treatment are faced with the task of adjusting to multiple physical, social, and psychological stress daily (Devins et al. 1981). These stressors not only stem from the challenge of dealing with a chronic condition but also from the actual dialysis procedure. As patients approach end-stage renal failure, they are usually confronted with many losses, including loss of physical integrity, reduction in capacity to engage in physical activities, unemployment and functional disability, and potential sexual dysfunction (Burton et al. 1984; Lefebvre and Norbert 1972; Rodin and Voshart 1987). This is followed by the stress associated with the realization of living with dialysis and fears associated with the dialyzing process, including pain, mechanical failure, clotting, death, and potentially witnessing medical emergencies and deaths of other patients in the dialysis units (Kocsis et al. 1990). Issues of extreme dependence on the hemodialysis machine and staff present patients with another psychological conflict; some patients react to this conflict by experiencing symptoms of depression and anxiety when they are away from the machine, while others may develop a phobic reaction to the hemodialysis machine (Israel 1986).

End-stage renal disease patients suffering from chronic medical conditions often yearn for the opportunity for respite through denial or frank avoidance of issues or situations that remind them of their illness. Dialysis patients are unable to readily experience this respite because they are faced with constant reminders of their condition. For example, the average hemodialysis patient must adhere to a rigorous dietary regimen including strict fluid restrictions. The majority of dialysis patients are only permitted five eight-ounce cups of fluid a day (fluids include anything in their diet that becomes liquid at room temperature, including ice cream and gelatins). Thirst must be quenched by sucking on ice chips or freezing fluids to satisfy dry mouth, without exceeding fluids allowed. Patients must be constantly vigilant regarding their intake of foods that may be life threatening, such as bananas, oranges, beans, potatoes, and salt. End-stage renal disease patients are typically dialyzed two to three times a week (for 3 to 5 hours each treatment), which significantly interferes with activities of daily living. Their daily routine must be arranged around their dialysis schedule, which can be disruptive for the entire family and subsequently can create marital and family conflicts. In addition, vacationing or travel needs produce much anxiety and stress, as it is often difficult to arrange for dialysis treatments in other facilities. Other significant stressors include disturbances in body image; specifically, male hemodialysis patients can experience disturbances in their masculine identity because of impotence, loss of hair, and their inability to produce urine. Finally, patients carry with them a constant obtrusive visual reminder of their condition: the shunt or fistula in their forearm.

It has been asserted that depression is the most frequent psychiatric complication or reaction to the above noted stressors among patients on hemodialysis. The prevalence of clinical depression in hemodialysis patients has been estimated at between 20 to 50 percent (Abrams et al. 1971). The wide range of reported prevalence rates may be partially due to differences in research designs and that somatic symptoms associated with medical illness such as sleep disturbances, anorexia, and fatigue can mirror those of depression (Black et al. 1987). As the dialysis population continues to age with an increase in concomitant illnesses such as diabetes and heart disease, the prevalence rates of depression in this population significantly increase in greater proportion than in the general population. Depression in this population can lead to a reduction in the quality of life and directly interferes with compliance to strict dietary and medical regimens. Compliance is essential to decreasing morbidity and mortality in this population.

Dialysis patients who are depressed tend to have an increase in mortality rate (Rodin et al. 1991) and a desire to discontinue to dialysis (Rand 1991). As has been noted, suicide rates in dialysis patients are 400 times higher than the general population when withdrawal from treatment and noncompliance with the complete medical regimen is included (Abrams et al. 1971). Furthermore, in a prospective study of fifty-seven patients with ESRD—forty-three of whom were treated with hemodialysis, fourteen with continuous ambulatory peritoneal dialysis—the role of depression on survival was closely examined. The Beck Depression Inventory (BDI), the Illness Effects Questionnaire (IEQ), and the cognitive item subset of the BDI (CDI), which controls for the possible confounding effects of the somatic items of the BDI, were used to assess depression. At a two-year follow-up, significant differences were found between the initial CDI scores of survivors and non-survivors. The authors concluded that depression might be a significant and early marker for a poor prognosis in patients treated for ESRD (Perez-Stable et al. 1990). These same investigators suggest that early recognition and aggressive treatment of depression might significantly modify the patient outcome. Whether depression is an independent risk factor for mortality or serves a mediating role by reducing compliance, it should be viewed as a treatable disorder.

Cancer

The diagnosis of depression in cancer patients is complicated, as in other medical illnesses, by the overlap between the physical symptoms of the cancer and/or its treatment and the vegetative signs of depression. In a study by Kathol and colleagues (1990) comparing diagnostic criteria (DSM-III, DSMIII-R, RDC, and Endicott) using 152 cancer patients who reported depressive symptomatology, prevalence rates for major depression ranged from 25 percent by RDC criteria to 38 percent by DSM-III. In a sample of 546 inpatient and outpatient consultations on cancer patients, Massie and Holland (1990) found major depression in 20 percent and adjustment disorder with depressed mood in 27 percent of the patients. They further reported that risk factors for depression in cancer patients include advanced stages of cancer, poorly controlled pain, comorbid medical conditions, medications used in chemotherapy that are known to cause depression, alcoholism, and history of mood disorder. Pancreatic cancer, in particular, has been associated with a high incidence of dysphoria as a presenting symptom of the illness (Holland et al. 1986). While it is common to have thoughts of suicide, particularly at the time of diagnosis and during advanced stages, estimates of suicide rates in patients who have cancer is around 8 percent (Breitbart 1987). Risk factors associated with suicide in terminally ill patients include previous history of depression and suicide attempts, uncontrolled pain, advanced stage of the illness, hopelessness, family history of depression, delirium, lack of social support, history of substance abuse, comorbid personality disorders, and recent other losses (Breitbart 1987).

HIV Disease

The chance of developing a secondary mood disorder increases as HIV-1 disease progresses. Rates of major depression ranges from 8 to 33 percent (Hintz et al. 1990). It is also noted that some groups at risk for HIV/AIDS such as gay/bisexual men and intravenous drug users, have a higher risk of developing major depression (Perkins et al. 1994). Patients with AIDS are 66 times more likely to commit suicide compared to the general population. Risk factors include poor prognosis, delirium, hopelessness, loss of control, prior history of substance abuse, prior suicide attempts, social isolation, and perceived lack of social support (Atkinson et al 1994; Marzuk et al. 1988). Systemic HIV disease and the medications used to treat its complications (interferon, steroids) contribute to major depression. Endocrine and metabolic disturbances in advanced stages of HIV-1 disease also contribute to depressive symptoms.

Chapter 4

Disorders with Depression as a Predominant Feature

Adjustment Disorder with Depressed Mood

When clinicians are faced with medically ill patients who are tearful and report feeling sad, the first concern is often whether this is a normal response to the illness or depression. In this context "normal" often refers to the clinician's belief that the emotional response is appropriate given the medical situation. Clinically, however, an "appropriate" or "expected" response is not enough to differentiate a temporary or transitional adjustment response from major depression. Assumptions are frequently made, based on nothing more than the clinician's biases, as to whether the clinical symptoms presented by the patient are normal and therefore do not justify aggressive treatment. Approximately one-third of all medically ill patients complain of mild anhedonia, difficulty concentrating or making decisions, tearfulness, discouragement about the future, and irritability (Cavanough 1983). Although many of these patients will experience improvement of their symptoms as they medically improve, those with significant mood disturbances have the same risk factors as those with major depression. That is, many of the patients diagnosed with adjustment disorders with significant mood disturbances demonstrated less participation in their medical care (Saravay and Larin 1991), had an increase in utilization of health care (Ormel et al.

1993), and had increased morbidity and mortality rates (Frasure-Smith 1993). Therefore, when considering a diagnosis of adjustment reaction, it is important to keep in mind that our own belief about "normal" and "appropriate" is not the means for making this diagnosis. In other words, this category should not conceptually be used as the "dumping" category when the patients symptoms do not fit into other categories.

When diagnosing an adjustment disorder, selection of the type is based on the predominant symptoms: depressed mood, anxiety, mixed anxiety and depressed mood, disturbance of conduct, mixed disturbances of conduct and emotion. Specifically, the following criteria must be met for a condition to be diagnosed as an adjustment reaction (DSM-IV):

Criterion A

Emotional or behavioral symptoms develop in response to an identifiable stressor occurring within three months of the onset of the stressor.

For many the development of a medical illness is one of the most stressful life events. After all, as the old adage goes, "If you have your health you have everything," and consequently, without your health, comes many different losses: loss of control over one's body, one's emotions and one's future. This loss of control can frequently lead to anger, feelings of demoralization, and depression. There is often a loss of job, sexual function, friendships, and previous lifestyle. Specifically, illness may result in dietary changes, which prevent the individual from feeling comfortable in social situations like dining out with friends. Medical illness often serves as a catalyst for change in the dynamics of relationships. Some patients respond to the illness by adopting a more dependent and needy style, which places great strain on those around them. Others struggle for independence and autonomy. These patients may often overtly reject efforts of help and support as they feel it will increase their sense of neediness.

Criterion B

These symptoms or behaviors are clinically significant as evidenced by either of the following:

- There is marked distress in excess of what would be expected from exposure to the stressor.
- There is significant impairment in social or occupation functioning.

This is often a difficult area to assess in the medically ill because the illness and not the emotional state of the patient may be interfering with functioning.

Criterion C

The stress-related disturbances do not meet the criteria for another specific Axis I disorder and is not merely exacerbation of a preexisting Axis I or Axis II disorder.

Criterion D

The symptoms to not represent bereavement.

Criterion E

Once the stressor (or its consequences) has terminated, the symptoms do not persist for more than an additional six months.

Bereavement

"Grief" is often interchanged with the terms "bereavement" and "mourning." These words are often thought of as an individual's reaction to a loss of a loved one, but grief reactions can be related to other losses. It is common to see grief reactions in medical patients who have suffered many changes and losses in areas such as employment, finances, physical functioning, appearance, and social relationships as a result of their medical illness. The higher prevalence rates of depressive symptoms seen in various medically ill populations is evidence of this. When the illness is devastating and produces either dramatic changes in the patient's life or the illness is likely to eventually lead to the patient's death, the grief reaction can be very similar to the phases of grief observed in those who have suffered the death of a loved one. The literature on theories of bereavement is vast and for the purpose of differentiating a normal grief reaction from a complicated grief or major depression, a summary of the phases usually seen in normal grief will be outlined below.

The Phases of Grief

There are many different theories describing the mourning process. A common theme running throughout these theories is the recognition that if feelings associated with grief and mourning, such as sadness, anger, loneliness, despair, and depression, are suppressed or inhibited, once they surface they are often more intense and difficult to manage. Most models of bereavement and adaptation to loss identify stages or phases of adjustment such as shock, denial, depression, anger (internalized and externalized hostility), acknowledgment/resolution, and final adjustment. Catherine Sanders (1989) discusses an integrative theory of bereavement, which includes in its underpinnings the work of several theorists including Sigmund Freud, Otto Fenichel, Harry Stack Sullivan, George Pollock, and John Bowlby. The theory takes into account internal variables such as age, gender, attachment to the deceased, health, and premorbid personality factors as well as external variables such as social support, sudden versus chronic illness as cause of death, and other concurrent stressors. Sanders contends that an individual suffering from grief will go through fives phases: (1) shock, (2) awareness of loss, (3) conservation-withdrawal, (4) healing, and (5) renewal. Each of these phases integrates psychological and physical symptoms and each level of change in the course of grief is seen as adaptive and not pathological.

The initial **shock** serves to protect the individual from the trauma of the loss. It is the reaction to an overwhelming experience and is often seen in those who suffer a sudden and severe injury (such as spinal cord injury or stroke) or when receiving a diagnosis of a life-threatening disease (such as cancer). Characteristics of this phase include disbelief, confusion, feelings of unreality, helplessness, and regression. Physical correlates include weeping, sleep and appetite disturbance, startle response, muscle weakness, and dry mouth and throat. Sanders recommends that a mild anti-anxiety agent can be useful during this period to calm the overstimulated central nervous system.

Typically the initial shock phase leads to the next phase of grieving, **awareness of loss**. Characteristics of this phase include anxiety (marked by a feeling of being close to a nervous breakdown), frustration, anger, guilt, sleep disturbance, crying, and fear of death. Anxiety in medically ill patients can be seen when waiting for results of medical tests, anticipating invasive procedures, experiencing side effects of some treatments, fear and uncertainty about the future, and other possible medical complications. Guilt and anger directed inward result when responsibility is placed on oneself for the onset of the illness or failure to improve medically due to past health behaviors (such as smoking or overeating). In some cases, the illness or disability is seen as punishment for past transgressions. Externalized hostility is often directed at the medical environment and others believed to be associated with the onset of the illness or when obstacles to recovery occur (Livneh and Antonak 1997). Behaviors associated with externalized hostility include demanding and critical attitudes, accusations, and passive-aggressive ways of blocking medical treatment.

Sanders describes the next phase of **conservation/withdrawal** as a period when an individual reports feeling despair, helplessness, and isolation from their social support. Physiologically, this is due to the prolonged period of stress they have experienced, and the body needs to conserve energy in order to recover. Isolation from social support results both from the individual withdrawing from others, and from others who give less support and move on with their own lives. In medical patients, behaviors such as reporting too much fatigue to actively participate in medical therapies, increased withdrawal from others, and a "giving up" attitude can signify this phase.

The last two phases are periods for **healing** and **renewal** when the individual makes a conscious decision and effort to build their lives again around the loss. In medical patients, this is evidenced by seeking new meaning and setting goals around the constraints of the medical problem. During this phase, patients are more willing to take responsibility for their medical care. They are more readily accepting of the roles they might have given up secondary to the medical illness.

Davis (1987) and Burke and colleagues (1992) describe the grief for chronically ill or disabled patients as "chronic sorrow" because the illnesses require prolonged and unpredictable periods of mourning. The individual must often cope with multiple losses that occur over a period of time, and the potential of death in the future. Burke further describes chronic sorrow as a grief that cannot ultimately be totally resolved, because the patient is reminded of the chronic nature of the illness on a daily basis.

It should be noted that any model of grief or adaptation to loss is mediated by variables such as social support and premorbid coping styles. It is also important to note that the phases of adjustment may often overlap. Some individuals may exhibit symptoms of grief that are debilitating and interfere with their medical care, whereas others may experience painful grief but still remain highly functional.

In summary, the process of grieving, whether it's mourning the loss of a loved one or of losses to oneself related to a medical illness, is a coping mechanism. The process allows healthy individuals to withdraw emotional attachment from a love object (a person or parts of the self) and to appropriately reattach to other objects and readjust life. Although a necessary process, it can be profoundly painful and is often accompanied by increased somatic complaints and increased morbidity and mortality. Moreover, the experience and clinical presentation can vary from person to person based on premorbid personality and coping styles, as well as the unique dynamics related to the loss. Careful examination and follow-up is imperative, however, as the medically ill grieving patient is particularly at risk for the development of a major depression and the related comorbidity that it carries for this population.

Distinguishing Depression from Grief

Several unique challenges are presented to the clinician when assessing bereavement in the medically ill. First, a depressed and often tearful state is normal and expected following a loss, whether the loss is death or losses associated with a medical illness. How then do we separate "normal" grieving from grief complicated by depression? The following guidelines can assist in making a differential of primary depression from normal grief.

- The first step is to recognize the normal process of grieving. During the first several weeks after a loss, difficulty with sleep, appetite, anhedonia, and decreased libido are normal. Depressed mood usually worsens during the first couple of weeks and may also be associated with increase use of alcohol and sedative medications. Vegetative symptoms that go beyond one to two months should raise a concern about major depression. In normal grieving, depressed mood typically shows major improvement by the sixth month and should be restored to normal by the first year. However, it is normal for the patient to experience episodes of depression when memories are triggered, but they are usually less frequent and intense. Although statistics do not demonstrate an increase in overt suicide related to bereavement, it is possible that hidden in the statistics are deaths related to alcohol abuse, particularly in bereaved men over 55 with a past history of alcohol abuse.
- Some researchers have noted that psychomotor retardation in behavior and as evidenced by speech latency may be suggestive of a grief reaction complicated by depression (Ruark et al. 1988).
- Freud (1917) characterized mourning as "a profoundly painful dejection, cessation of interest in the outside world, loss of the capacity to love, and inhibition of all activity." Although it is recognized as an intensely painful process on an emotional level, the individual maintains a positive self-concept. In contrast, patients with "melancholia," his descriptive for depression, suffer from a poor self-image on a chronic basis, which accompanies the emotional pain.
- Guilt experienced by patients who are grieving is usually specifically related to the loss. For example, guilt over actions that they should have taken at the

time of the death or loss. In contrast, patients with depression often experience more generalized guilt; this is usually accompanied by self-deragatory statements, negative perceptions of oneself, and preoccupation with feelings of worthlessness. There is also more variation in the guilt experienced by grieving patients in comparison to those with major depression, who experience more persistent negativity and guilty.

- In a grief reaction, the loss is recognized by significant others who subsequently provide support. In contrast, the loss associated with depression is typically not recognized or supported by significant others.
- Although the bereaved and depressed patients can have hallucinatory experiences, the quality typically differs. With depression the hallucinations are typically auditory and most commonly are consistent with the depressive themes such as being responsible for the death or illness of a loved one, delusions of being punished for inadequacies, voices that berate the person for shortcomings. In bereavement, the person may report transient experiences of seeing the deceased or hearing that person's voice.
- Patients who are grieving often see themselves as normal or without significant symptoms. They may also be resistant to discuss emotional pain related to grieving and instead may channel their distress somatically. Often it is much easier for people to talk about their physical pain as opposed to their emotional pain. Parkes (1972) found a 63 percent increase in physician visits by widows in the first six months after a loss with the primary complaint of anxiety, depression, and insomnia.
- Patients with grief that is complicated by depression typically experience a high death anxiety directed toward themselves and others and often tend to over-idealize the deceased. They can also experience intense anger, numbness, and ongoing restlessness. Behaviorally, patients with complicated grief tend to demonstrate some rigid compulsive behaviors as well as some self-destructive acts.
- Patients with complicated grief are also exquisitely sensitive to future losses. They may become preoccupied with the death or loss and are unable to reinvest energy into functional activities. Therefore, those with complicated grief tend to experience more prolonged functional impairment. They also may experience difficulties in their interpersonal relationships as they tend to fear intimacy and future loss. Therefore, those suffering with a complicated grief reaction may engage in either self-destructive relationships—where they remain emotionally distant and "safe" from loss—or replacement relationships—where they can engage in compulsive caregiving to manage the grief.

Delirium and Dementia

Among consultation requests to evaluate depression, 54 percent were diagnosed with an organic brain disorder (Boland 1993). The clinical presentation of depression among the medically ill and among organic brain disorders (such as delirium and dementia) can share similar symptoms making a differential diagnosis often difficult. Shared symptoms of these disorders can include an apathetic appearance, decreased concentration and memory, psychomotor changes, sleep disturbances, fatigue, loss of interest in activities, increased dependency, and other personality changes.

The term "delirium" is used to describe a disturbance of consciousness and a change in cognition over a short period of time. Hallmark symptoms include a reduced clarity of awareness with deficits in ability to focus, sustain, and shift attention. Patients are usually disoriented to time, then place, followed by person. Speech can be rambling, irrelevant, and incoherent at times. Thinking is often perseverative and tangential. There can be reversal of sleep-wake cycles, psychomotor retardation or agitation as evidenced by picking at bedding, attempting to get out of bed, or slowing in responses. Although in later stages hallucinations can be present, early perceptual disturbances can occur: misperceptions, illusions, bugs crawling. A hallmark symptom of delirium is the rapid fluctuations of symptoms, exacerbated in P.M. hours with more acute confusion and related behavior changes. For example, pulling out IV lines, getting dressed and attempting to leave the hospital, and cursing or screaming.

Emotionally, delirious patients can experience anxiety and depression. There is typically rapid fluctuations in these mood states, making it easier to distinguish from primary depression. In the early mild stages of delirium, however, these shifts may not be readily seen and subsequently may result in hospital personnel viewing the patient as depressed due to the apathetic and withdrawn appearance. In addition, fear typically accompanies delirium and in the early stages may be interpreted as being related to depression. That is, staff may view a fearful, emotionally labile, depressed patient as suffering from a primary depression. However, serial examinations may reveal fluctuations in this presentation that are more consistent with delirium. In addition to serial exams, review of the medical history and treatment may help to identify the underlying etiology, and information from family members regarding onset and history may assist with distinguishing dementia from depression.

A more difficult differential exists with dementia and depression. Dementia can be categorized as dementia of the Alzheimer's type (AD), vascular dementia (VaD), dementia due to HIV disease, dementia due to head trauma, dementia due to Parkinson's disease, dementia due to Huntington's disease, dementia due to Pick's disease, dementia due to Creutzfeldt-Jakob, dementia due to other medical conditions, dementia due to substance-induced persisting dementia, and dementia due to multiple etiologies. Although each of these disorders are differentiated base on etiology, they share common symptoms. An essential symptom of dementia is the development of cognitive deficits, particularly memory. There may also be disturbances in executive functions (planning, organizing, sequencing, and abstracting). For the purposes of this book, we will not review the difference in presentation for each of the above types of dementia. However, it is important to note that a diagnosis cannot be made during the course of a delirium. After the delirium has cleared, residual deficits can be evaluated to determine whether a patient suffers from dementia or depression.

Patients who are suffering from a major depressive disorder typically will not perform well on mental status exams or neuropsychological testing. This is particularly true among the elderly where cognitive and sensory deficits make the distinction between dementia and depression more complicated. In the evaluation process several issues can guide the differential process.

- Conduct a thorough evaluation of the medical chart, including history of onset for the symptoms of mood and cognitive changes, examination of changes in lab values suggestive of endocrine conditions such as hypothyroidism, hypercalcemia, and hypoglycemia, as well as evidence for structural lesions, infectious processes, and nutritional deficiencies such thiamin, niacin, and B_{12}. Each of these conditions can cause delirium, dementia, and can clinically present with depressive symptoms. Medical correction of these conditions will often improve the cognitive and emotional deficits. Once these conditions are treated, any residual deficits can be more accurately evaluated for a differential of depression.

- Evaluate the temporal sequencing of the deficits, the course of the clinical presentation, and any related family history. The premorbid history of patients with dementia should show a gradual and steady decline in functioning. Oftentimes subtle changes will go unnoticed by family members until the deficits begin to interfere with safety or management. On close examination, however, family members can frequently recall changes that predate the current onset. In contrast, the cognitive deficits observed in patients with major depression usually have an onset that coincides with the onset of the depression.

- Performance on neuropsychological tests demonstrates some differences that can aid in the differential between dementia and depression. Weingartner (1986) found that cognitive processes that to require greater effort are more impaired in depressed patients. Tasks that require great attentional capacity are termed *effortful* as opposed to those that require little attention, which are called *autonomic* (Hasher and Zacks 1979). Craik and McDowd (1987) found that recall memory requires more effort than recognition memory for both younger and older adults. Further, when depressed older adults were compared to age-matched controls, they were found to be more impaired on free recall tasks as compared to recognition. This data is consistent with the theory that there is decreased effort of memory processing among depressed patients (Blau and Ober 1988). However, mild to moderately demented patients of the Alzheimer's type (AD) demonstrated deficits in both recall and recognition (Corkin 1982). Therefore, comparison of recall and recognition memory tasks appears to be helpful in making a differential between mildly demented AD patients and those with depression.

- Rates of forgetting can also be an important indicator for depression versus dementia. Depressed individuals appear to learn and remember less well under situations that require effortful processing. However, depressed patients show normal storage as indicated by rate of forgetting once learning of the material has occurred. In contrast, mildly demented AD patients appear to show rapid rates of forgetting even when learning occurred under ideal conditions. This appears to reflect the damage thought to occur in the hippocampal region in the early stages of AD (Moss et al. 1986).

- Patients who are depressed and demented represent a rather heterogenous group, given the many different types of dementia. For example, some patients may have a primary dementing illness, such as Alzheimer's or a vascular dementia, coupled with depression and will continue to have cognitive deficits even after the depression is treated. Another group of patients may present cognitive deficits as a result of the depression and after it is treated may demonstrate marked improvements in their cognitive and emotional deficits.

- Cummings (1989) provided a review of suggested features to examine, which may assist with raising or lowering suspicion of either diagnosis. Keep in mind that a definitive diagnosis may not be possible as research to date has not clearly been able to differentiate the various types of dementia from depression. However, the following features can assist in distinguishing Alzheimer's disease from depression. First, for the depressed patients, the duration of time for seeking medical attention is shorter, and they tend to complain about their deficits, as compared to AD patients who are less likely to seek attention and often do not complain consistently about the deficits. A previous psychiatric history is more typical of depressed patients than those with AD. With a depressed individual, changes in mood are typically more persistent and all-pervasive regardless of the circumstances. In contrast, patients with AD have mood changes that are often responsive to environmental changes.

The prognosis for patients who suffer with concomitant depression and dementia remains unclear (Kazniak and Christenson 1994). Some investigators have reported that 89 percent of patients with concomitant depression and dementia who were treated for the depression, eventually developed dementia over an 18-year period (Rabins et al. 1984). However, others have found that when depression was successfully treated in patients with concomitant illness that mood and cognitive deficits remained stable over a two-year follow-up (Kral and Emery 1989). In part, the mixed findings may be due to the fact that an early indicator for dementia can be depression in the absence of cognitive deficits. Reding, Haycox, and Blass (1985) showed that over a three-year interval of time 16 of 28 depressed patients who originally did not present with a dementia, went on to develop dementia. Therefore, it is recommended that these patients be targeted for periodic reevaluations.

Personality Disorders

Certain personality disorders are characterized by feelings of worthlessness and guilt. The differential between a personality or depressive disorder is based on history. If these cognitive self-derogatory sentiments predated the onset of a depressed mood or anhedonia then they are most likely related to the character disorder and not to an affective disorder.

Post-Traumatic Stress Disorder (PTSD)

The clinical term used to describe the psychological sequelae that may follow exposure to a traumatic event is called post-traumatic stress disorder (PTSD). Although PTSD was recognized by the American Psychiatric Association in 1980 (in the DSM-III), it remains one of the least understood and appreciated psychiatric disorders (Matsakis 1994).

Typically PTSD is thought to be associated with combat veterans who experience flashbacks to battle. However, PTSD can be the result of trauma associated with natural disasters, domestic violence, rape, accidents, medical procedures (being intubated or cardioverted), medical illnesses (delirium, suffering a heart attack, surgery), sexual abuse, and working in professions with constant life-or-death situations. Matsakis (1994) argues that although the above group of victims appear to be quite divergent they all share the experience of having been rendered helpless in a situation of great danger. Although as with any psychiatric condition the presentation of PTSD can vary based on individual coping strategies, past experiences, predisposition to certain psychiatric complications such as anxiety and depression, symptoms of PTSD typically include insomnia, nightmares, depression, anger, anxiety, substance abuse, and increased psychosomatic complaints.

Langer (1987) found significant depression among 50 percent of those individuals with PTSD. It is a common presenting concern of individuals who have experienced trauma (Herman 1992). The depression may be a result of the trauma or may preexist the trauma. Matsakis describes trauma as a "wounding of the emotions, the spirit, the will to live, belief about the self and the world, one's dignity, and one's sense of security" (Matsakis 1994, p. 28). It is amazing that in a population that is frequently traumatized by invasive procedures, loss of security and self-image, and threats to a sense of logical predictability to life, that we seldom consider or recognize PTSD among the medically ill. Moreover, the medical environment is rich with potential triggers for patients who suffer PTSD.

In attempting to make a diagnosis of depression in the medically ill, a differential diagnosis of PTSD must be considered. Both conditions share symptoms of insomnia and related restlessness, difficulty concentrating, hypervigilance, anhedonia, suicidal thoughts, social isolation, guilt, self-blame, and depressed mood. Medical patients with a premorbid condition of PTSD may be continually exposed to triggers for the trauma, which may result in avoidant and noncompliant behavior. Consider the following case:

> John was a patient with end-stage renal disease who was undergoing hemodialysis treatments three times a week. During the process of hemodialysis, blood is removed from the patient's body through a visible tube, cleaned by the dialysis machine, and recirculated back into the body. The staff noted that John appeared depressed. He was withdrawn, agitated, tearful, and was frequently not showing up for his scheduled treatments. At first glance, John did indeed appear depressed and on examination of his life certainly had every reason to be depressed. For example, he was recently in the process of a divorce, started dialysis just six months prior and was physically not feeling very well. A diagnosis of adjustment disorder with depressed mood could have been made at this point. However,

> with a more thorough examination the following information was revealed: At the age of six, John witnessed the suicide of his mother who shot herself in the head while he stood three feet away from her. He recalls that "there was blood all over me and I couldn't breathe. I would have nightmares for years hearing the gun and seeing the blood." It became clear that the dialysis process was triggering flashbacks and that John had been suffering for many years with PTSD.

When making a differential of PTSD or major depression, inquire about family and personal history of depression that predated the trauma. Obtain information about substance abuse. Often patients who suffer with PTSD will abuse substances to manage depression related to the disorder. Finally, depression may be a response that medical patients who suffer with PTSD are experiencing as a result of numerous triggers in the environment. It is imperative to understand and recognize these triggers as they may increase morbidity and mortality via depression and noncompliant behavior.

Chapter 5

Other Mood Disorders

Bipolar Disorders

Bipolar disorders are classified as mood disorders with the essential feature of one or more manic episodes usually accompanied by one or more major depressive episodes. A manic episode is defined as a predominantly expansive, elevated, or irritable mood, which persists for at least a week. Hypomania is defined as a manic episode whereby the mood is not severe enough to interfere with functioning in social or occupational areas and does not warrant hospitalization. Delusions may be present with a manic episode but is never present in the less severe case of hypomania.

The DSM-IV distinguishes between four different types of bipolar disorders. These include bipolar I disorders, bipolar II disorders, cyclothymia, and bipolar disorders not otherwise specified (NOS). The essential feature of **bipolar I disorder** is the existence of at least one or more manic episodes. This is a recurrent disorder with more than 90 percent of patients experiencing subsequent episodes of mania after a single manic episode. Further, 60 to 70 percent of manic episodes occur after a major depressive episode (DSM-IV). The distinction between bipolar I and major depression is made based on history of at least one manic episode in the past that cannot be better accounted for as substance-induced or medically related, which is referred to as secondary mania. Secondary mania can occur as part of hyperthyroidism or during the course of a delirium whose etiology could be withdrawal or intoxication from a medication or infection. Obtaining a careful history is essential to ascertain if this manic episode was in relationship to the initiation or discontinuation of any medications, occurred during the course of a hospitalization, or was accompanied by other cognitive deficits.

Bipolar II disorder is characterized by the occurrence of one or more major depressive disorders accompanied by at least one hypomanic episode, not simple elation or euthymia, for several days following improvement of major depression. History from close friends and relatives may be necessary to diagnose a hypomanic episode, since many patients do not view their behavior or mood as unusual. As with all of the bipolar disorders, the symptoms must be severe enough to alter functioning in important areas of one's life. Among the medically ill, this disruption in functioning may affect management of medications, follow-up with medical appointments, and other related healthy behaviors.

The importance of accurately recognizing a bipolar disorder in the medically ill is underscored by the increased risk for suicide. The prevalence for completed suicide, usually during a depressive episode, is 10 to 15 percent for patients with a bipolar I or bipolar II disorder. This figure, coupled with the already increased risk for suicide among patients with chronic medical illness, highlights the need for aggressive treatment. The bipolar disorders are typically associated with eating disorders, substance abuse, and borderline personality disorders.

Cyclothymic disorder is characterized by a chronic, fluctuating mood disturbance involving numerous periods of hypomanic and depressive symptoms. Overall, the symptoms for both is not as severe or pervasive and the number of symptoms does not meet criteria for either for a major depressive or manic episode. Cyclothymia is diagnosed when after the initial two-year period of symptoms, the patient did not experience a major depression or manic episode. After the initial two-year period of time, manic or both depressive and manic episode can be superimposed on the cyclothymic disorder; then both diagnoses are given.

Bipolar disorder NOS is used when the clinical picture does not meet criteria for the above disorders.

For the purposes of this book, our focus in this section has been primarily on the differential between primary depression and depression which may be part of a bipolar diagnosis. For a more complete description of mania and secondary mania, which is diagnosed as mood disorder due to a general medical condition, with manic feature, the readers are referred to the *American Psychiatric Textbook of Consultation-Liaison Psychiatry* (Rundell and Wise 1996).

Substance-Induced Mood Disorder

There are several medications and substances that can be associated with depressive symptoms. It is important to note, however, that caution must be used when determining that a medication has caused a depression if you have not already ruled out that the depression is linked to the illness or an adjustment reaction to the illness itself. Depressive symptoms should remit when the dosage of the medication is decreased. It is more likely in some medically ill patients that depressive symptoms are a result of a combination of all three factors. It can be difficult to initially determine which of the above-noted factors is causing depressive symptoms. Addressing the potential contribution of a medication side effect to depression can be a good starting point in the treatment of depressive symptoms in the medically ill. The following is a description of medications and substances known to be strongly associated with depressive symptoms. If you or the patient suspect that a particular medication may be causing depressive symptoms, refer the patient back to the physician. The physician should be able to guide the patient in either exploring other medication options or possibly discontinuing the medication.

Steroids

The prevalence rate for steroid-related psychiatric side effects is around 6 percent (Kershner and Wang-Cheng 1989). Steroids have been associated with a variety of psychiatric reactions. Lewis and Smith (1983) found that, of patients who have psychiatric symptom-reactions to steroids, 40 percent have depression, 28 percent have hypomania, 8 percent have mixed symptoms of depression and mania, 14 percent experience psychotic symptoms, and 10 percent have delirium. The most important factor in steroid reactions is the dosage. Less than 2 percent of patients receiving under 40 mg/day of prednisone will develop psychiatric symptoms, compared to 4 to 6 percent who receive 41 to 80 mg/day and 18.4 percent who receive more than 80 mg/day (Rundell and Wise 1996). Symptoms may develop in the first week of treatment and usually takes about four to six weeks to resolve after adjustment or cessation of the dosage (Hall et al. 1979). A low dose of a psychiatric medication is helpful in treating an acute steroid-reaction episode, and sometimes lithium is prescribed as a preventive treatment for acute depressive reaction in patients requiring large doses of steroids (Kershner and Wang-Cheng 1989).

Antihypertensive Medications

Hypertension is usually treated using one of three drug classes, each of which attacks a different component of the blood pressure control system. However, the current antihypertensives commonly in use (greater than 80 percent of all hypertensive patients), calcium channel blockers and angiotensin converting enzyme (ACE) inhibitors, are rarely associated with depression. Diuretics can cause weakness and malaise secondary to electrolyte changes that can be confused with depressive symptoms (Beers and Passman 1990). The following antihypertensive medications have been associated with depressive symptoms as a side effect:

Reserpine

Although it is used in less than 2 percent of all hypertensive patients, approximately 20 percent of patients receiving reserpine for hypertension will have depressive symptoms. The period between exposure to reserpine and onset of depressive symptoms is about 4 to 6 months (Zelnik 1987). Depression symptoms are thought to be caused by depletion of serotonin, norepinephrine, and dopamine (Hall et al. 1980). Depression is seen more often at doses greater than 0.5 mg/day (Ganzini et al. 1993). Anxiety, lack of guilt, and lack of feelings of worthlessness distinguish reserpine-induced depression from major depression (Beers and Passman 1990). The most reliable predictor of reserpine-induced depression is a prior episode of depression, suggesting a predisposition for vulnerability to a medication-induced depressive reaction.

Pascualy and Veith (1989) found that this occurs in more than 50 percent of patients who experience depression as an adverse reaction. Prior family history is also a risk factor.

Methyldopa

About 10 percent of patients taking methyldopa (Aldomet) experience mild to moderate depression (Hall et al. 1980). Onset of depression is rapid, occurring within a few days of beginning the drug. Symptoms include agitation, anxiety, weeping, and suicidal ideation. The symptoms are thought to be caused by depletion of serotonin and dopamine (Beers and Passman 1990). Discontinuation of methyldopa brought relief of depressive symptoms within a week for most patients (Paykel et al. 1982). Once again, prior history of depression is a risk factor.

Beta-Blockers

There are mixed reports of depression induced by beta-blockers. Hall and colleagues (1980) estimated that some depression occurs in 30 to 50 percent of patients taking significant doses of propanolol. Petrie and colleagues (1982) reported that the severity of depression was related to dosage, but also reported that because fatigue and malaise are side effects of these medications, caution should be used when using these symptoms to diagnose depression. Zelnik (1987) concluded that patients taking b-blockers who became depressed typically had a past or family history of depression. Depressive symptoms usually cleared within a week after discontinuation of the medication.

Benzodiazepines

Benzodiazepines are associated with depression, particularly at higher doses (Smith and Salzman 1991). Patients receiving more than 40 mg/day of diazepam may experience some depressive symptoms: feelings of worthlessness, impaired concentration, anxiety, and suicidal ideation (Hall and Joffe 1972). Tiller and Schweitzer (1992) argue that this type of depression is seen because benzodiazepines uncover depressive symptoms seen in agitated patients with depression.

Oral Contraceptives

Depressive symptoms are associated with the amount of estrogen compared with progesterone in oral contraceptives. Current low-dose estrogen contraceptives usually do not cause major depression according to DSM criteria (Patten and Lamarre 1992). Women who have mood changes related to periods of hormonal shifts (such as premenstrual syndrome, childbirth, and menopause) are more at risk for mood reactions to oral contraceptives (O'Hara et al. 1991; Steiner 1992).

Chemotherapy Medication

A variety of chemotherapy medications such as vincristine, vinblastine, procarbazine, amphotericin, and interferon have been associated with depression (Rundell and Wise 1996). Physical changes to the body from these agents can occur, leading to adjustment reactions secondary to functional impairment. In addition, many cancer patients are also prescribed corticosteroids, thereby increasing risk of depressive reactions (Massie and Holland 1990).

Cimetidine and Ranitidine

Cimetidine (Tagamet) and ranitidine (Zantac), H_2-receptor agonists, are commonly prescribed for treatment of peptic ulcers and gastritis. There are some incidents of depression (1 to 5 percent) induced by these agents (Pascualy and Veith 1989). Onset of depression occurs within three days to several weeks after beginning the medication and resolves within 7 to 14 days after discontinuation.

Psychoactive Substances

Alcohol, opiates, and amphetamine withdrawal can cause a substance-induced mood disorder according to DSM-IV. Depression is common among those who abuse drugs. Major depression among substance abusers increases suicide risk, marital problems, and decreases prognosis for abstinence and recovery (Mueller et al. 1993).

Alcohol

Some individuals develop an alcohol-induced mood disorder that meets criteria for DSM major depression (Dackis et al. 1986). At higher doses, alcohol can cause dysphoric mood. Most alcohol-induced mood states resolve within one to two weeks following abstinence (Davidson and Ritson 1993). A thorough assessment from the patient and family members regarding the severity of alcohol use is the first step in making this diagnosis. Vitamin deficiencies can result from prolonged and heavy alcohol use, subsequently contributing to depressive symptoms.

Opiates

The use of opiates is associated with depressive symptoms, possibly as a result of changes in the neurotransmitter (endorphins, noradrenergic, and cortisol) systems in the brain (Dackis and Gold 1992). Opiate-related depression persists after abstinence, therefore antidepressant medication is effective (Dackis and Gold 1992).

Cocaine and Amphetamine Withdrawal

Withdrawal from cocaine and amphetamines begins within hours of abstinence, lasts for about three days, and is characterized by irritability, depressive symptoms, and anxiety (Satel et al. 1991). The depressive symptoms are caused by depletion of dopamine and norepinephrine (Dackis and Gold 1992). Even though symptoms of depression can range from mild dysthymia to major depression, antidepressant medication is helpful in treatment (Gawin and Kleber 1984).

A Note on Treatment of Substance Abuse

The use of substances should be assessed during the initial clinical interview. Many patients will deny that they abuse alcohol or other substances such as marijuana due to a belief that these are not harmful substances and are more socially acceptable. Patients will also underestimate how much alcohol by saying "I just have a couple here and there to unwind." A more detailed assessment should be done if substance abuse is suspected, particularly if the patient is referred for treatment of depression. The regular use of substances to cope with depressed affect will interfere with ability to participate fully in treatment. Many patients will also suffer from depression if they have a strong history of substance abuse, and the sudden onset of medical condition forces them to abstain from use. It is not uncommon to see patients in the medical setting appear depressed not simply as an adjustment reaction to being in the hospital but as a function of not having ready access to their substance of choice. If substance abuse is determined to be a problem, referral for substance abuse treatment is recommended. If the problem is severe, the patient, when medically stable, may consider entering an inpatient treatment program followed by an aftercare program. Outpatient support groups like Alcoholics Anonymous are important adjuncts to treatment.

Part III

Therapeutic Interventions for Depression in the Medically Ill

Chapter 6

The Patient's Introduction to Therapy

We have already discussed numerous reasons why depression is frequently not recognized or adequately treated by medical personnel; but why are *patients* so willing to suffer and endure the pain and despair of depression without asking or seeking help? In part, medical patients are often embarrassed about how they feel because they don't view depression as a "real" illness like they do their current medical condition. Subsequently, patients often minimize or deny depression for fear of being viewed as "weak." This belief is often expressed in statements like, "I just need to get it together and I'll be fine," "I'm just tired," or "I'm alive, so what do I have to be depressed about?" It is as if they have not given themselves *permission* to be depressed.

Another reason that depressed patients are often willing to suffer is the belief that there is nothing anybody can do to help. "Why bother? What's the point?" These feelings of personal helplessness and hopelessness are hallmark symptoms of major depression. This set of beliefs can actually prevent the patient from taking active steps to treat the depression. Ironically, clinicians often expect depressed patients—patients without hope, confidence, or energy—to actively participate in their medical care and work on improving their depression.

The very nature of depression leaves the individual feeling inadequate, overwhelmed, and pessimistic about the future. Therefore, when initiating therapy with a patient who is depressed, it is important and perhaps imperative that you provide direction and focus for the patient. The initial establishment of concrete goals and strategies will give the patient hope in the possibility for change, while also minimizing the patient's feelings of inadequacy to participate in his or her own recovery. This should not be interpreted as the clinician taking control and directing the patient to "well-being" as the clinician defines it. Rather, in the initial phase of treatment you should take an active, goal-oriented position at a time when the patient feels hopeless, directionless and incapable of making decisions. As the treatment progresses, control and energy can begin to shift slowly to the patient.

Understanding the Medical Patient's Frame of Reference

The first step in beginning to establish goals is to develop an appreciation for the general point of view of a medically ill patient. Remember, medically ill patients are often not requesting psychological services and may be, at the very least, guarded about the prospects of interacting with a "shrink."

Your evaluation of the patient's experience and frame of reference for the depression should include assessing the patient's degree of discomfort, identifying which symptoms are interfering the most with the patient's functioning, and understanding the style or personality of the patient. For example, a patient with an avoidant personality may have great difficulty revealing feelings of depression for fear of being rejected or criticized. You may find it easier to discuss the depression by focusing on the somatic symptoms such as poor energy, sleep problems, and bodily aches. A medical patient with an avoidant personality may become particularly overwhelmed and subsequently depressed as the medical condition forces them to rely on others, something which they actively avoid as a way of emotionally protecting themselves. An understanding of the patient's style, and the depressive symptoms which create the greatest distress for him or her, will guide you in the establishment of goals and treatment strategies.

By focusing on therapeutic strategies that deal directly with the symptoms that are the most troublesome to the patient, you reinforce that you understand the *patient's* experience of the depression. This connection serves to build trust and rapport. Once trust has been established, you can begin to treat the different symptom clusters of the depression starting with those symptoms that are least defended against and proceeding to those that are most defended. Most medical patients are more eager to discuss the physical aspects of their emotional discomfort because it more closely mirrors their medical illness, and therefore is more acceptable and "real." They may, however, be rather guarded and fearful of feeling out of control, sad, tearful, and inadequate. Therefore, a strategy in which the clinician *joins* the patient in establishing treatment goals to address the presented concerns, without imposing a need to treat all of the symptoms at one time or targeting those which the clinician deems most salient, is more likely to be successful.

Discuss Confidentiality

The patient's introduction into the therapy process should begin with a discussion of confidentiality. If treatment is initiated while the patient is in the hospital, issues regarding privacy and charting of information is a good place to begin. You and the patient should agree upon what information will and will not be included in the medical chart within the required limitations (for instance, suicidal or homicidal intent must be charted). Engaging the patient in a discussion about confidential information reinforces that the two of you are acting as a team in making important therapeutic decisions. This collaboration is critical; it both establishes a trusting therapeutic relationship and also empowers the patient to make decisions. For a patient, this sense of control is often felt to be absent in the physician-patient relationship. Patients who feel some sense of control typically cope better and experience less depression.

The following guidelines are recommended when approaching issues of confidentiality:

Be Selective with Labels.

Include information in the general medical chart which is deemed to be necessary and relevant for optimal care of the patient by the medical team. This may include information about the patient's *style* of interacting followed by recommendations for staff to facilitate optimal care and management of the depression. Do not use labels that may interfere with the staff's interaction with the patient. A label such as borderline personality disorder in a general medical chart is not only clinically limited but potentially harmful. Frequently, a label such as this may influence and alter the interactions of the general medical staff with the patient. An alternative strategy may involve simply describing the disorder as a "style of interacting" which is characterized by intense fears of abandonment and affective instability. This can then be followed by recommendations for the staff on strategies to minimize the affective instability and the coexisting depressive symptoms. This strategy provides a description of the behavior with strategies for care, as opposed to a clinical label that, to medical staff unfamiliar with psychological disorders, may result in doctors being *even more* distant with the already isolated patient.

Leave Off Sensitive Information.

Personal information such as sexual abuse history should not be included in the general medical charts. Only information that is judged to be related to overall care and the understanding of the patient's mood and behavior should be included. For example, if a female patient reveals that examination by a male doctor makes her quite anxious, tearful, and depressed because of a past sexual trauma, specific, detailed information regarding the trauma should not be included in the medical chart. Rather, information in a general format with specific recommendations is suggested: "Patient experiences increased distress when examined or left alone with male clinician. Would recommend female clinician examine patient if possible or a female to be present during male examination." This would be an example of maintaining the patient's confidence and privacy while the patient continues to function as a member of a team whose primary goal is communication of information that will improve the overall well-being of the patient. The specific information to be included in the chart should be discussed with the patient for approval. *This is essential if trust is to be maintained.* Therefore, this conversation offers a great means of connecting with the patient.

Only Provide Clinically Useful Information.

Information regarding progress and focus of the treatment process may be included in the medical chart. This may be documented as "depressed mood decreased, sleep improved, anhedonia and poor concentration still present." This will give the general staff information to guide their treatment and expectations of the patient. For example, if concentration and memory are still poor as a result of the depression, then the staff may need to present information regarding dietary restrictions or medication regimens in a concrete, written, and repetitive fashion to accommodate these symptoms. However, detailed information regarding feelings of poor self-esteem and inadequacies that are not influencing or being influenced by the current medical condition should not be included.

Examine the Patient's Expectations and Fears Regarding Therapy

Inquire about the patient's expectations and fears regarding psychological treatment. Medical patients are typically sensitive about participating in psychotherapy because their primary reason for being in a hospital or clinic is medical in nature. They usually have not requested help for any psychological problems and therefore may worry that someone has said that they are "crazy." It is important to focus on the depressive symptoms and how they may be interfering with their medical condition and overall quality of life. Educate the patient about the therapy process. An example for introduction to this process for medical patients is included below. It is not recommended that the information below be read to the patient or given to the patient to read but rather should be used as a guide for you, the clinician.

> "Depression" is a word used to describe negative emotions that can interfere with your relationships, your ability to enjoy life, and your physical health. It is also important for you to know that depression does not necessarily mean that you feel sad; you can feel irritable, anxious, or just plain disinterested with parts of your life. Depressed people often report feeling that activities, events, and even people in their lives that used to make them happy no longer do so. As a result, many depressed people feel that life is not worth living anymore and some attempt to take their own lives while others simply stop taking care of themselves. Many medical patients who are depressed admit to feeling that following their diet, taking their medication, and regularly following up for treatments is not as important to them as it used to be.
>
> Antidepressant medication and therapy are two forms of treatment for depression. The most effective treatment is the combined use of *both* therapy and medication, in much the same way that taking care of yourself *and* receiving treatment from your physician work together to provide the best treatment for your medical condition. Therapy is a collaborative process

between you and the therapist. This means that together you and the therapist need to identify your symptoms of depression and how they may be interfering with your life. The process of treating depression will involve you monitoring which thoughts, behaviors, physical symptoms, and social interactions tend to make the feelings of depression worse or better. Strategies for improving depression will include increasing your coping skills by enhancing social support and learning time-management techniques and problem-solving skills.

Identify Symptoms of Depression

The clustering of symptoms, as well as the level of impairment related to the symptoms, is often different for each patient. Some symptoms of depression are not even recognized by patients as related to depression. It is important for patients to be able to identify their personal symptoms of depression so that they will be able to monitor any improvements or exacerbation of the depression. This is another way to make the patient an active participant in the therapeutic process; monitoring symptoms can also serve as an objective gauge for therapeutic gains. To identify the pattern of depressive symptoms, ask the patient to check the symptoms in the handout (on pages 80–81) that they may be experiencing either related to their medical condition or to other low points in their lives. This checklist can be used at any point throughout the therapeutic process to monitor symptoms.

Organizing Symptoms

Which symptoms and feelings apply to you?

Physically Ill Pattern

- ❑ low energy
- ❑ difficulty with your sleep
- ❑ poor concentration
- ❑ poor memory
- ❑ frequent headaches
- ❑ poor appetite
- ❑ nausea
- ❑ get tired easily
- ❑ pain that you normally have seems worse
- ❑ decreased desire for sex
- ❑ want to sleep all the time

Anxious Pattern

- ❑ short-tempered
- ❑ cry more
- ❑ feel like you are "jumping out of your skin"
- ❑ worry a lot
- ❑ can't sit still
- ❑ poor memory
- ❑ no interest in activities
- ❑ feel an internal energy, but no desire to act on it
- ❑ trouble concentrating on reading or television programs
- ❑ can't get organized

Pessimistic Pattern

- ❑ feel hopeless
- ❑ negative expectations
- ❑ negative self-evaluation
- ❑ suicidal thoughts or wishes
- ❑ feel that you might as well be dead
- ❑ ambivalence about living
- ❑ dwell more on the past than the present or future
- ❑ feel worthless

- ❑ wish that you would just not wake up
- ❑ rarely smile or laugh
- ❑ lost sense of humor

Angry Pattern

- ❑ increased irritability
- ❑ extreme feelings of anger
- ❑ low self-esteem
- ❑ become enraged quite easily
- ❑ "giving up" behavior, stop taking medication, pay little attention to diet or medical limitations
- ❑ hypercritical of others
- ❑ reckless behavior
- ❑ increased alcohol use
- ❑ initiation of or increased substance abuse
- ❑ easily irritated
- ❑ recurrent nightmares

Isolated Pattern

- ❑ feel emotionally detached from others
- ❑ want to sleep a lot
- ❑ hide from others
- ❑ frequently call in sick to work
- ❑ feel content to sit alone
- ❑ feel irritated when others attempt to help
- ❑ not interested in talking to anyone

Dependent pattern

- ❑ feel scared
- ❑ cry easily
- ❑ feel insecure
- ❑ ambivalent
- ❑ difficulty making any decisions
- ❑ worry about decision making
- ❑ have a chronic knot in your stomach
- ❑ want others around all of the time
- ❑ afraid to be alone

Identify where the majority of symptoms cluster. Most patients are surprised to realize that these symptoms are indeed related to their depression. Once patients are able to recognize the presentation of their depression and the impact that it has on their relationships as well as their medical condition, they are more likely to engage in actively working on improving it. As part of engaging the patient into the therapeutic process, it is important to help them differentiate between the shared and unique symptoms of their depression with the depressive symptoms of their medical condition.

Depression is often under-diagnosed by clinicians because the symptoms overlap with many medical conditions. This can make a differential diagnosis difficult. Similarly, *patients* frequently struggle to identify what symptoms are depression. It is helpful for patients to understand that many symptoms of their depression are *shared* with their medical condition. Describe for the patient how symptoms of depression can be freestanding and can also exacerbate shared symptoms. As they become comfortable with recognizing their own unique pattern of depression independent of their medical condition, they will be in a better position to catch depression in the early stages. This understanding can lead to the patient feeling better, which in turn can lead to improving his or her physical functioning and overall quality of life.

Below is a list of several common medical illnesses that have shared symptoms with depression. This strategy of demonstrating shared symptoms can be utilized with other conditions as well.

Symptoms of Depression and ESRD/Dialysis

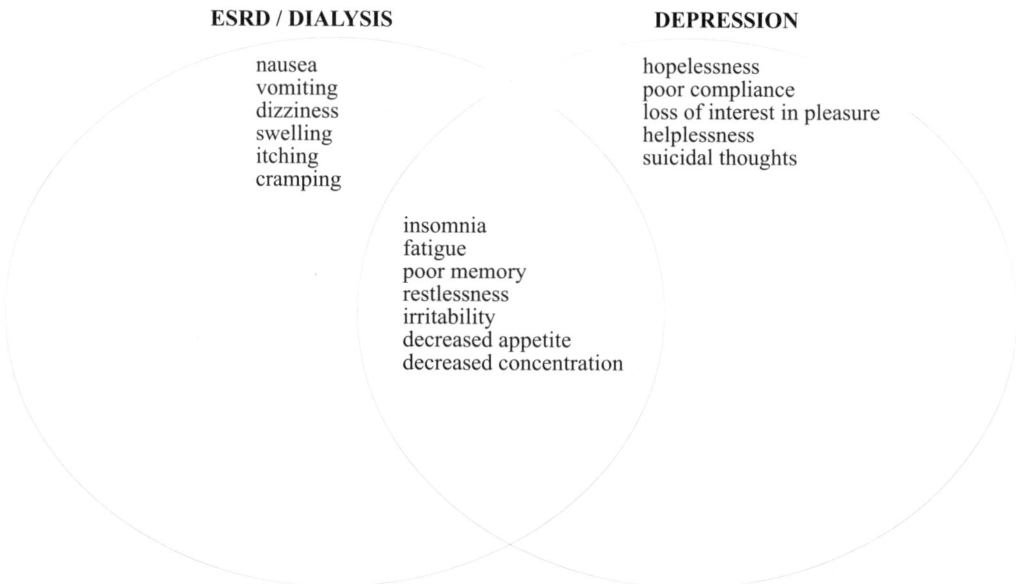

Symptoms of Depression and Coronary Heart Disease

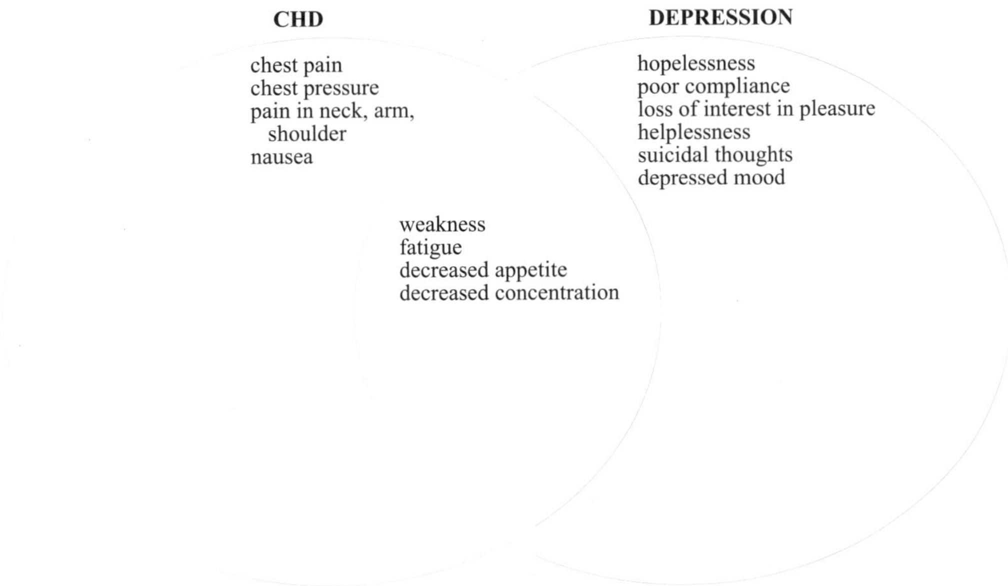

Symptoms of Depression and Hypothyroidism

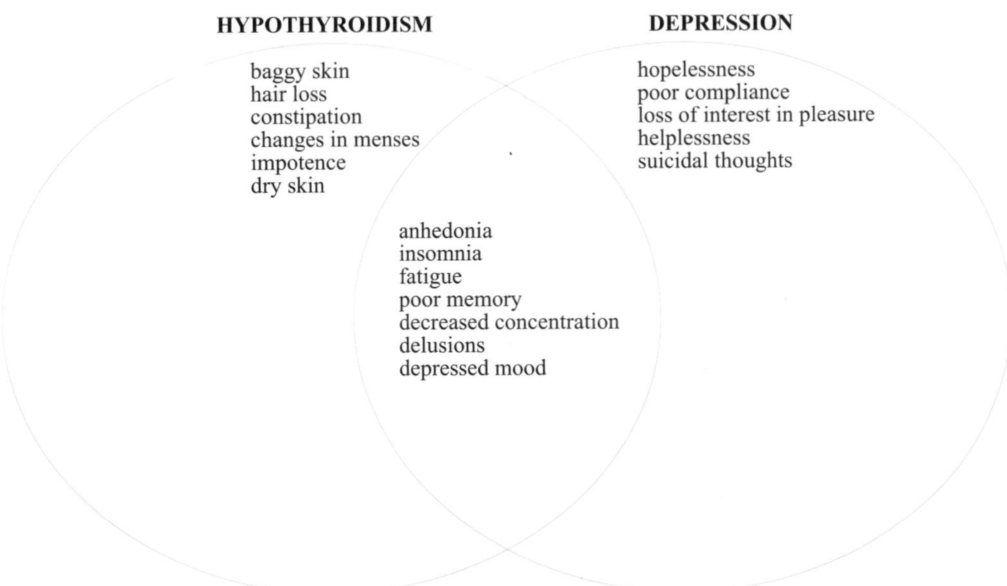

Establish Goals and Expectations of Psychological Treatment

Patients with major depression typically have lost hope, direction, and the energy to work at making things better. They can easily become overwhelmed and discouraged with minor setbacks. Therefore, it is essential to include the patient as an active participant in the formulation of goals for treatment. These goals need to be broken down into sub-goals with measurable objective indicators. The use of sub-goals allows patients to experience a sense of accomplishment, which serves to increase motivation, rally energy, and increase feelings of hope and confidence; moreover, it is important that these goals be personally relevant to the patient.

When formulating these goals, it is important to inquire about the impact that the depression is having on the patient's life and what is, therefore, most important to improve. Keep in mind that depressed patients are often not readily able to answer the kinds of questions necessary to setting practical goals. Depression often interferes with the patient's ability to evaluate their mood and its impact; and the resulting loss of hope makes it difficult to think about improvement for the future. Therefore, when evaluating the patient, the following questions can be used to guide your inquiry into areas of concern without directly confronting the patient about them. For example, asking patients about their life in the past (pre-depression) may provide much information about what triggers depression and what improves their mood without directly asking them about expectations for the future.

To formulate goals for the patient, inquire about the following areas:

- What would be better in your life if you were not depressed?
- How do you define good quality of life?
- Is your definition for quality of life realistic?
- How can you redefine quality of life in light of your medical limitations?

These questions will help you identify what constitutes good quality of life for the patient.

- Are you realistic in your expectations for "life after depression"?

In other words, does the medically ill patient believe that everything will be better when the depression is gone, including physical ailments. Obtaining this information will assist you in establishing realistic goals and expectations for the patient. For example, perhaps helping the patient see that when the depression is improved they may still have pain or still be physically limited but that their tolerance and perception of the pain will be better.

- What triggers depression?
- What makes it worse?

Understanding situational triggers to depression is imperative to preventing relapse. This information can be used with the patient when working on effective coping strategies to avoid or improve these triggers.

- How does depression interfere with relationships?
- How does it interfere with your medical condition?

Given that good social support and compliance is essential to good medical health, it is important to understand how the patient's depression may be interfering with both. Depressed patients tend to isolate themselves and consciously or subconsciously reject support from others. This behavior can also prevent the patient from complying with the medical regimen as they often believe their is no hope or no point in doing so. You need to understand *how* the patient may be rejecting help or passively sabotaging efforts to get them well. This information will lay the foundation for treatment strategies that will follow.

- What is the idiosyncratic meaning of the illness?

A person's body image, the importance placed on physical integrity, and personal beliefs about illness can be very different for each patient. If you are going to help the patient cope with their medical illness and the related depression, you need to understand the personal meaning that the illness has for them. For example, a dancer who can't walk may feel a particular loss in how she identifies herself now. Her entire self-definition may have changed. A patient who was given childhood messages that said "being ill is a sign of weakness or defectiveness" may struggle with issues of self-esteem. Also, if external appearance is particularly important to a patient and the illness has altered it in some way, he or she may be particularly vulnerable to depression related to poor body image.

Suggested Initial Goals

The following are suggested goals for you as the clinician. These goals are not necessarily sequential but rather are key points for you to keep in mind as therapy progresses.

Provide ongoing monitoring of potential overt or covert suicidal ideation.

This will be covered in detail in the suicide chapter. With depressed medical patients it is imperative to continually monitor and evaluate any potential changes in suicidal ideation at every session. The potential for exacerbation of the depression by changes in the medical illness, alteration of medication, or situational changes related to the illness can readily occur in this population. Realize that suicidal ideation can also masquerade as ambivalence regarding living and passive neglect of medical care.

Establish future orientation.

The internal frame of reference for a depressed person is often based on past failures, past pain, and the ongoing struggle with wanting help to feel better but believing that it is futile. As a therapist, you need to be able to tolerate what may be experienced as a passive stance from the patient. In reality, the posture may stem from the above-noted ambivalence or a simple mistrust in the belief or expectation that things can be better.

Non-threatening and indirect strategies can be useful here to anchor the patient to *your* belief that it can get better. In the therapeutic relationship, hope may be fostered. Specific strategies to instill future orientation may include framing the patient's beliefs and feelings as merely a consequence of the depression. This can be done through statements such as "That is your depression talking," or "Everyone who feels depressed views the future as you do." You can provide information about other cases as a way of modeling the normality of what they are feeling in light of the depression and how that feeling and belief system will change as the depression is removed. Below is an example of utilizing modeling and indirect strategies as a way of providing a future orientation of hope:

> Oftentimes patients with similar medical conditions will feel that there is no hope for the future in light of their physical limitations or related changes in their lifestyle. Sometimes they tell me that they feel weak, inadequate, and foolish for feeling depressed, when they should feel grateful for simply being alive. Have you ever felt like that? Once the depression was treated, and it *is* a treatable condition, they no longer viewed the future or their medical condition in the same way. Initially, it was hard for me to help them see that they are not unique or abnormal in the way that they are feeling. Many would say to me, "I know others can get better, but I am weak, and I know I won't be able to." This kind of comparison and evaluation of oneself as not as good or as strong happens to all patients who are experiencing depression. It is simply a symptom of the disorder of depression; it is not reality.

Providing this kind of information establishes your confidence that your patient can get better. Given that you may be the only one in the therapeutic relationship with hope, it is essential that you sabotage the patient's negative expectations and beliefs about social comparison from the onset. Such strategies will *normalize* what many medical patients view as a character flaw; telling a patient how others have improved can instill hope by helping them see that they are not unique in their experience of the depression. This in turn may set the stage for the establishment of a belief in the possibility for the patient's own improvement in the future. This seemingly minor shift in world-view can represent a major step toward mobilizing some energy to begin treatment.

Provide the patient with a brief and concrete strategy for the improvement of the symptoms that *the patient* has identified as most distressing.

Remember that the patient may identify symptoms of poor sleep and restlessness as the most distressing symptom because it is the safest or least emotionally defended. In therapy, you should proceed by addressing improvement of these identified symptoms first. This will reinforce the therapeutic relationship and prevent early termination by the patient. This does not mean that you should not be formulating your own list of distressing or concerning issues from a clinical standpoint. For example, you may have real concerns about the patient's tendency to isolate him- or herself from support and the level of anhedonia that is present. Although the patient may find it safer or easier to talk about sleep problems initially, you as the clinician need to respect and address them while maintaining your own therapeutic plan that you will be able to share with the patient as treatment progresses.

Before the first session ends the patient should leave with a prescription for the improvement of the most troublesome symptoms. This should be outlined in a brief and concrete fashion. The goal is to treat depression as a real disorder that carries with it a variety of problematic symptoms and behaviors. This focus will reinforce for the patient that

- depression is not "all in their head";
- as clinicians we understand the disorder and recognize that it is treatable;
- the treatment of depression is not a *frivolous* attempt to "make you feel better," rather it is imperative that the depression be treated to improve "your medical condition, interpersonal relationships, and overall well-being";
- depression is a biological, psychological, and social disorder, and treatment needs to consider all aspects.

The treatment approach should be outlined in a brief, written concrete format.

Keep in mind that medical patients who are physically ill *and* suffering from depression may struggle with concentration, poor memory, and difficulty making decisions. Subsequently, providing the patient with a written concrete strategy can minimize anxiety and facilitate collaboration with the patient. This treatment prescription should be viewed as a work in progress and should be developed in the first session with the patient. Below is an example of a treatment prescription:

Treatment for Your Depression

You have identified the following symptoms as most troublesome to you:

- difficulty sleeping
- crying a lot
- feel like jumping out of your skin
- restless and irritable
- trouble organizing your thoughts
- feel isolated and alone

The initial plan for treatment will involve starting an antidepressant to improve your sleep and feelings of restlessness and irritability. When we meet again we will talk about strategies to help you keep your thoughts organized and ways to make you feel more connected and supported by others. Your depression can be treated and you will feel better.

Issues Concerning the Therapist

Therapists working with the medically ill should be aware of several issues that confront them throughout their clinical work. You should always be mindful that the primary focus of medically ill patients is on their physical health, including symptoms, medical tests, and treatments. You will not be able to provide effective treatment for depression or anxiety without first having a working knowledge of the medical illness in question, including physical symptoms, treatment options, potential side effects, and common problems encountered by a patient. You should familiarize yourself with the important medical terminology used in each illness, such as "ESRD" for kidney disease, "CABG" or "Holter monitoring" for cardiac patients, and "autonomic dysreflexia" for spinal cord injuries. While it is not necessary to "study medicine," if a therapist does not understand the basic issues confronting the patient, it will be difficult to build trust and rapport. A therapist runs the risk of making potentially uncomfortable mistakes such as assuming a patient can physically engage in certain behaviors that they cannot due to the illness. For example, it would be important for you to understand the severe fluid restrictions that dialysis patients must endure or the problems with sexual functioning caused by certain medications. Lack of knowledge about treatment options can lead you to assume a worse prognosis for the patient than is appropriate. Furthermore, the therapist will not be able to deal with a patient's fears or give realistic reassurance and helpful coping strategies without some knowledge of the effectiveness of the medical treatments.

There are a few ways of obtaining this knowledge. If you don't have any medical background, you can read material written specifically for the layperson. The diagnostic sections of this book will help with some of these issues involving depression. Because patient education has become important in helping people adjust to and manage their illnesses better, there is a wealth of information available for many common illnesses such as heart disease, diabetes, and stroke. These materials are usually written in clear, easy-to-understand language and provide a fundamental understanding of the particular disease and its management. Of course, reading material directed at health care providers is also helpful. Literature searches for journal articles regarding management of issues related to each illness can provide additional useful information. Finally, communication with the treating physician and medical staff is important in order to obtain more accurate information about the individual's diagnosis, treatment, and prognosis. Patients are also sometimes happy to provide the therapist with specifics of their particular illness. If you set aside any feelings of needing to be "in control" or fears of not knowing something, the patient often gains a sense of mastery and control by "teaching the therapist all about the illness."

You also need to be prepared to have sessions with a patient that may only deal with physical symptoms related to the illness. Because this is of paramount importance to the patient, supportive therapy often involves what may seem like an endless focus on particular physical symptoms. Keep in mind that discussion of these symptoms and medical problems is therapeutic for the patient and it is your task, once the patient has vented his or her concerns, to assist in improving problem solving and positive coping. The patient may be coping quite well but still simply finds the therapy environment a place to confirm that he or she is doing "okay."

Countertransference

When working with medically ill patients, you should be aware of your own countertransference issues that may impede good care of the patient. Because patients facing serious and life threatening illness confront loss and death issues, it is essential that the you have insight into your own personal views of death as well as the ability to deal with losses. Just as the therapist may obtain a history of loss from the patient, it is important for the therapist to be aware of his or her own history of loss.

Unresolved issues such as grief about a death in your personal life can seep into the therapy with a patient who is confronting similar issues. In addition, choices about treatment options are ultimately a patient's personal choice, and it is important that you maintain objectivity. For example, the patient who is facing advanced terminal illness may have to make a decision regarding active treatment aimed at controlling the disease versus comfort care. As a therapist you should make efforts to contain personal feelings regarding the patient's choice regardless of whether the choice coincides with one you would personally choose.

A common trap that befalls therapists is the need to "rescue" the patient from their difficulties. You may feel a strong urge to save the patient from his or her suffering, or you may be pulled to respond to the patient's need to be rescued; feelings of helplessness easily arise, creating a sense of futility and discouragement, especially in cases of advanced illness or severe disability. It is not uncommon to have inner questions such as "Can I help this person?" You may even be tempted to withdraw from the patient prematurely. You need to stay focused on what serves the patient's needs, and while a therapist certainly cannot rescue the patient, it is possible for you to help the patient cope better with the illness and reduce depressive symptoms. Conversely, you may be tempted, due to feelings of frustration and helplessness, to push the patient to make changes or face issues he or she is not ready to address. When a patient appears to be denying his or her illness, it may just be a temporary coping mechanism to reduce distress about the reality of the situation.

Another fear that is sometimes of concern to therapists is the fear of causing more discomfort to the patient by bringing up painful or difficult topics such as maladaptive coping, resistance to treatments, or observations about family members interference with recovery. While the patient is already coping with a lot of emotional distress about their illness, issues that hinder recovery or that contribute to depressive symptoms should be addressed. For example, you may be reluctant to interpret marital issues when the presenting concern is the illness. This can be done through tactful and gentle questioning, or an interpretation of your observations: "I know that you have already suffered a lot, but it seems as though you are hiding your pain from your wife so as not worry her and thereby losing out on getting support for yourself."

Therapists can minimize countertransference reactions by seeking out support from other colleagues. You might want to discuss difficult cases or, when it's comfortable, your feelings about particular issues. Self-awareness and acknowledgement of sensitive areas will help you reduce emotional strain and maintain objectivity in treatment.

Chapter 7

Physical Symptoms

There are nine criteria for a major depressive episode according to the DSM-IV. A patient must have at least five of the nine described symptoms to warrant a diagnosis of major depression:

1. depressed mood
2. anhedonia (diminished interest or pleasure in previously enjoyable activities)
3. appetite and weight changes
4. sleep disturbances
5. psychomotor agitation or retardation
6. fatigue
7. feelings of worthlessness
8. diminished ability to think or concentrate
9. recurrent thoughts of death

Among medically ill depressed patients, however, the clinician may note related symptoms to the nine commonly discussed criteria. These related symptoms may include feelings of hopelessness, helplessness, loss of motivation and compliance with medical regimen, inability to effectively cope, poor problem-solving abilities, and decline in memory (there is a complete list in chapter two, Depressive Disorders).

The degree to which a patient suffers from these symptoms can vary. For example, some patients may suffer from a depressed mood, want to sleep all day and night, have poor energy, and lack motivation; another patient may feel depressed, restless, agitated, unable to sleep, and suffer from poor concentration. It is important to recognize that these symptoms are interrelated, so a significant problem with one symptom can exacerbate or lead to another symptom: insomnia can lead to fatigue and also exacerbate difficulty in concentration; excessive feelings of worthlessness and hopelessness can lead to a diminished ability to enjoy pleasurable activities, and can impair concentration, since the patient is preoccupied with negative thoughts.

Keep in mind that when we talk about depression we are referring not only to a major depressive disorder but also to depression as seen in the following diagnoses: dysthymia, adjustment reaction with depressed mood, grief reaction, delirium and dementia, mood disorders secondary to medical condition, post-traumatic disorders, and bipolar disorders. Although it is important to make an appropriate differential diagnosis among these disorders (because prognosis, course, and risk factors can vary), psychological treatment strategies covered in the remainder of this book can be useful for all of the above disorders.

For treatment purposes, it is useful to separate the symptoms into categories or clusters. These categories can include physical or vegetative symptoms, cognitive symptoms, and suicidal concerns. Changes in appetite, sleep, and sex drive are referred to in psychiatric textbooks as vegetative symptoms. Other related physical symptoms can include fatigue, loss of energy, and psychomotor retardation or agitation. Cognitive symptoms can include excessive feelings of worthlessness, hopelessness, helplessness and guilt, loss of interest in pleasurable activities (anhedonia), and diminished ability to think or concentrate. Treatment strategies to address these cognitive symptoms will be covered in chapter 8. We consider suicidal concerns to be a separate category, not only because of the potential danger of this symptom, but also because in a chronically ill patient, suicidal concerns include ambivalence about living and termination of care. This is more extensively discussed in chapter 10.

Categorizing the symptoms will help you monitor which set of depressive symptoms are exacerbating the underlying medical illness. This knowledge will reinforce to the patient that treating the depression will also improve symptoms of their medical illness. Remember that psychological treatment strategies for the medically ill need to be anchored to the medical illness; most medically ill patients are more motivated and compliant in the treatment of depression if they believe it will assist them in managing their medical condition. Before entering into treatment, it is important to identify the clustering of symptoms for your patient and then identify those that require primary attention. As you recall from chapter 6, The Patient's Introduction to Therapy, an examination of the patient's unique experience of depression will serve to guide the treatment process.

The categories approach is also useful for monitoring symptoms throughout treatment. For example, many of the vegetative symptoms may continue to exist even when depression has improved because they are primarily related to the medical illness; but cognitive symptoms (helplessness, hopelessness, feelings of worthlessness) that persist indicate a continued depression. Treatment needs to be holistic with a recognition that there is an interconnectedness of these symptoms and that strategies to assist one set of symptoms can also improve others. You should share this concept with the patient throughout treatment. Treatment of the symptoms should proceed in a parallel fashion. Vegetative, cognitive, and suicidal concerns can all be addressed simultaneously, but you will want to place primary emphasis on those symptoms that are causing the most subjective distress for the patient and interfering with treatment of the medical condition. For example, if your patient's physical condition is compromised because of a loss of appetite and a disturbance in sleep related to the depression, then your treatment should focus first on these symptoms with secondary considerations given to related cognitive symptoms.

Since the vegetative and physical symptoms of depression can also be caused or exacerbated by the medical illness, the following section will provide strategies for *managing* these symptoms. Because of your patient's medical condition, many of these symptoms may not completely remit as the depression improves, but by utilizing these strategies they can be improved. For example, a depressed patient with multiple sclerosis may continue to experience fatigue related to the illness, but he or she can learn to utilize new strategies to better manage the fatigue.

The physical symptoms of depression among medically ill patients include changes in sleep, appetite, and sex drive. These are often referred to as the vegetative symptoms—symptoms that are related to growth and nutrition. Although fatigue and psychomotor retardation or agitation are not typically viewed as vegetative, they are often categorized as physical symptoms. These symptoms can be particularly problematic since they are often caused by both the depression and the medical condition and related treatments.

Typically you'll want to address the vegetative symptoms first in the treatment process through combinations of medication and psychological strategies. This is because patients who are not sleeping, eating, and who have little energy or motivation are often at risk. Since these symptoms exacerbate the medical condition and the depressed mood, the patient is often unable to actively participate in therapy. Vegetative symptoms, therefore, should be aggressively managed, and you should consider an evaluation for adjunct therapy with a pharmacological agent. This will be discussed in detail in chapter 11.

This section will offer strategies for managing these often all-pervasive and distressing symptoms of depression. Discussion of the management of symptoms will be organized in the following manner. Initially, we will identify potential **sources** for the symptom and then provide **strategies** for treatment.

Sleep Disturbances

As we discussed in the assessment section of chapter 2, primary sources of sleep disturbances among the medically ill can come from the medical condition itself. Insomnia, for example, is associated with respiratory disorders, cardiac diseases, endocrine disorders, and neurological disorders including sleep apneas. This is more common among older patients, as sleep patterns often undergo changes in the later years with increased nighttime awakening (Prinz et al. 1990). Further, medications used to treat thyroid disorders such as synthroid can also interfere with sleep.

Sources of Sleep Disturbances

Although the medical condition is central to diagnosis, there can be less obvious reasons for sleep disturbances in a medically ill patient.

Hospital Milieu

Sleep can be interrupted for medical inpatients due to the noise and distractions frequently found in the hospital. These include periodic interruptions for monitoring of vital signs, administration of medications, or breathing treatments. Also, the experience of sharing a room with another patient may interfere with sleep. This can be particularly problematic if the roommate is confused, loud, in pain, sees numerous visitors, or has multiple medical problems. Other factors in the environment can include an uncomfortable bed and poor temperature control.

Development of Poor Sleep Hygiene

Many patients, even prior to the onset of a medical illness, have developed poor sleep habits such as taking naps, sleeping with the lights or television on, using the bed for activities other than sleep, and having irregular sleeping hours. With the onset of a medical illness, patients who had prior bad habits may find they experience more difficulty with sleep, and those who had no difficulty sleeping at night may develop bad habits in response to the illness. For example, if patients are required to rest in the afternoon during the acute phase of their illness, they may find it difficult to break the habit of napping.

Worry and Anxiety

If a patient is hospitalized, the unfamiliar surroundings can generate anxiety and thus interfere with sleep. Patients may keep themselves vigilant about when a nightly treatment—such as a wound dressing change or a check of the vital signs—will occur. A patient will have a hard time falling into a comfortable state of sleep if he or she is waiting for someone to enter the room. In addition, patients in the hospital may experience fear related to accidentally pulling out catheters and intravenous lines while sleeping. This fear may prevent them from relaxing and falling asleep.

Patients at home may continue to experience fears and intrusive thoughts related to their illness, pain, ongoing treatments, and prognosis. For many patients, nighttime often becomes a time for review of their above noted concerns. This fear and worry can create much anxiety and physical tension, which can ultimately interfere with sleep.

Strategies for Treating Sleep Disturbances

Regardless of the source, the management and overall improvement of sleep is important as sleep disturbances can interfere with all aspects of a patient's life. Poor sleep among medically ill depressed patients increases their risk for passive suicidal behavior—through noncompliance and poor management of their medical condition—as well as active suicidal gestures. The strategies below offer a number of ways to better manage sleep disturbances.

Assess Sleep Hygiene

A thorough sleep evaluation can be useful to identify factors that may be contributing to sleep interruptions. These factors can include intrusive thoughts, periodic awakening secondary to nightmares, and poor sleep hygiene. In order to determine the nature of sleep disturbances, the following questions can be asked of your patient:

- Do you nap in the daytime?
- Do you use your bed for activities other than sleep (eat, watch television, read)?
- Do you typically sleep on your back or your side?
- Do you snore?
- Do you lay awake at night and think about your problems or worries?
- Does pain keep you awake?
- Do you go to bed at a different hour each night and wake at various times of the morning?
- Do you eat before you go to bed?
- Did you begin to experience difficulties with your sleep at the same time you became physically ill?
- Does your sleep change when you feel more down or depressed?

Remember that many patients who report sleep difficulties are actually getting better sleep than they realize. When sleep studies are performed some patients who complain of insomnia and report little or no sleep are found to be sleeping more than they are aware.

Consider a Referral for a Sleep Study

Typically, an aggressive medical workup and a sleep study will identify any treatable psychiatric, neurological, or medical cause of poor sleep. For example, patients with sleep apnea may be instructed to lose weight, sleep on their side, or have a modified tracheotomy to improve breathing capacity. However, only 15 percent of patients seen in a sleep disorder center with chronic insomnia have a physical cause for the condition (Coleman et al. 1982). The majority of sources for the insomnia turn out to be related to psychiatric disorders such as depression, anxiety, delirium and psychosis, as well as poor sleep hygiene.

Limit the Uses for the Bed

Often medically ill patients may spend a great deal of time in bed whether in the hospital or at home. Although this may be medically necessary during the acute phase of the illness, it can also be the beginning of a bad habit. Examine with the patient how many hours are spent in bed and what activities are done there. A medical patient may struggle to get out of bed and therefore simply find it easier to stay in bed for much of the day. He or she may make a habit of eating and watching television in bed. If medically indicated, you should encourage your patient to get out of bed upon awakening in the morning. You should also strongly discourage eating, watching television, or engaging in non-sleep activities in bed. A mental image of the bed as a place to sleep and nothing else will reinforce thoughts of sleep when the patient lies in bed.

Establish a Routine

A medical illness is disruptive to all aspects of a person's life, and everything, body and mind, can feel out of sync. Sleep is often disturbed as part of this alteration in a rhythm. Part of restoring that balance is to find a routine and maintain it. Try to have your patient establish a schedule for mealtimes followed by a routine of preparing for sleep. Then maintain this routine. You may suggest limiting snacks after a certain time in the evening and beginning a relaxation or "wind down" period before lying down in bed.

Make Time for Worry

Depressed patients frequently complain about lying down in bed and finding themselves worrying about the events of the day, their plans for tomorrow, and their overall circumstances. During the daylight hours, distraction is possible by staying busy and purposefully shutting out intrusive, worrisome thoughts (strategies to counter negative thinking will be addressed later in the cognitive section). When our body and our mind rest, the subconscious begins to allow these thoughts into conscious awareness, and previously guarded material is left unprotected. To compound this problem, medically ill depressed patients can often be troubled by intrusive thoughts and dreams regarding pending or past medical procedures, as well as worries regarding their own mortality.

Working with patients on establishing a circumscribed time for worry can be useful. This may involve teaching the patient to become vigilant about their thoughts and only allowing relaxing pleasant images to be associated with the bed and related sleep periods. Instructions may include having the patient physically get out of bed when they find themselves plagued by distressing thoughts. You can teach them to give themselves permission to worry or sort out their painful thoughts in a circumscribed time and place. The goal is to remove the association of bedtime and sleep with an opportunity to worry and evaluate one's pain. That can be accomplished outside the realm of sleep time.

Avoid Stimulants Before Bed

For many it is common sense to avoid drinking coffee or other caffeinated beverages just prior to bed, but frequently alcohol and nicotine are overlooked. There is a misconception that since alcohol and nicotine are relaxing, they will aid sleep. In reality, both are central nervous system stimulants that can interfere with good sleep quality.

Stay Active During the Day

Depressed patients often lack interest and motivation to engage in activities. This lack of energy and activity contributes to feelings of isolation, poor self-esteem, and can leave the patient feeling chronically fatigued in the day, but with an inability to sleep at night. It has been suggested that when patients are physically active in the day that sleep is improved (Hauri 1985). Although medically ill patients may be limited by the physical activities that they can engage in, *depressed* medically ill patients also lack the *desire* to participate in activities. It is important to encourage patients to mentally and physically remain active in activities that are important to them. At first, it may be difficult for depressed patients to identify what those activities might be, as depression seems to render everything meaningless. Finding meaning and purpose through new activities or redefining the self in relationship to old activities is discussed in chapter 8.

Relax or Meditate

Preparation for sleep for many depressed patients requires a winding down or quieting of the mind for sleep to come. Therefore, utilizing the following meditation and relaxation exercises can also be useful when working with patients who have sleep disturbances related to their depression or their medical illness.

When patients are under a lot of physical and emotional stress, it is important to take built-in rest periods and actively withdraw from activities, decisions, and conflicts. This "shutting down" period should be viewed as an opportunity to recharge their battery. Teach the patient the difference between withdrawing for healthy rest versus isolating oneself due to depression. Help the patient resolve any fears of being perceived as weak or passive when taking time to rejuvenate or conserve energy. Instead of focusing on the things that are not getting done, help the patient focus on taking care of him- or herself, which includes getting rest. It is not unusual for patients to feel guilty when they are taking time for themselves.

As part of taking active rest periods, relaxation techniques are a useful skill for patients to learn. There are several forms of relaxation including progressive muscle relaxation, visualization, meditation, and deep breathing. Take time to teach the patient how to use these various relaxation techniques. The handouts on pages 98–101 can be copied and given to your patients to help them learn each technique, and practice it on their own.

Diaphragmatic Breathing

This is a process that helps people improve their ability to focus their attention on their bodies. Relaxation methods enable you to effectively reduce both your mental anxiety and its physical signs. As you become more relaxed, you will be able to listen better to important things you want to say to yourself. Relaxation is a self-control technique; you are in control of your level of relaxation. Like any skill, the more you practice, the better able you will become to relax more fully and in less ideal places.

An important step in achieving relaxation is to learn to breathe properly. This technique is called **diaphragmatic breathing**. It involves breathing from your diaphragm instead of your chest. Your diaphragm is a muscle that is located just below your ribs. Breathing from the diaphragm involves slow deep breaths where the diaphragm actually pulls and pushes air in and out of the lungs. Breathing from the diaphragm promotes relaxation in the body, as opposed to the shallow, rapid, and tense breathing that occurs in the chest when you are anxious.

Not only does this type of breathing make relaxation on a physical level much easier to achieve, it is also more efficient and subsequently increases the oxygen supply to the heart, brain, and other organs. By using this type of breathing you make the healing process smoother and more complete.

1. To begin the exercise find a comfortable chair in a quiet room.
2. Place your hand on your abdomen below your rib cage. This is where your diaphragm is located.
3. Concentrate on your breathing, taking slow, deep breaths. Breathe through your nose, inhale, and hold it.
4. Exhale slowly. You should be able to feel your stomach moving out when you inhale and in when you exhale.
5. Focus on your belly as it expands like a balloon when you inhale and deflates when you exhale.
6. Repeat several deep breaths. After you inhale, hesitate for a moment, and then slowly exhale.
7. Remember to *slowly* but deeply inhale and slowly but *evenly* exhale.
8. Avoid rapid, quick breaths. This can lead to hyperventilation
9. As you slowly blow all of the air out of you lungs, imagine all of the tension leaving.
10. Pause, and repeat this deep breathing until it has become a slow, comfortable rhythm.
11. As you concentrate on slowing down your breathing, let your body sink into your comfortable chair. Notice how relaxed your arms feel against the chair; so do your legs, your back, and your neck. Notice that your breathing is slow, deep, and regular. With each breath, you are becoming more relaxed and the tension is slowly fading.

12. You may wish to combine some imagery and positive self-statements with the breathing exercise. For example, when you exhale, imagine letting all of the tension in your body go with the breath; imagine that when you inhale, you are taking in energy and feeling stronger with every breath.

Progressive Muscle Relaxation

Another useful relaxation strategy is called progressive muscle relaxation. It was developed by Dr. E. Jacobson over fifty years ago (Jacobson 1974). He found that patients could achieve relaxation in their muscles by first tensing them. When you are working on tensing a particular muscle group, you need to try and keep all other muscle groups relaxed.

1. Begin by getting yourself in a quiet and comfortable position.
2. Take several deep cleansing breaths from the diaphragm.
3. When you tense a muscle group you need to do so in an intense manner and hold it for 7-10 seconds.
4. Release the tension from the muscle group in an abrupt way. You will feel a relaxed sensation. Enjoy the relaxation for 15-20 seconds.
5. Make a tight fist. Hold it (7-10 seconds) and then release it (15-20 seconds).
6. Tense the muscles around your eyes by tightly holding your eyelids closed. Hold then release.
7. Open your mouth as widely as you can. Hold it and then release.
8. Raise your eyebrows as high as you can by tensing your forehead. Hold it and then release.
9. Make a "muscle" and tense your biceps. Hold it and then release.
10. Stiffen your arms, extend them to your sides, and tense your triceps. Hold it and then release.
11. "Shrug" your shoulders by raising them up to your ears. Hold it and then release.
12. Pull your shoulder blades back as if you were sticking out your chest. Hold it and then release it.
13. Suck in your stomach. Hold it and then release.
14. Arch your lower back. Hold it and then release.
15. "Pinch" the muscles of your buttocks together. Hold it and then release.
16. Pull your toes up toward you and tighten your calf muscles in your legs. Hold it and then release.
17. Curl your toes down toward the floor. Hold it and then release.

Initially, the above exercise may take you 20-30 minutes to complete. With practice you will be able to reduce the time and will be able to achieve relaxation even in less ideal situations. You will need to practice this exercise in a quiet, relaxed atmosphere before you can learn to do this exercise under stressful situations or during periods of fatigue.

Deep Breathing and Visualizations

Your imagination and ability to daydream are powerful tools to reduce your stress. If you like, you can combine the breathing exercise with a visualization for deeper overall relaxation. You may want to remember a version of it, or to tape record it so that you can relax with your eyes closed. You might simply choose to create a scene of your own, once you get the idea. Remember to keep the details vivid.

As you relax, imagine this scene:

You are walking on the beach. Feel the cool breeze blowing off the water. As you walk slowly along the edge of the water, you can feel occasional droplets of water that spray up at you as the wind passes over the water. Feel the warmth of the sand between your toes. It feels coarse but smooth and gives way to your feet as you pass along. You feel the tensing and relaxing of the muscles in your legs as you walk along. The sun is warm and soothing on your skin, leaving you feeling safe and relaxed. Now and then, a bird calls out overhead, and you look up to see it gently soaring, sailing skyward. The smell of the water gently fills your nose and gives you a fresh cleansing feeling. Inhale deeply slowing your breathing down.

As you look out over the water you can see the gentle rhythm of the water. Gently lapping back and forth. The waves continue to gently roll with a smooth unhurried motion. You feel the beating of your heart with the same slow steady rhythm of the waves. Strong and sturdy and comfortable. You watch the free-flowing motion of the water and begin to imagine the same steady free-flowing movement of blood in your arteries. No barriers or blockages. Nothing preventing it from flowing comfortably and in an unhurried manner. You take in a deep breath of the fresh air filling your lungs. Your chest expands without pain or tension. As you exhale, you can feel the tension being released from your body. Remember to keep your breathing slow and even.

You sit down in the sand feeling the warmth of the sand on your body. You feel strong and refreshed. You see your heart beating regular and strong giving you the strength to handle life's stressors. You feel confident and proud of the control that you have over your body. You feel the improvements that you have made on your body. Your stress level is lower. You control the steady free flow of blood through your arteries.

You remind yourself of all your strengths. You focus your thoughts on the positive things in your life. You feel the strength of those who support and love you. Pay attention to how strong you feel with the support of others; it feels as if, at times, they're lifting and carrying you along like the waves. Remind yourself that you have control over your heart. You can protect it from breaking. You can keep it strong and safe. The clouds of pessimism and hopelessness are blown away by the steady wind. The only thing that remains constant and steady is your optimistic attitude, which shines like the sun. And like the sun this optimism reflects off the water, touches all that surrounds you, and then returns back to you.

Pause for a few moments while you repeat important things to yourself. Reflect on the steady and strong beating of your heart and the gentle comfortable and easy flow of the blood through your body. This blood carries energy, warmth, and strength to your mind. You are now more confident, content, productive, and happy as this rich blood bathes your mind with healthy substances.

Notice how much more relaxed and comfortable you have become and how much you have enjoyed being in this place. Focus on how relaxed your arms, legs, back, and neck feel. In a few moments you are going to bring yourself back. You know that when you want, you can bring yourself back to this spot.

Now while retracing your steps down the beach, count backwards from five to one. When you reach one, you will open your eyes, feeling relaxed, refreshed, alert and ready to do what you want to do.

Begin practicing these relaxation exercises twice a week for 30 minutes. If the example used here of walking on the beach is not particularly relaxing to you, then substitute some other place where you feel particularly relaxed and peaceful. The key to effective relaxation exercises is to make the imagery as vivid and real as you can. Therefore, when you are imagining this scene or your own, it is important to imagine as many sights, smells, feelings, and sounds as you can. Try to place yourself into the scene in such a way that you can feel the breeze and the sun, hear the waves, and the birds.

Your patient may wish to make a tape recording of the above imagery exercise to use. Many patients find it hard to listen to their own voices, so it may be helpful to encourage them to reach out to a family member, friend, or health care provider who's voice they find comforting and asking them to record it for them. This will also serve to foster support and connections with others which is essential in the treatment of depression.

Instruct the patient to practice these exercises on a regular basis in order to become better able to initiate relaxation prior to sleep. Make it clear that with any skill, time and practice will help them improve. The goal is to use relaxation as a way of *preparing* the mind for sleep.

Consider Sleeping Medication

If your patient continues to experience problematic sleep despite using the above strategies, the addition of a sleeping medication can be considered. If an already prescribed medication is acting as a stimulant and therefore interfering with sleep, the addition of a sleeping medication may be helpful. Selection of a medication should be considered in the context of the medical condition, age of the patient, nature of the sleep disturbance, and other medications that the patient is taking. It should be noted that generally tricyclic antidepressants can be sedating, whereas selective serotonin reuptake inhibitors can have a stimulating effect. Patients, however, may have individual responses to these medications. For example, an antidepressant such as Prozac may cause insomnia in some patients but not in others. There are over-the-counter medications that are typically used by patients to facilitate sleep, such as Benadryl or Tylenol PM. Ambien is a new prescription medication that shows some promise as a sleeping medication. It appears to have few side effects and complicating factors for medically ill patients.

You may also consider altering the schedule of already prescribed medications that may have sedation as a side effect. You could, for instance, suggest that drugs that are currently used by the patient and cause drowsiness be used as an evening dose, thereby *using the side effect* to facilitate sleep.

Changes in Appetite and Weight

Although appetite and weight loss are common among medically ill patients, it is the *poor motivation* and *lack of desire* to eat despite knowledge that it is essential for health that is the hall mark of depression. Depressed patients adopt the attitude "Why bother? I'm not getting any better." This is the voice of depression. Obviously the medical condition and the medications used to treat it can cause appetite and weight changes for the patient. Some medications, for example, can cause an upset stomach thereby affecting appetite, while others, such as steroids, can cause weight gain. Given that eating is an integral part of normal life, any change in appetite and weight can highlight the severity and impact of the illness on the patient's life, thus contributing to the depression.

Sources of Appetite and Weight Change

Apart from the illness or the depression, there are other more subtle issues that can contribute to weight and appetite problems.

Environmental Factors

Many patients, when hospitalized, avoid eating the food as a result of either the poor quality of hospital food or their own individual food preferences. This can then contribute to poor appetite and a decline in food intake. The medically ill outpatient may struggle with financial constraints, which make it difficult to follow the recommended diet. Physically weak patients may have difficulty cooking for themselves and may lack social support to help assist them with meals. Patients in pain may have difficulty opening food items or using the stove or microwave. These inconveniences can make the patient less motivated to cook and subsequently can contribute to changes in appetite and weight.

Worry and Anxiety

Anxiety and worry about the medical illness and pending treatments can easily interfere with appetite by leading to overeating or avoiding food. A vicious cycle can develop with anxiety, worry, and depression about weight loss leading to further decline in appetite and desire for food.

Issues of Control

Concerns about eating and weight loss can become a focus of control for the patient and the family. Constant focus on the body because of the medical illness leads to feelings of loss of control and for some patients eating becomes a way of regaining control. For example, a patient suffering from multiple medical illnesses such as diabetes, hypertension, and cardiac disease may feel resentful of the dietary restrictions placed upon them and subsequently overeat or avoid eating as a way of maintaining control.

Strategies for Treating Appetite and Weight Problems

Psychological treatment should focus on improving symptoms of anorexia whether related to depression, the primary medical illness, or both. Improvement in appetite and weight is healing for both conditions.

Assess Appetite Changes

As the clinician it is important for you to help guide the patient toward a better understanding of the patterns and problem areas contributing to the appetite disturbance. An in-depth understanding of the contributing factors to their appetite changes can be helpful in managing this problematic symptom. The following questions can be asked of the patient to assist them in identifying patterns and changes that may be helpful in differentiating contributing factors:

- Do you experience anxiety about pending medical appointments?
- Does this anxiety interfere with your ability to eat?
- Are there certain smells or images that change your appetite?
- Do you feel fatigued when trying to cook?
- Do you have a hard time using the microwave or stove?
- Does anyone assist you in food preparation?
- Are you able to go to the grocery store?
- Do you experience nausea in the presence of food?
- Does your stomach get upset after taking certain medications?
- Are you embarrassed or uncomfortable eating in the presence of others?
- Do you start telling yourself that you will be sick if you eat and then find that you do get sick?
- Do you have any financial difficulties that interfere with your ability to purchase food items for your diet?
- Do you have limited food preferences?
- Despite knowing that you have to eat, do you sometimes simply not want to be bothered eating?

The following strategies can be used to address the issues or contributing factors to the appetite changes.

Be Mindful of Meals

Instruct the patient and the family to pay attention to the setting or atmosphere of a meal. Eating a meal with the family is symbolic of normalcy. The loss of "feeling normal" along with the frequent reminders of the medical illness contribute to alienation and depression. Encourage the patient and the family to share meals together, use candles or prepare a favorite dish. Teach the family to be careful to avoid foods that are likely to increase feelings of nausea or those that are restricted.

Lessen Anxieties at Mealtimes

When a patient has no appetite but is intellectually aware of the need to eat, he or she can often begin to experience anxiety around mealtime. This anxiety and worry over an inability to eat, a lack of desire to eat, or nausea becomes linked with the sight, preparation, or initiation of a meal. In this case, behavioral strategies such as self-hypnosis or relaxation training can be useful in treating this anticipatory distress. The symptoms may be worse in social situations where the patient may feel embarrassed that others will potentially witness the eating problems. Altering the milieu for eating may be an effective behavioral strategy to prevent anticipatory anxiety from escalating into total loss of appetite, which will only serve to worsen feelings of depression.

Use Visualization

The use of imagery exercises, which focus on the benefits of food for the body, can help sustain motivation for healthy eating and can decrease anticipatory anxiety. The use of visualization in medical patients helps them imagine that their efforts and behaviors will be worthwhile and ultimately lead to an improvement in well-being. Encourage patients to imagine the food they're eating working in their body to make them feel stronger, more energetic, and happier. If these exercises are used in appropriate and realistic ways with patients, they begin to feel a sense of control over their eating and an ability to motivate themselves to *try* despite a poor appetite.

You and the patient can collaborate to come up with an eating visualization based on the relaxation techniques you learned earlier in the chapter. Here are some images that promote visualization for healthier eating:

- To prepare for any imagery exercise, you may need to first instruct the patient to use some of the relaxation exercises learned earlier. This will help prepare the mind for the imagery exercise by relaxing the body.
- Instruct the patient to imagine food entering their body as if the body were transparent and they could visualize what the food was doing.
- Ask the patient to imagine the food breaking down and providing the body with a burst of energy.
- Have them imagine this energy strengthening red blood cells and increasing oxygen which in turn will increase their strength and energy.
- Imagine their immune system becoming stronger and fighting with the disease and winning.
- Instruct them to imagine watching the body respond in a healing and comforting way to the food that they have eaten.
- If nausea is a concern, you may need to alter the imagery exercise to include statements focused on the stomach and intestines. For example, helping them to imagine the stomach being quiet, calm, and serene and them taking in the food and enjoying its calming effects.
- If no appetite is a concern, the imagery can include messages of the body being hungry for nourishment and using it to increase energy and strength.
- The imagery exercise should be tailored to the individual appetite concerns of the patient.
- The exercises can be done in a step-wise fashion actually leading up to eating while doing the exercises.

Consider Pharmacological Intervention

If appetite changes are significant and are interfering with the patients well-being, then antidepressant therapy should be considered. Similar to the effect that drugs have on sleep patterns, different antidepressants have varying effects on appetite. Prozac has been shown to decrease appetite and lead to weight loss, whereas Paxil has been found to do the opposite. Keep in mind, however, that people may have varying degrees of side effects to medications.

The choice of an antidepressant will depend not only on the course of the depression but on other symptoms that the patient may be experiencing, such as sleep disturbances, poor appetite, restlessness. The issues of side-effect profiles will be discussed in greater detail in chapter 11.

Improving Environmental Factors

You may need to take an active role in improving factors in the patient's environment that are contributing to changes in appetite and weight. For example, you may need to consider meals on wheels, a home health aide to assist with cooking, meeting with family members to educate them about the patient's struggles in an effort to rally support, and connect the patient with agencies to assist with financial concerns.

Refer the Patient to a Dietician

You may also want to consider a referral to a dietician for education on a healthy diet, including information regarding high calorie foods, ways to serve them to make them more visually appealing, and recipes for small and frequent meals. This is also helpful for "picky eaters" who may need to expand their diet.

Loss of Sexual Desire

Sexual difficulties, or dysfunctions, include problems in one or more stages of sexual responsiveness. In women, difficulties include low sex drive, lack of physical arousal (less moisture or lubrication in the vagina), pain during intercourse, or problems achieving an orgasm. Men may also experience low desire as well as problems achieving an erection or ejaculation. Problems with desire and related dysfunctions can be caused by depression, medications, or certain medical conditions. Psychological sources of lessened desire include a number of interrelated causes.

Sources of Loss of Sexual Desire

The loss of sexual desire is often a symptom of depression and in the medically ill can also be related to the medical condition, treatments, and medications. Psychological sources of lessened desire can include a number of interrelated causes.

Change in Appearance

Changes in appearance as a result of the medical condition including loss of hair, weight gain, scars, skin changes, and the presence of prosthetic devices can leave the patient feeling unattractive. Sexual self-image in part depends on how attractive a person feels physically and how capable he or she feels in satisfying a partner's needs. If a patient feels damaged or less attractive as a person because of a medical condition, then self-esteem and the ability to enjoy sex can suffer. If they have had a heart bypass operation, for instance, they may feel self-conscious about the scarring on their chest and leg. Women are especially vulnerable to anxieties about their body image. Rather than avoiding sexual contact and intimacy because of this, they can be encouraged to make some adjustments to enhance their comfort and confidence levels. For example, if a woman has had a heart bypass operation, she may consider wearing romantic lingerie to conceal the scars until she feels more comfortable with herself.

Fatigue

Fatigue or pain associated with heart disease may lessen sexual desire and enjoyment. Fatigue is a common symptom of depression and is related to many medical illnesses and can interfere with sexual desire. Even when physical symptoms are controlled, feelings of disappointment, depression, and discouragement can persist. At these times, it may be useful for the patient to simply engage in intimate acts such as hugging, kissing, or being silent together as a way of restoring desire.

Anxiety

Decreased desire can also be associated with anxiety related to exacerbating the underlying medical condition. For example, patients who have suffered a heart attack often fear that engaging in a sexual act may trigger another attack. Patients with cancer can have irrational fears that they may be contagious and hence avoid sexual contact.

Relationship Tension

Stress and depression related to medical illness can create a great deal of tension in the patient's intimate relationships. Fears, resentments, and prior marital discord can be exacerbated by a medical illness and can then be easily channeled through their sex life. Given that sex is not simply a physical process, the psychological state of the relationship should be closely evaluated. For example, patients may have concerns that the illness has radically altered who they are and their ability to perform sexually. This type of performance anxiety can create avoidance of sexual interactions and interfere with performance when sex is initiated. It is important to remind patients that if their mind is preoccupied with fears about their performance, they won't be able to enjoy the experience as much. If these anxieties are persistent, they are also more likely to have difficulties like impotence or problems achieving orgasm, because anxiety distracts them from focusing on the pleasurable side of sex.

Moreover, poor performance experiences can leave the patient feeling demoralized, which exacerbates depression; and the vicious cycle continues.

Pressure to Resume Sexual Activities

Remind patients that there is no need to pressure themselves into rushing into sex prematurely. Some patients are worried or curious about how their medical illness may affect sexual abilities, so they test it out too quickly. This can put unnecessary strain on the patient physically and emotionally and set the patient up to feel like a failure, leading to an increase in depression. To avoid this, encourage both partners to openly discuss their feelings of being pressured. It may be pressure that the patient is putting on him- or herself, or it may be felt from the partner. An open discussion and recognition of the source of this pressure may help to decrease anxiety by clarifying mistaken beliefs. Cognitive restructuring of intrusive thoughts related to performance may also be necessary to decrease anticipatory anxiety.

Avoiding Sex Due to Fear

It is also important to encourage patients not to wait too long before engaging in acts of intimacy. Many heart attack survivors err on the side of caution and postpone sex due to fears of physical harm coming from this exertion. Sometimes the longer patients wait, however, the more likely they are to be exceedingly nervous and worried, leading to difficulties with performance anxiety. Remind the patient to start slow; this will help build confidence and minimize irrational fears and thereby relieve some of the pressure that maintains avoidant behavior.

Strategies for Treating Loss of Sexual Desire

After the immediate crisis for a medically ill patient passes—after recovering from a heart attack, completing chemotherapy, or adjusting to a disability—concerns about sexual function may occur. It is important for you to remind the patient that sex is not simply a physical process demanding medical stability. To enjoy a healthy sex life a person also needs to be emotionally stable. For example, concerns about performance, fears about aggravating the medical condition, decreased desire due to depression, and conflict within the patient's primary relationship can all affect the sex drive and related performance. It is important to remind patients that their depression can not only be a source of their poor sexual desire but sexual fears can also contribute to depression. The following strategies are designed to address these concerns.

Learn about Sex and the Medical Condition

Encourage the patient and the patient's partner to educate themselves about sex and the medical condition. This will serve to calm fears and misperceptions related to sex. Given that discussions of sex are often difficult not only for the patient but at times for health care providers, the handout on page 110 can serve as guide for patients on how to approach the topic.

How to Discuss Sexual Issues with Your Doctor

Your doctor should be the one to initiate a discussion about sex related to your medical illness. This in itself, however, is not an easy endeavor. Many doctors avoid or neglect doing this, perhaps due to discomfort in discussing the area of sexuality. Additionally, many doctors have not been formally trained in dealing with this important issue with their patients. Sometimes, physicians focus exclusively on the physical recovery of your body and neglect issues pertaining to your lifestyle.

Whatever the reasons, a lack of attention to this area can be very detrimental. You may mistakenly assume that if your doctor doesn't bring it up, then this means that sex is either not an important issue for you or that you won't be able to, or shouldn't, resume a healthy sex life. If your doctor does not include sexuality when discussing what to expect with your illness and related depression, then it will be up to you to ask. Below are sample questions you can use to guide your discussion with your doctor:

1. How will my medical condition, and my medications, affect my sex life?
2. When can I resume sexual activities with my partner?
3. Are there any sexual activities or positions I should avoid?
4. When should I take my medications (in relation to timing for sexual activities)?
5. What should I do if I have chest pains, or other symptoms, during sex?
6. If I have problems with (choose one or more of the following) what does this mean and what can I do about it?
   - pain during sex
   - low or no sexual desire
   - pain with erections
   - becoming physically aroused
   - pain during ejaculation
   - soft erections
   - premature ejaculation
   - no erection
   - achieving orgasms
7. I had problems with (choose one or more of the above) even before my depression or physical illness. What does this mean and what can I do about it?
8. Can you suggest a professional I can see to offer help with sexual counseling?

Be Mindful of Side Effects of Medication

Keep in mind that many medications can have sexual side effects. These include antihypertensive medications (Lopressor, Inderal, Tenormin), cardiac medications (Mexitil and Norpace), antihistamines, sedatives (including alcohol), antidepressants, drugs used for peptic ulcer disease (Tagamet), and some pain medications (such as narcotics). If a patient feels that their medications may be interfering with a normal sex life, encourage a talk with the doctor. Remind your patient never to adjust doses or stop taking their medications without first speaking with a physician. Often alternate medications with fewer sexual side effects can be substituted.

Encourage the Partner's Involvement in Medical Care

If a partner has fears that sex may trigger a heart attack or sexual activity may increase pain, he or she may avoid the topic of sex altogether. This avoidance may be misinterpreted as rejection, leading to further loss of self-esteem and concerns about sexual activities. A partner of someone with heart disease, cancer, kidney disease, or any serious medical condition should participate in related rehabilitation programs. Participation may put to rest anxiety and fears related to the patient's physical capabilities. To encourage this participation and to address any potential misperceptions, it is essential for you as the clinician to meet with both the patient and partner and discuss their points of view.

Debunk Myths and Misconceptions

Sexuality is one of those areas clouded by myths and misconceptions. Some of these myths are particularly damaging to the elderly or to those who have had a serious medical problem. A patient's beliefs can interfere with his or her sexual adjustment by preventing new skills and attitudes. Working with a couple to clarify myths from facts regarding sexuality can improve communication and intimacy, which in turn can increase desire.

Here are some examples:

Myth: Sex is only for the young and beautiful; older people can't enjoy sex.
Fact: Though there are changes in your sexual reactions that occur with age, sexual interest and activity are common for people in their sixties, seventies, and may continue into the eighth and ninth decades of life.

Myth: Lovemaking must involve intercourse; lovemaking must lead to orgasm.
Fact: Lovemaking includes a range of activities, not all of which include intercourse. Hugging, cuddling, kissing, caressing, and body massage are important expressions of intimacy that do not include a focus on orgasm or intercourse. Petting and caressing of erogenous areas (genitals and breasts) may be done with or without a focus on orgasm.

Myth: Sex saps your strength and therefore is harmful to those not in perfect health; too much sex is unhealthy.
Fact: Sexual activity can provide a healthy workout for your heart. During

the vigorous exercise associated with sex, you can burn four or five calories per minute. This is roughly equivalent to dancing, hiking, or playing tennis. Not only does sex feel good, but it can also reduce a sense of isolation, improve your relationship with your partner, and strengthen a sense of intimacy—as well as your physical health.

Myth: Engaging in masturbation (self-stimulation) is dirty and only for those "hard-up" individuals who can't get a partner.
Fact: Masturbation usually begins in childhood, continues throughout life, is enjoyed by both sexes and by people with or without a regular sexual partner. It is not "dirty" or deviant but a common, natural, and healthy part of sexual activity. It is often a "safe first step" back to sexual function.

Improve Couple Communication

With the patient's permission, it is often helpful to include the partner in some sessions to work directly with both parties on improving communication. It may be necessary to meet individually with the patient, individually with the partner, as well as with the two parties together. The goals for both the individual and joint sessions should be thoroughly discussed with both the patient and the partner to prevent any misunderstandings or hidden agendas. Work on teaching both patient and partner how to talk openly about their feelings, fears of changes in their sexual responses, as well as about worries about their health. Sharing feelings and concerns will make both parties more relaxed and accepting. Encourage open dialogue regarding what is pleasurable for the patient and what is painful. Many couples have never talked about sex openly before, so this may be their first opportunity to share their desires, pleasures, likes and dislikes more fully.

Start Slowly

Medically ill patients may need to resume lovemaking gradually by starting out with low key but enjoyable contact, like cuddling, kissing, and caressing. One technique, which has been used successfully to remove pressure associated with performance anxiety and to enhance a focus on whole body erotic feelings, is called "sensate focusing." It involves sensual kinds of touching that allow you to improve your ability to give and receive pleasure in a gradual, relaxed progression (see the handout on page 113).

Sensate Focusing

1. Agree to begin by having a ban on intercourse. The focus initially will be on touching and caressing each other without anticipating or worrying about sexual performance or intercourse.
2. Set the mood. Make the atmosphere as erotic and romantic as possible by including candles, soft music, or other props you enjoy. Even though the focus is not on intercourse or arousal, it should be on romance and sensuality.
3. Begin by lightly touching or massaging your partner's body, covering all the areas from head to toes, front and back. Experiment with different kinds of touch, using different parts of your body (for instance, your mouth or lips in addition to hands) to do the touching. This is not a typical back rub or body massage. Though you want to be relaxed, no one should be so relaxed that they fall asleep! Keep a focus on the sensual, erotic aspects of your touching.
4. Avoid touching genitals the first few times you do this. The goal is not arousal or orgasm but to increase pleasure and sharing that go along with whole-body touching, and to enhance intimacy and closeness.
5. Keep talking to a minimum. The exception is sharing about what feels good or uncomfortable. Sharing sexual fantasies, or memories of past rewarding experiences can also increase closeness and sensuality. After about 15-30 minutes, switch places, and have your partner touch you in a similar fashion.
6. During later interactions, gradually include caressing of genitals and breasts. But don't rush to include intercourse. It's better to take it slowly. With time, and when you feel ready, then let intercourse happen.

Robert Ornstein and David Sobel provide a wonderful description of these techniques and others in their book, *The Healthy Mind, Healthy Body Handbook.*

Try Different Positions

When couples progress to including intercourse among their sexual interactions, they may need to be open to trying different positions. The "missionary" position, with the male on top of the female facing each other, is the most common position for intercourse. Patients may find other positions are more comfortable—possibly even more stimulating and exciting. For example, a patient who had heart failure may notice greater shortness of breath when lying on his or her back; men using the missionary position can experience greater fatigue from supporting themselves on elbows or hands and knees. As an alternative, the female-on-top position may reduce this discomfort or strain. In addition, a side-by-side, face-to-face—or a side-by-side, female-back-to-male-front—position can avoid any weight-bearing burdens and lessen the strain of either partner supporting him- or herself.

Start with Masturbation

If the patient is concerned and self-conscious about how their first sexual interaction will go after a heart attack, a medical procedure, surgery, or initially after a diagnosis, you can suggest that they experiment first with masturbation. If the patient is comfortable with this activity, it can put some of their fears to rest and make the first experience with a partner less anxiety-provoking.

Encourage a Realistic Outlook

Remind couples that, generally speaking, if they had a good sex life prior to the medical illness, then they can most likely return to a good sexual life during and after their recovery. And even if they had sexual problems before their illness, sexual counseling can be helpful in overcoming problems like impotence, premature ejaculation, loss of sexual desire, difficulties reaching orgasm, or painful sex. Patients need to be educated that even if their difficulties stem from a medical disorder or condition, or from their depression, there are treatments which can help restore sexual functioning. Remind the patient not to minimize the importance of a healthy sex life. It can lead to a positive sense of well-being, an improved intimate relationship, and an improvement in their depression.

Fatigue

One of the most frequent complaints heard by a clinician is that of fatigue or low energy. As discussed in the assessment section, criteria for depression includes loss of energy and feeling slowed down. A thorough assessment that includes history, physical examination, and laboratory tests is essential to finding potential medical causes of fatigue. Similarly, a thorough evaluation of a patient's depressive symptoms is also essential in determining the contribution of depression to the overall clinical picture.

Sources of Fatigue

Physical Illness

Some illnesses in particular have fatigue as a primary symptom such as multiple sclerosis, lupus, chronic fatigue syndrome, and Epstein-Barr. Fatigue can also occur as a side effect of treatments such as radiation, chemotherapy, and dialysis. The most significant impact of fatigue, regardless of etiology, is a reduction in the patient's quality of life and lack of energy to participate in medical care. Therefore, management of fatigue is important in improving not only well-being, but also overall compliance.

Strategies for Treating Fatigue

Assess Fatigue

You should help the patient determine his or her own individual pattern of fatigue and the role of emotional factors. Asking the patient the following questions can serve as a guide in determining the effect of fatigue on well-being and the extent to which it affects daily life.

- What does fatigue feel like to you?
- What seems to make the fatigue worse?
- What seems to make it better?
- How does fatigue interfere with your daily activities?
- How does it influence your mood?
- How do others respond to your low energy?
- How does it make you feel about yourself?

Starting an Energy Log

One method that is useful in gathering information about a patient's individual pattern of fatigue and its impact is to teach the patient how to keep a log of when fatigue is triggered. The patient can rate his or her fatigue level before and after any event using a rating scale of 1-10. Rating fatigue forces the patient to examine concretely just how tired he or she is instead of making global statements such as "I'm so tired all of the time" and "I never get anything done"; these ratings will educate the patient on the link between emotional stress and fatigue and how even a relatively minor event can exacerbate symptoms of fatigue. Monitoring levels of fatigue, even for a week, can help you and the patient become aware of when fatigue is most problematic. The patient can then learn to pace activities and also avoid unnecessary activities. The log also helps the patient understand the link between depressed mood and fatigue.

Daily Activity and Fatigue Log

Date and Time	Activity	How you felt	Level of fatigue	
			Before	After
Fri. 10:30 A.M.	going to the doctor	worried, helpless	4	8
Sat. 2:00 P.M.	seeing a movie	relaxed	4	3

Activity Pacing

The daily activity and fatigue log can be used as the starting point to begin teaching the patient about pacing activities. Since patients with medical illnesses may have limited energy relative to their previous functioning, a useful strategy is to conserve energy and pace their activities. Too often, patients become frustrated and focus only on what they are not accomplishing, instead of what they are able to accomplish. For individuals who led a very fast-paced and active lifestyle, this reduction in level of energy can be particularly difficult to accept. If the patient is depressed, this only adds to negative self-worth. Goal setting can be important in helping the patient structure the day and feel a sense of accomplishment. Setting more realistic and flexible goals will build confidence in their ability to manage a very difficult symptom.

Outline Activities

Using the activity and fatigue log, outline the patient's current level of activities. Also determine whether there is a pattern to their fatigue. For instance, do periods of low energy typically occur in the beginning of the day, midday, or later in the evening? Do periods of fatigue occur after therapies such as chemotherapy or physical therapy and, if so, for how long? How long can the patient perform a typical activity before fatigue sets in: one hour or twenty minutes? And finally, does fatigue tend to be at its highest when strong negative emotions are present? The log should provide an individualized record of daily activities and periods of low and high energy for each patient.

Fluctuation is Normal

Remember to tell the patient that there is no "correct" amount of activities he or she "should" or "should not" be able to do, that there will be natural periods of high and low energy that may fluctuate daily and weekly. Learning to take advantage of periods of higher energy without overdoing it will help compensate for periods of fatigue when any type of activity seems impossible. Include in the log all necessary medical treatments and doctor's appointments. Medically ill patients often become fatigued just with the time spent taking care of their medical needs and then feel they have little energy left to manage their other activities.

Organize the Activities

Instruct the patient to reduce his or her overall activity level and then build stamina by gradually increasing activities. After the activities have been broken down in the previous assessment, help the patient go back and examine what steps can be taken to slowly begin increasing tolerance. For example, instead of cleaning the whole house, begin by doing just one room; or if further pacing is needed, clean for ten minutes one day and slowly increase to twenty minutes. Sometimes, patients will have a difficult time accepting this, especially if they were used to fulfilling multiple responsibilities. Explain to them that this exercise will allow them to develop a sense of confidence in their ability to control their life, even if it is not in the same manner to which they were accustomed. In addition, a reduction in activities may be part of recommended medical advice. Overall functioning may improve by the patient dividing activities into more organized, manageable chunks instead of feeling overwhelmed. With fewer activities on the schedule, the patient can be selective about what is most important.

Learn to Ask for Help

Help the patient learn how to request assistance when needed. This can be a difficult task when asking for help is equated with a loss of independence. Resolving this issue is important when fatigue is a concern, because the strain required to complete certain activities can be alleviated by simply requesting assistance from friends and family. For instance, if heavy housework or yard work can no longer be done because of physical limitations and related fatigue, hiring someone else or asking for some help when doing these tasks can help to conserve energy. The act of reaching out can also improve social support, which is discussed in chapter 9.

Add Pleasurable Activities

In his book on chronic fatigue syndrome, Friedberg (1995), discusses the importance of adding pleasurable activities to the daily schedule and applying the idea of pacing activities levels to pleasurable activities as well. Patients may feel guilty even considering pleasurable activities when doing the daily routine is difficult, but since loss of interest in pleasurable activities is a symptom of depression, incorporating pleasurable activities into a daily routine is important.

Ask the patient to make a list of pleasurable activities he or she used to enjoy as well as list of activities they may enjoy currently. If the activities include physical exertion or dietary considerations, please request that the list of activities be reviewed with the physician for any special precautions. Have the patient schedule pleasurable activities along with other activities as discussed earlier. These activities should also be broken down into concrete, manageable steps. For instance, if a patient used to enjoy bicycle riding for long periods, he or she may modify the length and frequency of the riding.

The following is a checklist of pleasurable activities that can be used as an exercise for the patient. This list is by no means exhaustive and the patient should be encouraged to add his or her own:

- ❑ taking a walk in the park
- ❑ going to a movie
- ❑ going out to eat
- ❑ shopping
- ❑ watching sports
- ❑ watching television
- ❑ reading a book or magazine
- ❑ working on arts and crafts
- ❑ playing golf
- ❑ going to a bar or nightclub
- ❑ listening to music
- ❑ tinkering on cars and other machines
- ❑ going for a drive in the country
- ❑ going to or hosting a party
- ❑ restoring antiques
- ❑ going to church
- ❑ taking a new class
- ❑ cooking
- ❑ being with animals
- ❑ working at your job
- ❑ playing an instrument or singing
- ❑ visiting with friends
- ❑ getting a massage
- ❑ doing volunteer work
- ❑ writing
- ❑ making love

Chapter 8

Coping Skills

The way an individual copes with stress is important when dealing with patients with medical illness. Holmes and Rahe (1967) defined stressful life events as "undesirable changes in the usual activities of an individual that require substantial behavioral readjustments" (p. 214). Examples of such stressful life events include bereavement, job loss, divorce, and acute illness. While positive life changes can also be defined as stressful, typically they do not lead to long-lasting psychological distress.

Chronic strains are persistent conditions that require daily readjustments and interfere with ordinary daily activities. Chronic illness is an example of this. The entire experience of being diagnosed with a medical illness, living with the symptoms, and keeping up with the medical treatments can be one of the most stressful experiences in an individual's life. Chronic illness can lead to further stressors including fear about death, physical and sometimes cognitive difficulties, alterations in body image, financial strain, conflicts with family secondary to the illness, and pain or discomfort associated with the illness and its medical treatments.

The way individuals cope with stress can affect whether they seek medical care, how well they adhere to medical regimens, and to what degree they seek social support. An individual's response to a medical illness is influenced by subjective interpretations about it: appraisals made about the illness and the individual's own needs for information, control, and level of optimism about recovery.

The Transactional Model

There is a wide body of research devoted to health, stress, and coping, which is relevant to the treatment of depression in the medically ill. Someone who suffers from depression—either as a premorbid condition (the depression existed before the illness) or as an adjustment reaction to the illness—uses patterns of coping similar to those used when dealing with other stressful life events. Coping has been defined by theorists as an individual's attempt to meet environmental demands to reduce negative consequences (Lazarus and Folkman 1984; Pearlin and Schooler 1978). Lazarus and Folkman (1984) further described coping as "constantly changing cognitive and behavioral efforts to manage specific external and/or internal demands that are appraised as taxing or exceeding the resources of the person." (p. 13)

The Transactional Model of Stress and Coping is based on the work of Lazarus and Folkman and provides a guide to understanding the processes of coping with stressful events. The impact of the stressor (the event or situation that causes stress) is mediated by the individual's appraisal of the stressor and the psychological, social, and cultural resources at his or her disposal (Lazarus and Cohen 1977; Cohen 1984). The individual first evaluates the potential harm of the stressor—this is referred to as *primary appraisal*—as well as his or her ability to change the situation and manage negative emotional reactions—*secondary appraisal.* Coping efforts are strategies used to manage the problems and regulate emotions. These efforts then lead to the adaptation to stress, including psychological well-being, functional status, and adherence to healthy behaviors.

Primary Appraisal

Primary appraisal refers to the individual's evaluation of the significance of a stressful event. If the event is evaluated as positive, irrelevant, or benign, then it will have little negative impact. Health problems are usually evaluated as threatening. Three basic primary appraisals take place: the perception of **susceptibility** to the threat, the perception of the **severity** of the threat, and the perception of **responsibility** for the threat. If an individual makes an appraisal of personal risk and severe threat, then he or she will make efforts to cope with the stressor. For example, if a person perceives herself as at risk for a heart attack, then she may be motivated to see a physician for an assessment of risk factors and seek social support to cope with her worry. However, heightened perceptions of susceptibility can cause enough psychological distress that the result is avoidance behavior. For example, Schwartz (1995) found that women who had a family history of ovarian cancer and who perceived themselves at high risk, were more prone to experiencing psychological distress; and Lerman and Schwartz (1993) found that women who were highly distressed about their personal risk for breast cancer were less likely to adhere to recommended breast cancer screening guidelines. Conversely, if an individual minimizes the potential impact of a health threat (especially if the health threat is uncertain or ambiguous), then distress can be reduced. This type of appraisal can also decrease motivation to practice positive health behaviors, as is often the case with smokers, who are less likely to perceive themselves as highly susceptible to the long-term consequences of smoking. The final component of primary appraisals is the perception of responsibility for the stressor. If a person perceives himself or herself as responsible for their illness, then feelings of guilt and depression can occur (Smith et al. 1993). For example, a smoker who develops lung cancer may feel particularly responsible for the illness and become angry with themselves, which can ultimately trigger feelings of depression. A less obvious example involves the patient who is injured in a car accident and makes self-deprecating statements about his stupidity for driving at that time of night, on that particular road. This type of perceived responsibility may not be obvious initially and may only be uncovered by a thorough evaluation.

Secondary Appraisal

Secondary appraisal is the evaluation of an individual's coping resources, perceived ability to change the situation, ability to manage one's emotional reaction to the stressor, and expectations about the effectiveness of one's coping resources. Perceived control over an illness has been associated with improved psychological adjustment (Taylor et al. 1991; Taylor 1992). Individuals vary in their perceptions of control, thereby influencing what actions they may take. For example, a woman who perceives herself as having high sense of control may be more likely to consult a physician immediately after having discovered a lump in her breast than a woman who has a low sense of control. Related to this concept is *self-efficacy*, the belief in one's ability to manage a particular situation (Bandura 1977). Self-efficacy can be specific to one situation and is not a global trait such as self-esteem; a man can have high self-efficacy or belief in his ability to manage exercising but may have low self-efficacy when it comes to resisting the temptation to smoke.

Coping Strategies

Coping strategies are typically classified as *problem-focused* coping and *emotion-focused* coping. Problem-focused coping strategies include problem-solving, information-seeking, and using strategies to manage the problem. Emotion-focused coping strategies include expressing emotions, seeking social support, denial, and avoidance; it can also include changing how a person feels about a situation. When a stressor is threatening and uncontrollable, an individual may use disengaging coping strategies (Taylor et al. 1991) such as distancing, distraction, avoidance, and denial. These techniques serve to minimize distress, especially in the beginning, when the individual needs to regroup and gather energy for further planning. However, too much avoidance and denial can lead to increased distress (Schwartz 1995). When a stressor is evaluated as controllable and an individual believes that they have abilities to cope (positive self-efficacy), then he or she is more likely to use engaging or problem-focused coping strategies (Aspinwall and Taylor 1992). Other coping strategies include acceptance, humor, self-distraction, and using religion or spirituality (Carver 1993; Reed et al. 1994).

Literature on coping strategies, adjustment to illness, and health behavior generally point to the psychological benefits of using active coping strategies and acceptance over avoidant and disengaging strategies (Lerman and Glanz 1997). Three recent studies examining the effect of coping on mood in cancer patients were consistent in their findings that using active strategies such as focusing on the positive and using social support were associated with lower levels of distress (Carver 1993; Dunkle-Schetter et al. 1992) Research indicate that persons with diabetes mellitus who use more constructive coping modes such as problem solving, seeking out professional help, and being persistent show better adherence to a medical regimen and better metabolic control compared to people who use nonconstructive coping modes such as wishful thinking, avoidance, and denial (Jacobson et al. 1990). Feifel and colleagues (1987) examined the relationships between coping strategies and health-related and personality variables. They found the following:

1. The use of avoidance was linked to negative self-esteem and to reduced self-directed life orientation.
2. Heart attack patients coped more successfully with their disability when they minimized the use of avoidance and resignation coping modes.
3. The use of resignation and acceptance coping modes was associated with negative self-esteem, lower expectations for chances of recovery, longer duration of chronic illness, and expression of negative affect.

The ability to use a variety of different strategies is also helpful in maintaining healthy behaviors. Health behaviors such as communicating with medical staff and adhering to medical regimens are obvious outcomes of efforts to cope with illness and are heavily influenced by emotional factors such as depression and anxiety. An individual's particular coping style and perception of social support are also influential in how effective coping strategies are.

Dispositional Coping Style

Some coping styles are defined as stable personality traits rather than an actual coping behavior. Lazarus (1993) further distinguishes dispositional coping style as a generalized style as opposed to coping strategies used for specific situations. An individual's particular style of coping can moderate the impact of stress. The most widely studied coping styles are optimism, information seeking, and locus of control.

Optimism is the tendency to have a positive outlook on life's outcomes as opposed to a pessimistic outlook. The expectation of a positive outcome has shown to be relatively stable across situations and over time (Scheier and Carver 1992). Several studies of cancer, coronary, and HIV-positive patients have shown positive effects of optimism on psychological adjustment (Carver et al. 1993; Scheier et al. 1989; Taylor 1992). Dispositional optimism was associated with active coping, planning, problem solving, and acceptance, and it was inversely related to avoidance.

Information seeking is another coping style involving the level to which an individual seeks or avoids information related to a stressor. Those individuals who become too vigilant can experience a heightened perceived risk of disease and excessive worry about health threats. However, information seekers also receive health information that could have significant benefits and adhere better to medical regimens (Lerman et al. 1994; Steptoe and Sullivan 1986). Conversely, those who avoid information related to their medical condition may experience less distress in the short term by being able to avoid and deny the reality of their situation. However, chronic long-term avoidance can lead to non-compliant behaviors such as missing appointments and not taking medications.

Finally, **locus of control**, another factor influencing coping style, is a generalized belief about one's ability to control events through one's actions (Rotter 1966). People who have an external locus of control are more likely to believe that their own actions do not have much impact on events that happen to them and they are therefore more likely to be influenced by others. People with an internal locus of control believe that their own actions can influence events and are therefore more likely to take action on their own. In turn, this leads to more active coping and greater efforts directed at controlling the environment. Applied to health behaviors, people with internal locus of control may participate strongly in trying to recover quickly and use vigilant coping strategies (Wallston and Wallston 1978). Those with an external locus of control might believe that what happened to them was due to chance and might not participate as aggressively in recovering or using preventive behaviors (Wallston and Wallston 1978). Many individuals who are depressed have an external locus of control where they believe that they are powerless to change what is occurring, thereby leading to feelings of helplessness and hopelessness. Depressed medical patients may believe that because they had no control over the illness befalling them, taking an active stance will not really help them manage or cope with the illness.

Strategies to Improve Coping Skills

Interventions that aim at teaching and promoting adaptive methods of coping are likely to help alleviate some depressive symptoms. In general, we encourage you to support any positive methods of coping the patient may already use. Patients will typically use coping strategies that have been learned over their life span, both from previous experiences and from their family of origin. As stated in the previous section, the use and benefit of coping strategies is influenced by the individual's personal needs for information, locus of control, and level of optimism or pessimism (Lerman and Glanz 1997). Interventions that take these dispositional coping styles into account will be more effective in helping the depressed medical patient cope better. Information regarding your patient's coping styles and strategies can be obtained through clinical interview and questionnaires such as the Ways of Coping Checklist (Lazarus and Folkman 1984) and the Psychosocial Adjustment to Illness Scale (Derogatis and Lopez 1983).

Coping strategies can also include maladaptive patterns such as chronic avoidance and denial or substance use. The issue of substance abuse will be discussed briefly in a later section. A note about the use of denial in medically ill patients is warranted here. Denial, in an extreme form, can result in a person failing to seek medical consultation for a problem, or even ignoring an acute symptom. However, denial is commonly seen in medically ill patients when it serves a protective function, giving them time to "regroup" and face the changes at a slower pace. Patients may actually be suppressing the overwhelming information rather than actually denying its existence. It is difficult for any person to live with the hopelessness of a serious illness such as cancer on a daily basis, so denial may serve to make reality more tolerable. When the use of denial interferes with necessary functioning, then it becomes maladaptive.

The structure of the following interventions should be based on the information gleaned from your clinical evaluation. Most depressed medical patients will benefit from working on all of the coping skills addressed here. Those areas that appear to be more problematic should receive more focused attention, practice, and review. Although an individual may have the ability to engage in active coping, the presence of depression may interfere with his or her ability to actually use these strategies.

Therefore, reviewing particular strategies during treatment, and encouraging the patient to practice them between sessions, can help structure and guide the depressed patient toward a more active self-management plan.

Education about the Illness

Any intervention that educates the patient about their particular illness is crucial to increasing coping ability and sense of personal control during the struggle with illness. When faced with the unknown, patients tend to feel powerless and overwhelmed and subsequently are at risk for depression. As mentioned previously, information seeking is a useful coping strategy in reducing overall distress when a crisis or stressor occurs. The first step is to clarify information about the medical condition, treatment, side effects, and other issues with the medical system such as insurance coverage. Many patients become overwhelmed when they hear the first preliminary diagnosis of an illness; depressive reactions can begin at this point, interfering with their ability to fully understand the volume of information being presented to them. Other patients may fear bothering their doctor or medical staff with what they perceive to be unnecessary questions. These people then tend to suffer in private while maintaining a facade of strength and positive adjustment. The following steps are useful in helping the patient gain the information pertinent to their condition.

Understand That Lack of Knowledge Is Troubling.

Explain to the patient that sometimes when confronted with information that is overwhelming, especially when it is a threat to physical health, people can shut down and be unable to comprehend all of what the medical staff is telling them. As a result, making decisions regarding the next step in treatment becomes difficult and confusing. In addition, information can be misperceived, creating negative feelings counterproductive to treatment. For instance, it is not unusual for patients to feel that their condition is hopeless and therefore not be motivated to participate in healthy practices which reduce the likelihood of recurrent symptoms. Furthermore, denial that a problem exists, whether because of fear of further medical procedures or fear about the meaning of the results, can be potentially dangerous to health.

Participate in Health Care.

Encourage the patient to think of themselves as active participants in their health care in order to increase a sense of control.

Write Down Questions.

Encourage the patient to prepare a written list of questions and concerns they may have. It is difficult to remember everything they might want to ask the doctor in the midst of life-altering news. Taking a notepad and asking the doctor to make a sketch of the medical procedure or diagram the particular organs affected can also be helpful. The following is a list of sample questions for the patient to ask:

- Could you describe my medical condition in specific terms?
- What did my test results reveal?
- What are the expectations for recovery?
- What are my risk factors?
- Could you describe all of the potential interventions?
- What kind of symptoms should be reported immediately?
- Which hospital should I go to in case of an emergency?
- What activities am I restricted from and for how long?
- What other resources do you have available to further educate myself on this condition? Are there pamphlets, books, or tapes available?

Write Down Information.

Encourage the patient to write down the information presented to them for later review. It is helpful to write information down because depressed patients often suffer from impaired concentration. The written information can then be reviewed later at a slower pace, giving the patient an opportunity to formulate further questions for the doctor.

Take Time to Reflect.

Remind the patient that except in an emergency, no decisions need to be made without some chance for reflection. You might suggest ways to gather more information as needed.

Discuss with Loved Ones.

Encourage the patient to consider bringing a family member or friend to appointments, both for support and because the other person can ask additional questions. This can also help alleviate some of the family's concerns by having someone get the information firsthand.

Organize Medication.

Medication issues are another area where patients often feel overwhelmed. It is likely that the patient may be prescribed more than one type of medication. Remembering when and how many to take of each can sometimes be difficult because some should be taken with food to avoid an upset stomach and others before a meal on an empty stomach. A further complication is that many of the medications may resemble each other in size and color. Helping the patient learn how to educate him- or herself about medications is another step in increasing self-efficacy. The information in the handout on pages 126–127 can be given to the patient to be used as a reference at home.

Minding Your Medications

The following tips will assist you in remembering to take your medications at the right times and in the right dosages. The effectiveness of your medications will depend on you taking them properly.

- **Same Time**—Plan to take your medications at the same time every day so that it becomes routine. It is often helpful to take them either right before or during your meals as advised by your doctor. Try to take them on time as well. If you miss a dose by several hours, ask your doctor if you should skip the dosage or go on to the next time. *Do not double up without first consulting your doctor.*
- **A Chart or Checklist of Medications**—A checklist will help you remember the amount and time of day that you need to take your medication.
- **Color Code**—You may want to color code your medication bottles if you have trouble reading them. Make a note on your chart or checklist of what color you choose to mark each drug.
- **Use a Pill Organizer**—Pill organizers are available at your local drugstore; they are little plastic containers divided into compartments. You can get seven-day pill containers that are marked for each day of the week and for morning, noon, and night; you can also get smaller-sized pill containers for travel if you plan on being away for the day. Electronic pillboxes are also available at a local drugstore or electronics store. These pillboxes can be set with alarms that remind you when it is time to take your medications. Using the alarm on your wristwatch can also be helpful.
- **Backup Supply**—If there are places away from home where you spend time regularly, plan to keep a backup or emergency supply of medications. For instance, you may be prescribed nitroglycerin in case of chest pain or discomfort. You should carry a supply with you at all times, have some in your car, work, and any other place where you regularly visit.
- **Know Your Pharmacist**—Select a pharmacy near you and get to know the pharmacist. A pharmacist can be very helpful in providing you with information about medication dosages, interactions with other medications, side effects, and so on. Make sure that the pharmacist is accessible and willing to answer questions. Also select a pharmacy, or backup pharmacy, that is available at night and during weekends.
- **Payment Options**—Some of the medications prescribed for you will be expensive. Ask your pharmacy about payment options. Do they accept your prescription insurance plan? Can you pay by credit card? Can you be billed monthly? Some of your medications may be available at a discount through mail order if you purchase them in larger quantities or repeatedly over time. The American Association of Retired Persons (AARP) has a list of mail order pharmacy services. Their phone number is (202) 434-2277.
- **Ask Your Doctor Questions**—Use the following guidelines to help you manage your medications. Begin by asking your doctor the following questions

about your medications. Writing down the information will be useful for later reference. Your doctor may also have some printed literature on some of the medications that are prescribed for you.

Questions Regarding Medications

1. What is each medication for and what is it supposed to do? What are the generic or brand names of each medication?
2. How much should I take at one time? How often? When? With food or on an empty stomach?
3. Do I need to avoid any foods or alcohol while taking these medications?
4. What over-the-counter medications, like allergy medications, or prescription drugs do I need to be careful about when taking this medication?
5. What are possible side effects? What are the treatments for any unpleasant side effects?
6. What symptoms should I report immediately? How long should I wait before calling you if I have any problems?
7. Will it be safe to drive or operate other heavy machinery?
8. Will any of the medications affect my ability to perform at work?
9. Are there any psychological side effects like depression or anxiety?

The medication containers may not be labeled with all of the instructions, so keep the information from the above questions handy as a reference if needed.

Problem-Solving Skills

Medical illness can cause a wide array of problems. The individual can face lifestyle changes involving daily routine, finances, work, and family functioning. Simply coping with the overall threat to physical well-being presents an imposing challenge for most people. The resulting feeling of helplessness can be further compounded when depression is present, since this feeling is also a symptom of depression. Effective skills in problem solving and increased confidence in problem-solving abilities have been found to be associated with lower rates of self-reported depression in disabled individuals. Furthermore, maintaining goal-directed behaviors and a higher level of hope was also associated with less distress (Elliot and Harkins 1991).

Since problem solving is believed to be responsive to clinical intervention, addressing these skills in the depressed medical patient can be useful in alleviating feelings of helplessness. Tackling a problem in a systematic manner will make it seem more manageable and less overwhelming.

There are times when a depressed patient must make important decisions about treatment options. As a therapist you can assist the patient in considering the options and deciding on a course of action. A woman with breast cancer, for instance, might be overwhelmed by the need to decide between a mastectomy and radiation therapy and partial resection. It is helpful to review the steps involved in both actions and encourage the patient to imagine her feelings taking one course of treatment, then the other. The therapist can help the patient explore personal feelings about a particular treatment, which the patient feels are too trivial or embarrassing to discuss with the physician

The extensive work of D'Zurilla (1986) and Nezu (1986) in the area of problem-solving therapy has provided much of the framework for teaching problem-solving skills. These techniques can be applied to any type of problem, including those related to coping with medical problems. You can begin improving the patients problem-solving skills by focusing on the basic principles below. The following list of steps can be given to the patient as a handout, but should first be practiced in the session to help understand the process. Begin by asking the patient to discuss a problem that is currently on his or her mind and then go through the following steps:

1. Recognize that there *is* a problem. The first step in problem solving is to acknowledge that a problem exists and decide that you are not going to avoid dealing with it.

2. Define the problem in as much detail as possible. Be specific and include how you feel about the situation.

3. Brainstorm some solutions. This means making a list of possible solutions *without* evaluating whether they are good or bad. The more ideas that you can generate, the more likely it is that you will find one that works. This is a good time to get ideas from other people as well.

4. Evaluate each of the solutions. Go back and rank them in terms of what you think is plausible. Think about the positive and negative consequences of each option. There is no perfect solution, but there may be one or two solutions that will work best for you.

5. Try out one of the solutions. You may have to try it out a few times before it works. Evaluate it to see what worked, where the problems were, and make adjustments as needed. If it was not effective, go back to steps 3 and 4 and try out another solution. Remember, there is no perfect solution, but one of the options should be fine.

Communication Skills

Frequently, depressed people experience stress during interactions with others because they do not feel equipped with the skills to effectively communicate. Yet medically ill patients are continually forced to communicate with the medical team as well as their families. Poor communication skills can lead to misunderstandings with the medical staff and conflict at home due to the increased stress of dealing with a chronic illness. In order to reduce potential for conflict, you should address communication skills when treating a medical patient. These skills are also important for the family members and medical staff to practice. There are many skills involved in interacting with people in general. Here are four important skills that may help the patient and family feel more at ease when interacting with each other and the medical staff. Poor communication with doctors, family members, and other caregivers is often at the root of much unnecessary pain and distress for the patient. You may need to work with the patient to improve communication skills by teaching the patient the following technique.

Learn to Read Non-Verbal Cues.

Part of the discomfort that people experience in social situations is often a result of their misinterpretation of others' body language. Inquire if the patient has ever said to themselves, "the doctor looks bored when I am talking" or " They seem like they are evaluating me." These statements can stem from the patient's misperceptions of body language. For example, a nurse may be yawning or not making great eye contact because he or she is lacking sleep or is uncomfortable in social situations and not because the nurse finds the patient boring. It is important for patients not to base all of their interpretations on the medical worker's body language alone. It is also important to pay attention to *their* own body language. Perhaps the patient is not aware of the signals that he is sending to others. For example, he may be physically separating himself from others based on where he stand. Or perhaps he tends to make poor eye contact with others or crosses his arms in front of himself as a way to keep distant from others. If the patient is doing these things he may be feeding into his own sense of isolation, discomfort, and feelings of being negatively evaluated by others. Reading another person's non-verbals and recognizing our own is a skill that takes practice.

As a way of becoming more aware of body language, you may suggest that the patient get together with a friend or a family member whom they trust. Instruct the patient to ask the other person to observe the non-verbal behavior and then give the patient feedback on what the person observed. Likewise, have the patient reverse roles and provide the friend or family member with feedback on what the patient observed. This information can be processed in a session. This is an excellent way for you to give the patient feedback on your observations of the non-verbal behavior you have observed.

Develop Active Listening Skills.

Good listening skills will help the patients interact more completely with others, which will in turn make them feel more comfortable in social situations. Although most people believe they are good listeners, they usually are not. Listening is a skill that, like any other, requires *practice.* To be a good listener means more than just hearing what the other person is saying; it means fully understanding the content of what the other person is saying in a non-judgmental way. The following information on improving listening skills can be given to the patient as a handout. You may need to practice these exercises with the patient by giving them examples related to interactions with the medical staff. For example, if a common complaint of your patient is that the doctor never seems to explain things well, then you may want to use the handout on page 131 as an example to teach active listening skills.

Ways to Improve Your Listening Skills

Avoid being judgmental and evaluative when listening to others.

Avoid planning your next response while the other person is still talking. If you are thinking about how to respond, you are probably not listening very well.

Avoid assuming that you know what the other person is saying. Once you start assuming you understand, you stop listening to the content.

Repeat back to the other person what you understood he or she has said but in your own words. Don't repeat verbatim like a parrot, but summarize the essence of what you heard. For example:

> Joe: My doctor told me today that I am at risk for another heart attack, but he didn't really tell me what to do before he left the room.
>
> Response: You seem upset with the doctor.
>
> Joe: Well, I'm irritated that the doctor gave me this serious news and left before I could ask any more questions about it. The whole thing is scary to me.

In order to repeat what you have heard, you need to pay close attention to what is being said to you through active listening. Moreover, by repeating back to the other person the essence of what you have heard, you give them the opportunity to clarify any misunderstandings. In the example above, the response was correct that Joe was upset, so the listener was able to get further information that Joe was specifically upset not only about the news of being at risk for another heart attack, but that he also had further questions to discuss with the doctor. By repeating back to the person what you understood you give them the chance to more fully explain their position. This helps the listener more accurately and fully understand what is being conveyed. The next step can be to problem-solve together. The listener, for example, could then help Joe formulate his questions for the doctor for the next time.

Initiate and Maintain Conversations.

It may be difficult for depressed patients to initiate conversations with other patients or health care providers. They may feel awkward and unsure where to begin. You may want to instruct and model for the patient ways to initiate conversation by beginning with open-ended questions. Remind them that these are questions that can not be answered with a simple yes or no answer. If they ask closed questions, or questions that can be answered with a yes or no response, the conversation is often over shortly after it begins: after the other person has responded the dialogue is limited. Open questions are those that ask what, when, where, and how. Remind the patient to avoid overusing why questions, as this can put people on the spot or make them feel defensive. Below is an example that you can share with the patient of a conversation using closed and open questions:

Closed Questions

Jack: Do you like red wine?

Sue: Yes.

Open Questions

Jack: What kind of wine do you like?

Sue: I usually like red wine but on certain occasions I drink white.

Jack: They serve an excellent white wine here.

Sue: How do you know so much about wine?

Jack: I took a wine tasting class.

You can see from this example that conversation flowed much smoother and with greater ease when there were open-ended questions asked. It provided the opportunity for more dialogue and interaction between the two people, leaving less room for stress.

Improve Assertiveness Skills.

Medical patients can often struggle with feeling insecure about asserting their feelings or needs to health care providers. Part of treatment should focus on teaching the patient appropriate assertiveness skills. To keep your patients motivated to learn these skills you may need to remind them that asserting their needs, feelings, and opinions will ultimately help them keep their stress level down. Patients may report that they feel socially awkward because they have nothing to contribute to a conversation. They may believe that the opinions and views of other patients, their family members, or the doctors are better or more interesting than their own. Teaching them to assert their opinions, thoughts, and feelings will make them feel more confident in themselves. This will be reflected in the way that they handle themselves in social or group situations with others. As a result, they will feel more relaxed, in control, and capable of coping with the medical condition. The handout on page 133 is a list of exercises that can be used with the patient in the sessions and then taken home for review.

Ways to Improve Your Assertiveness

Keep in mind that assertiveness is not aggressiveness. Assertiveness is a balance between the extremes of aggressiveness and submissiveness. People who act in an aggressive style demand and expect others to do exactly what they want. Those who act in a submissive style give up their own beliefs, opinions, and wants to the demands of others. They feel guilty to ask for what they want as if others' needs are more important than their own. An assertive person respects others' views and feelings but also values and respects their own.

Look others directly in the eyes when talking to them and maintain an open posture. This will be easier to do if you reinforce for yourself that what you are saying is important. Don't assume a posture that says you are absolutely right—such as glaring at others when speaking, and ending your statements as if there is no questioning or doubting your words.

Be specific when making requests. Vague requests or comments can often be misinterpreted by others or simply ignored. If your request is very specific and direct, there is little room for confusion. For example, instead of asking for someone's help in general, specifically state *what* you want help with, *when*, and for *how* long.

When discussing an opinion or making a request, use statements that begin with I. For example, "I feel . . ."; "I want . . ."; or "I think . . ." When you use I-statements, it is more likely that others will be receptive to hearing what you have to say. Statements that start out with "you," such as, "You said . . ." or "You think . . ." tend to make the other person defensive and less likely to be open to what you are saying.

Observe the behavior, non-verbals, and conversations of others who appear to be quite comfortable in social situations. Examine how your non-verbals, behavior, and conversation are similar and different from their style.

- List a few people you know who seem attentive and at ease when interacting with others.
- Which of their characteristics gives you the impression that they are at ease with others and able to truly listen
- What similarities do you notice between your style in social situations and their style?
- What differences do you notice between their style and yours?

Practice modeling the characteristics that you feel helps them interact with others without becoming stressed. For example, if they seem to assume a certain body posture, practice that posture when you are alone and then when you are in a social situation.

Alter Negative Thinking

The use of cognitive therapy principles and techniques to address thought patterns that contribute to depression is well established by Aaron Beck (1979) and others. These techniques can help medically ill patients *manage* their responses to very realistic stressors such as dramatic changes in daily life, chronic pain, and physical dysfunction. Caution must be used, however, in interpreting justifiable depressive reactions to traumatic illness as dysfunctional thought patterns: *People suffering a medical illness may need time to adequately grieve their losses before they are receptive to learning better thought patterns.* Pace these sessions gradually while carefully monitoring and giving the patient ample opportunity to express his or her emotions. You can use cognitive techniques to adapt the patient's *coping* thoughts about medical illness.

The first step in cognitive therapy is to identify negative thoughts. Explain to the patient how negative thoughts can increase anxiety and depression and a sense of helplessness. The following is a list of examples of different styles of negative thought that can undermine the ability to cope and manage an illness:

- "I can't cope." (emotional filtering)
- "Poor me; everything bad happens to me." (catastrophizing)
- "I'll never get better." (polarized thinking and catastrophizing)
- "I should have gotten better faster than this" or "I'm not cured yet." (polarized or black-and-white thinking)
- "I'll never be able to enjoy life again." (polarized thinking)
- "The doctor is not giving me the best treatments." (blaming)
- "This is all my fault that I got sick." (blaming)
- "I shouldn't feel sorry for myself." (should statement)
- "The treatment isn't working at all." (polarized thinking)

Teach your patients to identify their own list of negative thoughts about their ability to cope. Instruct them to try to think of what thoughts were going through their mind as they began to feel more depressed. Many of these statements will become apparent during the treatment sessions, particularly during the supportive phase, where the clinician is primarily and listening providing emotional support to the patient. You may want to lead in by telling the patient, "I notice that you often make comments about your inability to cope, or focus on the negative aspects of the illness. Let's discuss how you can change some of those negative statements into more positive ones to help you feel stronger."

The following is a list of positive coping statements that can be used by the patient. Help the patient specifically match a positive statement with the negative one. The patient may have to practice these statements by writing them down and repeating them to themselves often.

- "I can cope."
- "I have managed difficult situations before; I can manage this one."

- "I am learning new ways to cope."
- "The doctors are doing the best they can."
- "Some people's treatment takes awhile to work."
- "I did nothing to cause my illness; and even if I did, I have to forgive myself."
- "Bad things sometimes happens to people; I have had lots of positive things happen to me."
- "I am going through a difficult time right now; I deserve to feel some emotions about it."
- "I may not be able to do some of the same things I did before, but I can still enjoy life."
- "Although I may never be completely well, I am making some headway slowly but surely."
- "Forget about blaming, hindsight is always clear."
- "I can cope with whatever happens."
- "I am not helpless; I have the power to improve my situation."
- "I do not always have to be in control."
- "I have the skills, friends, and resources to cope."
- "I know that I have the right to be upset, so I will let myself feel sad for a while."
- "When my emotion subsides, I will look at my situation again."
- "Even though I have suffered some losses, I will find new things to do that will put meaning in my life."

In summary, depressed medical patients will suffer from the same cognitive distortions that depressed non-medically ill patients have. These thought patterns are part of the overall coping style and set of strategies that each individual chooses to use in periods of stress. Almost all depressed medical patients can benefit from a review of their coping skills, pointing out the ones they already use effectively and improving on the others that are not as strong. Improving their thought patterns around the illness to focus on positive coping statements will improve self-efficacy and decrease feelings of helplessness and hopelessness.

Coping with Loss

Medical illness has a profound impact on an individual's life, creating an interruption and threat to the tasks of living. The magnitude of loss for patients with chronic and life-threatening illness is tremendous, because it encompasses multiple areas of their lives. These areas include physical integrity and body image, changes in interpersonal relationships, vocational and achievement issues, and loss of independence. The impact of these losses and changes can be understood using a developmental life-cycle model.

Understanding the Life Cycle

Life-cycle theories seek to place people in the context of their particular ages. Each age range, such as adolescence, early adulthood, or late adulthood, are characterized by certain **tasks of life**; these are areas of primary concern such as defining a career, finding a partner, beginning a family, which can become areas of vulnerabilities if these tasks are disrupted. Medical illness often disrupts the tasks of living, and subsequently leads to depressive symptoms.

Although, as stated above, there are common areas of disruption, the point at which an individual is in their life cycle can influence the relative impact of certain changes. For example, an unmarried thirty-two-year-old with a diagnosis of a cancer that is life threatening and causes an alteration in body image and possible sterility from chemotherapy may be profoundly depressed about the fear of not finding a partner and the threat of not being able to bear children. An individual with a family to support financially may be primarily depressed because his medical illness has forced him to resign from his full-time job. Many life cycle or developmental tasks will overlap over an individual's life span: nonetheless, understanding the tasks that are prominent at each phase will be useful in helping the patient understand his or her particular depression. Poor adjustment to the changes caused by medical illness not only leads to depression, but also manifests itself in noncompliance and decreased quality of life.

Further detailed reading regarding the life cycle is available in the developmental psychology literature; theorists such as Erikson (1963) discuss the whole life span, while others specialize in certain age ranges (Jacobs 1991). Since this book's focus is primarily for adults with medical illness, discussion of life-cycle stages will be limited to the tasks of adulthood. It is noted, however, that the life cycle is a continuum, and understanding the whole cycle is useful, especially when intervening with family members of all ages. Medical illness in one member will affect the entire family. Family issues are discussed in chapter 9.

The developmental phases are outlined below:

The Young Adult (19-30 Years)—One of the developmental tasks of the young adult is identifying a vocational path and making plans to pursue career goals. Formal education and training is often done during this time. Socially, the young adult's primary life task is centered around achieving intimacy and closeness with others. Sexual identity is usually solidified and establishing a strong relationship with a partner becomes a major goal. Milestones during this period may include commitment to another through marriage or cohabitation and entering into parenthood. Erikson (1963) marked this period by intimacy versus isolation. If something occurs to disrupt the goal of forming close and intimate ties, the result can be isolation.

A diagnosis of a major illness at this stage can bring about fears of intimacy with another person; even an already established relationship can become strained because of the fear and guilt about the potential consequences of the illness. An individual may feel isolated at this time when peers are not experiencing similar stress. The young parent will be concerned about leaving behind young children if the illness is life threatening. Self-esteem is affected as an individual may become dependent on others. If the illness and treatments cause alterations in body image and sexual functioning, confidence in the ability to maintain satisfying relationships is undermined. Expectations and goals for a career may become severely curtailed leading to feelings of disappointment, and ultimately depression.

The Mature Adult (31-45 Years)—This period is characterized by a consolidation of goals, both career and social. This is usually the most stable stage in the life course but one that is marked with multiple responsibilities. For many, this time is the peak of intellectual ability, with career goals being accomplished. Socially and emotionally, life tasks center around parenting and maintaining stable relationships. Roles are specifically defined at home and at work. Erikson (1963) characterized this period as balancing generativity (marked by productivity and caring for the next generation) and stagnation.

Disruptions at this stage can result in a failure to achieve a sense of productivity and meaning. Body image issues and threats to physical integrity have the same consequences as described above and are further compounded by the normal process of aging. The reversal of roles to one of dependency on others and the partner assuming more can be very difficult on the individual and family. Relationships that had difficulties can crack under the strain of a serious illness. Therefore, the diagnosis of a medical illness during this period can again contribute to feelings of despair and hopelessness because of the disruptions to all aspects of an individual's life.

The Older Adult (46-65 Years)—Individuals in this phase are adapting to a variety of changes both physically and socially. Physical changes during this period include changes in skin, bone density, and muscle mass, and for some, a redistribution of fatty deposits. Women face menopause and the accompanying changes caused by a shift in hormone levels. These changes create an awareness of physical vulnerability. Socially, the adult is establishing new roles with adult children and the relationship with a partner without children in the home. Others may be establishing a second marriage or may still have children in the home if they started their families later. Vocationally, this is a period of career peak where goals are either achieved or adjusted to meet reality.

An illness during this period disrupts a sense of independence and accomplishment, both financially and socially. Illness can disrupt a chronically unhappy marriage and create conflict between a healthy couple, who may have difficulty adapting to the sudden changes in roles after many years of marriage. The patient may fear becoming dependent on others (such as older children) while not being able to bear the financial burden. If early retirement is needed secondary to a disability, there can be disappointment about a career cut short and financial concerns as well. People can become so despairing at this time, worrying about the future welfare of their family, that they may contemplate suicide as an option to draining the family. Finally, depression can be seen at this point because life review may result in disappointments about missed accomplishments and struggles about the purpose of one's life. The further threat that illness brings results in an increased awareness of one's mortality.

The Aging Adult (66 Years and Older)—With the increasing life expectancy, the population of adults that will enter into late adulthood is increasing. The issues they face will mostly be influenced by the health and physical integrity they have. While there is a general decline in physical status as part of normal aging, the variability in the condition of an eighty-year-old who is still active in his or her own home is vastly different than the seventy-year-old who suffers from a chronic medical illness. The aging adult faces an increasing sense of isolation as their peers die.

The aging adult who has been successful in taking care of themselves and others will have difficulty in suddenly relinquishing this role and asking for help. It is not uncommon to hear of older adults having difficulty letting caregivers into their home for assistance. Financially, the burden of an illness is a strain on a fixed retirement budget. People may feel anger at having finally retired to enjoy life and then having a chronic illness befall them. The aging body is more fragile and vulnerable to the secondary complications of, and treatments for, illness. The aging adult also engages in life review, and if it does not meet expectations, this can lead to despair and feelings of failure and guilt. A depressive response to illness is seen during this time because of the overload of the multiple loss and changes (such as physical, possible move to nursing home, isolation from family). Individuals who are ill also fear a long protracted period of suffering preceding death.

Strategies to Cope with Loss.

As described above, the tasks of living become significantly disrupted as a result of medical illness. These disruptions can lead to feelings of prolonged depression characterized by feelings of despair and hopelessness. It is important to help the depressed medical patient understand the connection between experiencing all of these changes and subsequently feeling depressed. A review of losses and changes specific to each individual patient is important to address how he or she can cope with the emotions and then later develop active cognitive skills such as problem-solving.

You can set the foundation for this work by first asking the patient to determine what changes have occurred in his or her life as a result of the illness and what feelings these changes have generated. For instance, has the illness caused a drastic change in physical appearance as in a spinal cord injury, or has the illness forced a dependency on others? Use the list below as a prompt but explore all aspects of a patient's life and encourage additional responses as needed.

Physical Problems

- significant weight loss or gain
- skin discoloration
- weakness
- fatigue
- itching
- sexual difficulties
- nausea

- headaches
- hair loss
- bone pain or other pain
- changes in diet
- sleep difficulties
- increased medications
- loss of a body part
- loss of ability to walk or be physically active
- other ________________

Psychosocial Changes

- loss of job
- can only work part time
- loss of financial security
- more dependent on others
- dependent on treatments
- feelings of helplessness
- more anxious and fearful
- more irritable
- loss of control over your schedule
- marital problems
- family having problems coping with your illness
- can't parent your children the way you would like to
- don't feel as masculine anymore
- don't feel as feminine anymore
- afraid that your loved one will leave you
- afraid that your loved one won't take care of you
- loss of personal freedom with multiple hospitalizations
- loss of ability or time to enjoy previous hobbies
- the reality of decreased life expectancy
- other ____________________

After the patient has come up with a personal list of losses and changes, ask him or her to list the changes that are most painful and difficult to cope with. Some of the changes can be coped with by addressing coping skills such as increasing social support and problem-solving skills. Explore the feelings that are generated by these changes such as depressed mood, guilt, frustration, anger, and poor self-esteem. Be sure to educate the patient on the link between these very real losses and changes and the patient's normal emotional reactions. Assist the patient in learning to express emotions appropriately by providing a supportive non-pressured therapeutic environment. In times of exacerbation of illness, you will probably want to return to providing support rather than active interventions. What is often very therapeutic for the medically ill patient is to allow them ample opportunity to vent their concerns. Once the emotion has subsided, more active coping efforts can be initiated.

For some patients, their medical condition may affect their previous ability to express themselves; changes in facial expression due to Parkinson's disease or loss of ability to move limbs with normal function because of multiple sclerosis or paralysis can hinder emotional expression. The expression of emotion can be done through alternative methods such as music and the creative arts or writing. Encourage the patient to explore which venues are the most comfortable. Encourage the patient to try their hand at an art or craft project of some type as an experiment if they have not done so in the past. Many patients report that the soothing nature of other forms of expression has been very helpful to the patient, particularly when attempting to cope with unchangeable medical conditions.

Coping with Chronic Pain

Many medical illnesses are accompanied by chronic pain, which can be unremitting for the patient. Pain becomes a frequent reminder that the illness is still present and a signal for many that they might not recover their health. Further, the physical hardships caused by pain force people to withdraw from others, contributing to feelings of isolation, loneliness, and depression. Depression is a frequent related condition of chronic pain and it bears addressing as a clinical issue.

A detailed discussion of the assessment and treatment for chronic pain is beyond the scope of this book. Catalano and Hardin (1996) offer a more detailed discussion of managing chronic pain in their *Chronic Pain Control Workbook*. They provide detailed step-by-step instructions on how to cope with chronic pain.

For the purpose of this book, the following section will summarize pain management strategies that can be used to augment your treatment of depression. It is strongly encouraged that you make a referral to a pain specialist for comprehensive treatment if chronic pain is significantly interfering with the patient's mood and ability to function.

Obtain a Comprehensive Pain Evaluation.

A comprehensive pain assessment will help clarify the psychological and physical components of the pain. This will aid in the development of appropriate strategies to improve pain. These strategies typically will involve a multi-modal treatment plan designed to address the pain and associated physical, psychosocial, behavioral, and emotional problems for the patient. Multi-modal approaches may include surgical procedures, anesthetic approaches to numb the pain, pharmacological management with pain medications, and psychological approaches.

Try Relaxation Techniques.

Tension and stress can increase the sensation and experience of pain. Therefore, teaching the patient how to relax and reduce physical stress is important. Consider teaching the patient how to use progressive muscle relaxation and guided imagery. Please refer to the sleep section in chapter 7 for a detailed description of these exercises.

Use a Graduated Exercise Program.

This involves providing the patient with an exercise plan that gradually increases from simple activities to more strenuous ones. Ask patients to keep a diary of their level of pain with each of the activities. Swimming, walking, and stretching can be good exercises for a person challenged by a medical condition.

Decrease Negative Thoughts.

Help the patient decrease the level of pain through psychological management techniques such as learning to manage difficult situations and addressing negative thoughts and anxieties. This can be accomplished by improving communication skills and altering negative self-talk as was discussed earlier in the chapter.

Set Small Achievable Goals.

Pain can interfere and at times prevent the patient from engaging in many activities. It is important to help the patient return back to partial functioning by assisting in setting small achievable goals. For example, encouraging the patient to simply get out of bed and sit in a chair for limited time periods or to walk outside for a short time. By making the goal achievable and then expanding the activity or lengthening the time, you improve the patient's sense of control. This in turn will improve management of the pain and reduce feelings of depression.

Use Humor.

The well-known example of using humor as a pain reliever is provided by the former *Saturday Review* editor Norman Cousins. When fighting the effects of a chronic illness, he found that laughter was the most effective painkiller. He found that ten minutes of hearty laughter from watching funny movies would provide him with several hours of pain-free sleep (Cousins 1990).

Research has shown that laughter relieves pain by reducing muscles spasms. When we laugh, physical tension in the body dissipates and the spasms relax. Also, laughter stimulates the brain to release endorphins, which are the body's own painkiller. It is estimated that endorphins are two hundred times more powerful than morphine. Endorphins also reduce inflammation and can stimulate the immune system, which fights off diseases and infections. Laughter appears to improve the immune system by reducing the stress hormones secreted by the body, which generally suppresses the immune system (Ornstein and Sobel 1989). One hundred good belly laughs have the same health benefits as fifteen minutes on a stationary bicycle (Fry 1997).

Not only is laughter healing for physical pain, but also for emotional pain. The psychological benefits of laughter include diminishing fears, calming anger, and relieving depression. Humor relieves depression by managing pain and stress and by offering a new perspective for coping. So, encourage your patients to laugh more often. At first this may be difficult and they may need to learn to give themselves permission to laugh in the face of pain and sadness. Once they are able to recognize that laughter is really good medicine, you can offer some of the following suggestions for using humor to cope:

- Watch funny movies.
- Make weekly contact with a friend who makes you laugh.
- Start a humor collection by clipping out cartoons, jokes, etc.
- Use sticky notes that have funny sayings.
- Do something silly at least once a week.
- Remember to choose humorous material that is suited for you. Much of what makes for good humor are those books, movies, or sitcoms that allow you to laugh at yourself or the social mistakes of others. This type of humor can give you social cues about appropriate behavior and can teach you that it is acceptable to make mistakes at times. This attitude will lead you to be more tolerant of others and yourself.

Find Meaning in the Illness

The old adage, "If you have your health you have everything," highlights the importance that is placed on physical integrity. Consider that a simple cold can influence a person's ability to work, enjoy a meal, engage in pleasurable activities, and quite often can interfere with mood: it is difficult to be happy and energetic when feeling physically ill. If these changes in an individual's day-to-day existence can occur with a mere cold, it is not hard to understand that more serious, chronic, and debilitating illness can have profound effects on every aspect of one's life. The effect of a physical illness on your patient's mood, behavior, and ability to cope is frequently influenced by the personal meaning of the illness. How has the illness altered their view of themselves? Do they feel they have become *nothing* without their health? Patients who are able to find meaning and coherence in their illness tend to feel more in control and therefore less depressed. Factors that influence meaning may include the self-image of the person, the nature of the illness, and early dynamic issues.

The personal meaning of a physical illness has long been recognized as an important and central factor in the emotional response and adjustment of the individual. Robert Shuman (1996) in his book, *The Psychology of Chronic Illness*, poignantly writes about illness from his own personal experience with multiple sclerosis. He states that for most people, the body is experienced simply as background, but for those with medical illness, the body becomes a dominant figure. We exist through our bodies from birth to death and, when in good health, we take for granted the routine actions of day-to-day living. When physical illness occurs, the patient can no longer take things for granted. They are faced with the task of making sense out of what has happened and defining the meaning of the illness in an effort to more effectively cope.

The goal for the clinician is to assist the patient in recognizing the meaning—the idiosyncratic, highly personal impact of the illness in an attempt to improve coping. Explore the meaning of the patient's body prior to the illness and subsequently the way that the illness has altered that view.

Individuals whose self-esteem prior to the illness was directly related to their bodily appearance, physical strength, and stamina are often more vulnerable to depression as a result of a physical illness. Patients who, prior to the illness, viewed themselves as weak and inept may view the illness as a reminder or reinforcement of that belief. Further, the patient who struggles with a negative self-image may view the illness as a punishment. That may be the meaning of the illness for the patient. Assisting the patient in recognizing the meaning of the illness and its effects on their self-esteem can facilitate integration of the illness. This can be accomplished by direct examination and discussion of the effects and meaning of the illness or by using metaphors to indirectly explore the meaning.

Healing Through Metaphors

A wonderful strategy to help patients explore emotionally guarded material and subsequently uncover the meaning of the illness is to use metaphors. Metaphors allow people to express the inexpressible and to communicate something intangible through a tangible image. It is the side-door approach of therapy. An opportunity to explore feelings, images, and thoughts in a safe, symbolic, and comfortably distant yet intimate manner.

The use of metaphors should be used in therapy by experienced clinicians who feel comfortable with psychodynamic theories and techniques. For more extensive information on using metaphors in therapy, read Ellen Siegelman's book, *Metaphor and Meaning in Psychotherapy* (1990).

Medically ill patients are not always willing to admit or discuss feelings of depression. The primary thought is often on their medical condition and the related image of themselves as medical not psychiatric patients. Also, depression can often leave patients feeling overwhelmed and thereby unable to process information directly. In the process of integrating an illness into one's psyche, metaphors allow us to attach creative new feelings and sensations to an old familiar image or context.

Metaphors can use other people to make a point about a patient's circumstances in a non-threatening way. It is important when utilizing metaphors focusing on other people, that you are sensitive to the level of the patient's feelings of personal helplessness. That is, if a patient feels that others can succeed but they personally are unlikely to, the use of metaphors may not be therapeutic (Yapko 1988).

Metaphors can be effectively used to identify and highlight the underused aspects of the self. With physical illness comes loss, change, and transformation, so the goal of treatment is to help the patient recognize that the whole self is not lost, only parts of it. This loss gives the patient an opportunity to reclaim other parts of the self that can bring happiness and completeness. It is an opportunity for the patient to reconnect with parts of the self that have been lost. Illness disrupts the familiar life narrative and forces patients to retell their story using other characters or parts of themselves. The following metaphor can be used to begin the process of integrating parts of the self when illness has altered the image:

> I worked with a woman once who felt that her illness had robbed her of her opportunity to be happy. She felt that her happiness came from feeling good about the way that she looked and the way that others responded to her looks. She felt angry when others would tell her that she was still the same person. When she looked in the mirror, she saw a very different person from the one whom she felt like before the illness. She didn't really believe that she could ever feel comfortable and happy in her changed body. Throughout the course of therapy she was able to recall other times in her life when things changed without her consent. She felt out of control and angry but later was able to realize new potential within herself. She felt stronger and more in control. The challenge for her was to feel attractive in a new way. A disconnected part of herself was her intellect: she learned as a child that she would get praise and recognition for how she looked and rarely for what she thought. Unconsciously she led her life focusing on her appearance, the attention and how it would make her feel good about herself. She continued to read and write but rarely shared that part of herself. After she got sick she found herself "forced" to communicate with others differently; she began to share her thoughts, ideas, and writing with others. She had rediscovered a part of herself and surprisingly found herself receiving attention and recognition from others. It was this undiscovered part of herself that allowed her to feel attractive and happy again.

Triggers for Meaning

Sometimes a person's ability to cope is influenced not only by the general meaning of the illness but by triggers for meaning. This may include smells, sounds, or sights related to the medical illness that may not have meaning unto themselves but may call back something else in a person's life. A sight or smell, for instance, may trigger an old memory or feeling from another painful event and, by association, the trigger becomes painful. Consider the following example:

> Joe was fifty-six and had received a heart transplant. He was experiencing increased anxiety and depression when undergoing his endomyocardial procedure used to detect early signs of organ rejection. The procedure is performed with the use of a small catheter with pincers on the end, called a bioptome. The bioptome is inserted into the internal jugular vein via a small incision into a fully awake and alert patient. The bioptome is then

guided into the right ventricular chamber of the heart where pieces of tissue forming the myocardium are removed and examined microscopically for early evidence of rejection. The patient can often feel the bioptome "tugging" at the heart while the tissue samples are removed.

After working with Joe and exploring the meaning of this procedure and his strategy for coping, his distress became clear. In a particular session he disclosed that his twenty-two-year-old son had been stabbed to death at a party six months ago. When Joe felt the initial incision during the biopsy procedure, he would make an association to his son's suffering and death: he would begin to imagine the excruciating pain that his son must have endured and to experience his own guilt for being unable to save him. These thoughts would become so intrusive and distressing that Joe would experience high levels of physiological arousal while on the surgical table. This would make the procedure medically more complicated. These negative thoughts of his son's suffering and his own unconscious wish to share in the pain as a way of punishing himself became associated with the biopsy procedure. Individual treatment focused on addressing his own guilt and anger over having had no control over what happened. We helped him establish a different association with the biopsy procedure and learned to use cues in the environment to trigger alternative strategies to coping.

The Process of Becoming a Medical Patient

The meaning of an illness is not only related to the illness and its treatment, but also influenced by the mere process of being a patient. Becoming a medical patient is not always an easy transition. The following statement from a patient poignantly describes the hospital experience for many:

> I am a sixty-three-year-old woman and have never been really sick a day in my life. When I was told I had heart disease and needed to check into the hospital I became somewhat nervous. I did not know what to expect. When I arrived at the hospital I was told to get undressed and to put all of my belongings in the locker. I felt as if I were hanging up my identity. As I was lying there in bed, something I would never dream of doing in the daylight hours, I began to feel nervous and embarrassed. Strangers would enter my room and see me in my pajamas. I felt demoralized. As the days passed, I found it difficult to adjust to having my meals chosen for me, or to be told when to bathe, to sleep, and to rest. The *me* that I knew was ebbing away and being replaced by a sick, incompetent, child-like person. I was no longer allowed to make decisions for myself and felt my independence and privacy were gone. I could deal with the pain, the procedures, and even the hospital food, but to be unable to work, to think clearly, and to have my motivation and energy for life gone was more than I could handle. Several months ago I was sitting in business meetings with people who respected my opinions and knowledge. Today I'm being asked if my "bottom" is sore or if my "tummy" hurts. I have also been called "dear" and "honey" twice today. In the business world, this would be considered

> sexual harassment. Is it acceptable because I am lying here in bed in my pajamas and not in a suit? My depression began slowly with feelings of hopelessness and fatigue, and as time passed I began to feel pessimistic about ever being healthy, competent, and worthwhile again. I had always thought that depression was something that only the weak could "catch." What happened to me?

In summary, before a patient can search to find hope, purpose, and meaning in an illness, they need to understand what effects the illness has had on them. Often patients may be aware of some of the meaning of the illness, while other issues may be less clear. To help a patient find meaning and purpose, you will want to use strategies that deal directly with conscious material, like having them describe how they feel about the illness and the process of being a patient, as well as indirect strategies, such as using metaphors, to help uncover issues that may not be in the patient's awareness.

Spirituality

We have been impressed by the number of medically ill people who have been successful in making difficult lifestyle changes as well as successfully coping with medical illness by relying on spiritual beliefs. Patients and their families seem to come out of the crises with renewed vigor, purpose, and meaning to their lives. They do not spend an overly large amount of time being bitter about what happened to them, nor do they stay stuck in an endless cycle of repeating the same lifestyle patterns they had before their medical illness. Rather, they go about systematically changing their life without a lot of need for outside attention. They seem to gather strength from elsewhere, from a place they call spirituality.

Spirituality or spiritual health has been defined by some

> as a state of well-being—not just the absence of disease; something that gives meaning and purpose to life—finding a meaning and wisdom in the here-and-now difficulties;
>
> a sense of connectedness to one's deepest self and others;
>
> or simply a sense of hope and positive expectations.

Dr. O. Carl Simonton, a renowned radiologist oncologist who spent years of research on the connection between the mind and the body, wrote,

> I believe that beyond the mind and the body, there is another aspect of healing that needs to be addressed: the spiritual aspect. . . . the dictionary defines *spirit* as the life principle, especially in humans, and the feelings and motivating part of our lives. . . . our work with patients has demonstrated that health involves body, mind and spirit. And while the mind alone can be used to influence the physical state, it is used most effectively when it is aware of spirit. (Simonton & Henson 1992, p. 13)

Religion and spirituality are important components in the lives of many. Approximately 95 percent of adults in the United States express a belief in God and 88 percent pray (Hoge 1996). A number of studies have linked religious coping with greater overall mental health and well-being. A study of medically ill elderly patients found religious coping related to fewer depressive symptoms and lower scores of depression at the six month follow-up (Koenig et al. 1992). Among kidney transplant patients, religious coping was related to less distress among significant others and more life satisfaction in both the patient and family (Tix and Frazir 1998). Similarly in a study of three hundred terminally ill and non-terminally ill hospitalized patients, spirituality was significantly related to low death fear, low discomfort, decreased loneliness, and better emotional coping and adjustment (Reed 1987).

The search for purpose or meaning in life has plagued people for centuries. The process of this quest can leave people feeling either exhilarated and renewed at the realization of meaning or empty at their inability to find this meaning or purpose. Think about some of the language that we use when we talk about meaning and purpose in our lives. We refer to it as "something being missing." While we may not be able to put a label on what is missing, we are aware of an incomplete feeling. Patients will sometimes refer to the feeling that they do not have a sense of purpose or meaning in their life. These feelings are usually triggered when people suffer a life-altering crisis or even a brush with death as is the case with many medically ill patients. They may ask themselves questions such as "Why did this happen to me?"; "What am I going to do now?"; and "What if I have another set back in my illness?"

The spirit is traditionally believed to be that vital force within living beings that gives us vigor and energy and provides us with a sense of determination and courage. This spirit or energy can come from many different avenues. This feeling of being complete and energized can come from organized religions, prayers to whomever it is that you believe in, or from meditation that focuses our energy and attention in the present. Each of these different sources of spiritualism share a common goal of increasing our internal energy source that allows us to live more fully in the present. By more fully experiencing the *process* of living, we end up feeling more complete, less stressed, and happier at a core level of our being. Spirituality can help many patients cope more effectively by helping them

experience peace of mind—a deep feeling of safety and calmness;

find some purpose or meaning to their life when something bad happens;

give strength and support during a crisis;

and help them feel more connected to others.

For patients who wish to develop their spirituality or strengthen it, the following strategies are offered:

Practice Meditation and Relaxation as Often as Possible—Exercises are offered in the sleep section of chapter 7.

Do for Others—A dimension of spirituality is the feeling of connectedness to others—the willingness to do more for others than for yourself. Research has shown that doing good deeds for others may actually have a positive effect on the immune and nervous systems (Rockefeller and Luks 1988). James Lynch, a researcher at the

University of Maryland School of Medicine, wrote in his book, *The Broken Heart: The Medical Consequences of Loneliness,* "One thing you get from caring for others is you're not lonely. And the more connected you are to life, the healthier you are" (Lynch 1977, p. 42).

The antithesis of doing for others is having self-centered thoughts and behaviors. Engaging in acts of kindness for others also serves as a great distraction from our own distress. Our focus shifts from dwelling on our own distress toward helping others. When we focus more on others than on ourselves we begin to develop qualities of altruism. These qualities include optimism, sense of purpose, and spirituality, each of which has been identified as an important component to effective coping and decreased depression.

Subsequently, therapeutic efforts should help the patient focus on acts of kindness toward others as a way to distract from their own distress and to keep them connected with others:

- Encourage your patients to do volunteer work.
- Ask them to pace themselves and only offer services to others that they think they can reasonably handle
- Remind them that giving to others is important, but it is equally important to recognize their own limits to avoid feeling overwhelmed. If the patient has physical limitations, assist them in finding alternative ways to volunteer by phone or written correspondence.

Chapter 9

Social Support

Social support can be defined as supportive personal relationships. Also known as structural support, these relationships may include being married, belonging to groups, or just having frequent interactions with others resulting in a strong and cohesive social network. It can also be defined in more qualitative terms, such as the feeling of being connected to others and subjectively feeling supported (Heitzmann and Kaplan 1988). This measure of support assesses an individual's *perception* of the availability and quantity of support; some patients may have many supportive friends and family members but do not *feel* supported by them.

Isolation and the related perceived lack of social support is both a contributing and a resultant factor of depression. Individuals who have limited social support have a higher prevalence rate of depression and those who are depressed tend to further isolate themselves. Research has clearly shown that social support and depression predicts survival in patients with coronary artery disease (Frasure-Smith et al. 1993; Barefoot 1997; Ruberman et al. 1984; Berkman 1995). Behaviorally, low social support and depression have been associated with health damaging behaviors such as smoking and noncompliance and subsequently can influence morbidity and mortality. Oxman and Hull (1997) found that the perceived adequacy of social support among heart surgery patients at one month after surgery predicted depression scores five months later.

However the concept is defined, there is substantial evidence that social support has direct effects on psychological and physical well-being as well as indirect "stress-buffering" effects (Cohen and Wills 1985). There have been numerous studies outlining the benefit of social support in the health and well-being of medical patients. Studies have shown that having strong support from family and friends can keep blood pressure down when performing a stressful act (Uchino and Cacioppo 1996). Naturally occurring support has been shown to have a positive effect on adaptation and recovery from a heart attack, and spinal-cord injured patients who reported satisfying support demonstrated fewer depressive symptoms than those without good support (Wallston et al. 1983). Further, women with breast cancer who had undergone surgery with a cohesive family and a reported confidant were found to be less depressed or anxious as compared to women who had poor social support (Bloom 1982). Poor social support systems have also been identified as a major risk factor for depression and suicide.

Assessment of Social Support

House (1981) has defined social support as consisting of four different types—emotional, instrumental, informational, and appraisal.

- *Emotional support* are the people who offer expressions of love, empathy, trust, and genuine caring. For example, the support person would listen when the patient needs to talk, and offer words of encouragement and gestures of affection (bringing flowers, books, or special pillows).

- *Instrumental support* provides the individual with tangible services like providing the patient with meals, rides, money, laundry services, grocery shopping, or assistance with paying bills.

- *Informational support* provides advice, suggestions, and information, which influence the thoughts and behaviors of the patient. This type of support includes helping the patient make medical decisions by reviewing medical information and engaging in intellectual decision making. Informational support does not usually involve emotional support on a personal level and may come from a physician or other "expert in the field" who can simply provide the necessary facts and information for the patient to make decisions regarding medical treatment and care.

- *Appraisal support* offers feedback, affirmation, and social comparison information that allow the individual to engage in self-evaluation. This type of support may involve giving the patient feedback on their behavior and how it is influencing their medical condition. For example, telling the patient that he or she appears depressed and does not seem to be motivated in rehabilitation and therefore is not progressing. This type of support may come from a loved one who is also providing emotional support, or it may come from a physical therapist who is simply noting the behavior and attempting to motivate and support the patient's physical progress.

Just as there are a variety of ways to conceptualize and define social support, there are also a variety of personal styles and needs regarding social support. Social support can mean different things to different people. For example, some people are most comfortable alone, others may feel more comfortable with one-on-one support, and still others may enjoy the dynamics of a group experience. It is important to identify what *kind* of support works best for each individual. To evaluate the personal needs and comfort level of the patient with regard to social support, the following questionnaire is offered as a guideline. These questions can be used to guide your dialogue with the patient about their social style:

- During periods of sadness, depression, or simply feeling down in the dumps, does the patient feel better when around others?
- Does the patient feel comfortable confiding personal information in just one good friend?
- Does knowing that others are having similar feelings or experiencing the same thing make the patient feel supported?
- Does the patient tend to feel awkward in social situations and generally feel uncomfortable in groups?
- Does listening to other people's similar concerns make the patient feel worse instead of better?
- Does the patient cope better with concerns when left alone?

If the patient's answers to the questions above suggest a tendency to cope better when left alone, you will need to educate the patient about the different types of social support networks. For example, a loner may not benefit from support groups or the use of a buddy system, but may benefit from instrumental or informational support. That is, although receiving emotional support may not be valued, obtaining available resources, advice, or suggestions may be useful and easily accepted by a loner.

Conversely, if the patient's answers to the above questions suggest that he or she is generally more comfortable confiding in one person or that they tend to feel awkward in social groups, then a one-on-one support system will need to be established or a pre-existing network strengthened. For example, a buddy system network, which involves two people working together to support each other through similar stressful situations, may be useful.

If the patient's answers suggest comfort in social settings and in sharing feelings and experiences with others, then support groups may be useful.

In addition to the patient's social style, you need to keep in mind the stage of adjustment with the illness when working to increase overall social support. For example, some types of support are better suited for different stages of adjustment. A patient who is newly diagnosed with ESRD and has just begun dialysis may need emotional support. However, as a patient begins to settle into life on the dialysis machine, more informational or instrumental support might be needed. This type of support could include providing travel, meals, or advice on how to maintain a healthy diet.

The relationship between lack of perceived support and emotional distress is well documented, so you should not only ask the patient about social support, but also inquire with the primary providers. Understanding the point of view of both parties will help to facilitate communication and thereby improve social support. Adequate assessment of the support network is important: often patients may feel that a friend has abandoned them when in reality they may have asked that person—either overtly or covertly—to leave.

Evaluate the Social Support Network

A person's social style will give you important information about what *kind* of support will be most useful to the patient. Evaluating the patient's social network will provide you with important information about *who is actually available* to the patient. Treatment strategies can be designed to develop new social networks or improve existing ones based on your evaluation of the patient's current network of support. The following list of questions can be used to guide you in the evaluation process:

- Who does the patient generally rely on for emotional support?
- Is this person or persons consistently available to the patient?
- Does the patient have tangible support (travel, adequate finances, etc.)?
- Is the patient capable of recognizing when support is needed?
- Can the patient readily access the support system?
- Is the patient connected to extended community networks?
- Is the patient able to assertively ask for support?
- Does the patient believe that good social support is essential to physical and emotional well-being?

Techniques to Improve Social Support

Therapeutic efforts should be designed to reduce feelings of isolation and improve meaningful social contact with others. Some of the techniques outlined below are designed to help the patient get the most from existing support networks. This is accomplished by increasing the patient's assertiveness skills and providing him or her with information and skills to help them make connections to existing social groups. Other techniques are geared toward the supporters and are designed to assist them with improving the way that they offer support to the patient.

Collaborate with Patient

Enlist the patient as a collaborator in improving his or her social support network. This can be accomplished by outlining to the patient the benefits of having good social support systems:

- Improvement in physical health
- Improvement in emotional contentment
- Increased energy and motivation when supported by others
- Opportunity to obtain information about medical condition and the experiences of others who share similar situation
- Decreased feelings of loneliness and isolation when connected to others

Be Attentive to Social Style

Establish what type of social support would be most useful to the patient given their social style and current stage of adjustment to their medical illness. Follow the assessment from above.

Include Family in Medical Care

Increase emotional and instrumental support of family or friends by including them in the care of the patient. Family members or friends who are well educated about the patient's medical needs and concerns are usually better able to provide emotional support. Also, they can provide instrumental support by becoming more involved in the care of the patient by taking his or her blood pressure, giving medications, or helping out with other daily routines.

Examine Existing Social Networks

Educate the patient about existing social networks of others who have been through similar situations. Provide information on community resources and local support groups. Discuss advantages of interacting with other medical patients who may be experiencing similar concerns. Some patients find comfort and support being around patients with similar conditions; they use these interactions to share coping techniques, practical information, and emotional experiences. Others find group experience with similar patients to increase their feelings of depression and despair. Therefore, it is important to help the patient make a choice about support groups.

Encourage the Buddy System

Teach the patient how to develop a buddy system. A buddy system typically involves two patients with similar medical concerns who join forces to support each other with their medical regimen, limitations in physical activities, and changes in life style. Patients may wish to choose someone in their own community or to be connected with someone from a different medical facility. Ask the patient to make a list of possible candidates and then examine with them the advantages and disadvantages of their choices. Also, discuss in concrete terms how to approach someone to be part of a buddy system.

Teach Patient How to Ask for Help

Teach the patient how to be assertive when asking for support from others. Oftentimes medical patients will report not wanting to "be a burden to their family or friends" or appear to be "whining or complaining all the time." Have the patient make a list of what is needed from individuals in their support system. Then teach how to ask for those needs without feeling like a burden or complainer. This can be accomplished by having the patient follow the steps outlined below:

Aid vs. Dependence

Frequently, family members and friends of chronically ill people do not know what to say or do to be helpful. Finding a balance between helping without making the person totally dependent on them is a struggle for supportive family members and friends. Similarly, the patient may be struggling with the same issues. Therefore, begin by having the patient outline what is needed and from whom and then teach more effective communication skills so that these needs will be addressed.

Assertiveness vs. Aggressiveness

Discuss the difference between assertiveness and aggressiveness. Assertiveness is the balance between two extremes of aggressiveness and submissiveness. People who act in an aggressive style demand and expect others to do exactly what they want. Those who act in a submissive style give up their own beliefs, opinions, and wants to those of others. They feel guilty asking for what they want, as if others' needs were more important than their own. An assertive person respects others' views and feelings but also values and respects his or her own. This is discussed in greater detail in chapter 8.

Specific Requests

Teach the patient how to be specific when making a request. Vague requests or comments can often be misinterpreted by others or simply ignored. If your request is very specific and direct there is little room for confusion. For example, instead of asking for someone's help in general, specifically state *what* help you want, *when* and for *how long*.

Meet the Supporters

In addition to working directly with the patient, it may be helpful to offer some guidance to those who will be providing the support. Studies have shown that support efforts intended to be helpful are often perceived to be unhelpful (Davidowitz and Myrick 1984; Maddison and Walker 1967). In part, support efforts may fail because when face to face with someone who has experienced a loss or life crisis, feelings of intense anxiety can interfere with the delivery of supportive messages (Wortman and Lehman 1985). The anxiety may result in support attempts that are ritualistic, like stating platitudes such as "things will get better" (Lehman et al. 1986). Providing some guidelines and education of those who will be providing support to the patient can alleviate this anxiety and hence improve the support effort. Below are a few guidelines that you can offer to the patient's support network.

Reminders to Give to Supporters of the Patient:

- Tell the supporters not to overemphasize or ignore the patients disease (Wortman and Lehman 1985). Keeping things normal and reality based decreases the stress of the social interaction for both the patient and the supporter. For example, kiss the person if that is normally how you greet them. If humor and bantering is part of the usual exchange, don't try so hard to avoid it. Talk about the illness in present-day language. For example, "How are you feeling today?" If others avoid the topic of the illness completely, the interaction may feel less than genuine and may increase the distress for the patient. However, hovering or focusing only on the illness discounts the rest of the person. Balance is the key.

- Let the patient take the lead in the conversation. It is hard to predict what the emotional state or current needs of the patient may be from visit to visit. Be a good listener and learn to tolerate quiet moments in the conversation. Ask the patient specifically what he or she wants to talk about or if they simply want you to just be physically there with them. Caregivers often try to hide their anxiety by needing to do something at all times and often forget that sometimes what is needed is nothing but physical contact.
- Teach the members of the support network how to recognize that the needs of the patient may change over time. They need to realize that there may be times when the patient needs to be alone and other times when perseverance is necessary as the patient may avoid needed help because of feelings of pride.
- Provide information to members of the support network about agencies and assistance that may be available to the patient. In addition to emotional support, patients may benefit from assistance with home health care needs, connection with transportation services, alternative housing arrangements (such as assisted living or nursing home placement), special adaptive equipment needs, assistance from financial agencies (Social Security Disability, Medicaid), and recreational support through programs at the YMCA or YWCA, senior citizen centers, or state sports associations. The support network can also be useful in making the arrangements with these services.

Family Adjustment

The role of the family in the adjustment of the medically ill patient is an important one and becomes even more so when depression is present. Family members are likely to be the ones providing the most support to the patient. The support can take many forms from emotional support to actual caregiving. The endless barrage of stressors—feelings of loss of control, dependence on the medical staff, disruption of daily activities, worry about the future, and fears about suffering and death—are often shared by the family, especially the partner of the patient.

The changes that the patient must face will also result in changes that the family must make. For instance, during a period immediately following a heart attack, the spouse or partner may have to assume the responsibilities of both people in the household, keeping up the finances, parenting, and management of the home. If the illness is chronic, these changes in roles may be long lasting.

While the patient understandably receives the most attention, reassurance, support, and treatment, family members are often left to struggle with their fears and stress without any support. The family is expected to provide support for the patient and contain their own feelings. This can be overwhelming, especially when the partner is simultaneously trying to cope with his or her own set of fears. The adjustment that the family makes and how well they cope can have direct impact on the patient's adjustment. Many patients report that their concern about the burden of the illness on their families was even greater than their concern about the burden on themselves.

This can be due to the patient's fear of being a burden on the family, or related to the reality of hardships that the family will incur. It can also be explained by patients needing to focus their fears and worries on something less threatening and frightening, in order to take their minds off their own fears. This is a common form of denial and can serve as a respite from the distress of the illness. While focusing on the family, patients can give themselves distance from worrying about themselves, which allows them time to delay actually integrating what is happening to them. In this way patients can benefit from interventions aimed at supporting the family unit. This will help to reduce stress and worry about the family and will slowly allow the patient to begin to focus on the reality of the illness.

Family Response to Illness

The way in which a family chooses to cope with the stress of illness is unique to each family. Some styles of coping are unhealthy while others are healthier. The patterns of coping are determined, in part, by the way family members related to each other prior to the illness. Family theory (Minuchin 1974; Satir 1972) conceptualizes the family as a system with members relating to each other in hierarchical lines and functioning in certain roles. For instance, the spouse may be the "caretaker" while another member the "peacemaker." The rules of the family include how emotions are expressed, how conflict is handled, and how the values and beliefs of the family are enforced. Families will do what they can to maintain their system, whether healthy or not. A diagnosis of a major illness destabilizes the family system and families will often revert to patterns that worked previously, because it is the easiest thing to do (Minuchin 1974).

The family should ideally respond by becoming flexible and most families find a way to achieve this. But the process of this adaptation is not always smooth and signs of distress can appear. Because the bulk of the attention is being given to the sick patient, problems the family members may be experiencing are not always easily seen. A family can rally in the beginning of their loved one's illness, providing active help and support, and then gradually become distressed over time in response to the multiple changes caused by a physical illness.

The following are examples of signs of distress in family members and patterns of interacting that may lead to increased dysfunction during the long periods of stress caused by chronic illness. These signs of distress do not have to be permanent and can be addressed. Minuchin (1974) stated that the pathology lies in whether or not the family shows any capacity to change and adapt under stress. If the family is amenable, family members can be included in therapy sessions. This may be particularly useful when addressing strategies to improve coping skills, discussing effective ways to provide and receive social support, and teaching both the patient and family to communicate their needs. If the difficulties between the patient and family persist, you may need to consider a referral to another mental health professional for family members.

Physical Symptoms

Many partners of chronically ill patients may suffer from health problems of their own, which can worsen during this period of acute stress. If a lot of time and energy is being devoted to taking care of the sick family member, then the partner's own health needs become ignored. In addition, stress responses in the form of sleep and appetite disturbances, chest palpitations, headaches, and gastrointestinal upset can plague family members.

It will be important when meeting the family to assess any symptoms of stress that may be occurring as well as their ongoing health concerns. Urge the family member to seek out medical advice and care as needed.

Depression

When the family member appears to be grieving for too long a period, depression should be considered. It is not unusual to see family members of depressed patients become depressed themselves. A medical illness that causes tremendous strain also contributes to the increased risk of depression for the family. At this time, outside support for families tends to drop off as people "move on." The family can become increasingly isolated at a time when it needs the most help.

Try to assess the level of depression in the family by asking tactful questions regarding how they are coping, and inquire as to any problematic symptoms. Educate the family that symptoms of depression are often not restricted to the medical patient only, but can include family members, who are affected by the illness. Typically family members do not feel that they have "the right" to be depressed since they are not the one "suffering from the illness." Simply educating family members about the impact that the illness can have on loved ones can free them from guilt and will give them permission to seek out treatment for themselves.

Many times *patients* will recognize that a loved one is depressed and as a result may feel that he or she is to blame. This feeling of guilt usually will cause the patient to pull away or avoid asking the family for help to prevent increasing the burden or stress on the family member. Interventions at this point may need to focus on helping the patient and the family in establishing boundaries for help and assistance. Specific needs and methods for getting needs met will reduce excessive guilt and blame.

Denial of the Illness

For some family members the threat of illness and possible loss of their loved one becomes too frightening, so they use denial as a coping mechanism. They may minimize the significance of symptoms and join the patient in denying potentially serious problems rather than urging the patient to actively seek medical care or adhere to the medical regimen. Denial can also take the form of the family member's resistance to getting educated about the illness or participating actively in the care of the patient. This resistance makes it extremely difficult for the medically ill patient to make necessary lifestyle changes.

Address issues of denial and minimization of symptoms with the patient and family if possible. Education about the illness and continued emphasis on the importance of adhering to medical regimens is useful.

Anger

Persistent anger about the changes that chronic illness has brought to the family's life can also lead to dysfunction. Increased irritability, moodiness, and temper outbursts are behavioral signs of anger becoming a problem. This anger can also be directed at the medical staff for "not doing enough" and may lead to strained relationships with the very people who are needed to provide consistent medical care.

Teaching effective communication skills and problem solving can help reduce the level of anger in a family member. Increasing social support or providing options for respite can help ease the strain of caregiving as well. This is covered in more detail in the communication skills section of chapter 8.

Overprotectiveness and Overworking

Often partners or family members will assume all of the caregiving responsibilities. They attempt to alleviate all of the stress the patient is experiencing by taking over all of the responsibilities of the household, the finances, and child-rearing so that they can protect the sick patient from experiencing any stress. The result can then be overwork, fatigue, depression, burnout, and ultimately resentment. This pattern can leave the patient with an increased sense of helplessness since he or she appears to have no control over any aspect of his or her life.

While it may be necessary for the caregiver to take over many responsibilities, particularly during the patient's recovery period or if there is a permanent loss of some functional abilities, it is also important to allow the patient to begin slowly to do some things for themselves. The patient needs to gain some mastery over activities and chores: for example, dressing themselves, preparing a meal, or feeding themselves. Slowly easing back into doing "normal activities" will promote healthy coping and adjustment.

Walking on Eggshells

A variation on the pattern of overprotecting the sick patient, this pattern is seen often in families affected by cardiac illness. Many cardiac patients have personality styles that include hostility and feeling pressured by time. Spouses and family members will hold back their own feelings so as not to provoke the sick patient for fear they may cause another heart attack. This too can lead to resentment and depression in the family. Interventions that focus on teaching assertive communication in a calm, non-defensive manner can address this pattern. For further discussion on communication, please refer to the communication skills section in chapter 8.

Withdrawal

In families where the members are disengaged from each other, illness poses a crisis where emotional and other needs may not be adequately met. In this type of family pattern, members become used to taking care of themselves. Since illness creates a dependency situation, this pattern results in the patient feeling reluctant to ask for support and the family members suffering their own emotional stress about the illness without strong support.

As discussed above, social isolation has been linked with increased morbidity and mortality in illnesses such as heart disease and cancer among others. Interventions should focus on increasing communications skills between family members.

Life-Cycle Issues

Another conceptual way to view how illness affects families is to use the life cycle as a frame for understanding the developmental tasks that are disrupted by the chronic illness. These developmental tasks refer to goals that individuals at different stages in their life need to accomplish. Eisenberg (1984) discuss in detail the effects of chronic illness and disability throughout the life span. (This concept was introduced in chapter 8.)

The New Couple

The developmental task of new couples is to create a strong, enduring system while separating from the family of origin. A medical illness in one of the pair can often push the patient back into dependency and intimacy with parents and siblings, while excluding the spouse. This can lead to tension between the family and the partner, which can lead to problems in the management of an illness, particularly when decisions must be made about treatment such as in terminal care situations. If the illness is chronic and a strong bond has not been created between the couple, the resulting stress can lead to a breakup, with the ill patient then losing a much needed source of support.

The Young Family

The developmental tasks of the young family center around child-rearing while negotiating the needs of the couple and each partner. The family is also still dealing with families of origin, friends, work, and the community at large. An illness then creates a huge stressor where the bulk of responsibility becomes shifted to one partner. Without adequate supports, the strain can be overwhelming.

The Family with Young Adults

The developmental tasks at this phase include helping young adults separate from the family and consolidate their identity. An illness at this time can interrupt this task, since focus becomes shifted to the ill patient and the young adult may have to direct energy to caregiving responsibilities. The young adult may choose to act out, become depressed, or assume the changes with little difficulty noted.

The Aging Family

Older individuals face the developmental task of focusing their goals toward issues of aging. This may involve role reversal of parent and adult child when illness strikes, thereby creating stress around the dependency issues. If the parents live too far apart from their children, there may not be family available for support during the illness. This forces the medically ill older adult to look to outside resources for assistance and, often in later stages, disrupt his or her established life to move closer to adult children to facilitate caregiving. The need for consideration of placement in assisted living or nursing care facilities secondary to medical illness is an acute stressor for the family.

The Family and Medical Staff

Chronic illness presents a unique situation where the patient and family must come to rely on the health care team on a regular basis. Cassileth and Egan (1979) point out that the medical team is given a powerful role, where their words are overinterpreted and their actions are scrutinized for covert messages about the patient. Families are also expected to conform to the team's "rules" about interactions with the medical system. Many families are intimidated by hospitals and all of the complex medical information that is brought to them. Furthermore, in the current health care delivery system, families deal with a larger number of highly trained and specialized professionals who may give seemingly conflicting reports about the patient's diagnosis and recommended course of treatment. Families can become easily overwhelmed with caregiving responsibilities either due to lack of resources or because they are emotionally unprepared.

Based on how a family chooses to be involved in the care of their sick loved one can often determine a label that the treatment team places on a family. When a family is seen as supportive and also "compliant" with the treatment team, the family is seen as a "good family" from the perspective of the staff (Rait et al. 1988). Other families seem to be cooperative with the staff initially, but when something does not "go right," their feelings change to hostility, blame, and unrealistic expectations for treatment. Some families are labeled as "difficult" from the beginning, questioning the staff at every turn, demanding increased attention for their loved one, and being difficult to satisfy. Some of these families may engage in "doctor shopping" and alternative forms of treatment (Rait et al. 1988). Finally, some families appear to "abandon" their sick loved one by avoiding or resisting involvement with the medical team. Families will also approach individual members of the medical team, bonding with those they feel more comfortable with and weighing this staff person's opinion more heavily irrespective of whether this staff person is the primary treating physician. If a family dynamic is to be guarded and private, then all outsiders including the medical staff will be kept at a distance (Rait et al. 1988). No single style of interaction between staff and families is the "right" one, but rather represents a range of responses to severe stress brought by chronic illness. Understanding the patient's unique family style is important as it will guide you in your interventions with the patient and the family.

Interventions for the Family

As we have discussed, the stressors affecting the depressed medically ill patient also often face the family as well. Therefore, many of the same interventions used to treat the patient can potentially be useful in helping the family cope as well. Any improvement in bolstering the strength of the family will lead to better social support for the medically ill patient, which is extremely important in treating depression. Interventions can focus on providing an emotional outlet for families to express their fears and concerns about the illness, educating the family about depression and aspects of the illness itself, improving coping skills by teaching problem solving and fostering open communication, and bolstering outside sources of support. Support groups are particularly helpful in imparting some of the information needed to cope better and providing needed emotional support as we discussed earlier in this section.

Providing Emotional Support

Encourage the family to first share their feelings and concerns about the illness with their loved one. Often, families will keep their concerns to themselves because of a fear of burdening the already sick patient. The depressed medical patient is typically feeling isolated and withdrawn and is therefore less likely to share or inquire how a partner or family member is coping. Facilitating communication in the family, particularly between partners and between children and parents, is particularly useful (Worby and Babineau 1974). Communication skills, as discussed in chapter 8, can also be taught to the family. The following explanation can serve as a guide for educating the patient about the need for open communication:

> Sharing your feelings with family and friends will help you cope with this overwhelming experience. Keeping it all inside by pretending that it will go away will not be helpful to you or your loved one. Talking about traumatic events soon after they have occurred can help prevent a more serious reaction at a later date. Stress reactions are natural when dealing with a loved one who is chronically ill. You may find yourself crying, not sleeping well, eating too little or too much, being more irritable, having trouble concentrating, or feeling very sad. Remember that your loved one will need your support and encouragement at this time. So it is important to take care of yourself by getting support from others and also by communicating with your partner or family member.

Educating the Family

Another intervention aimed at improving the family support of the depressed medically ill patient is to educate the family members about depression. Using similar explanations as given to the patient in chapter 6, explain to the family common reactions the patient may have to the illness. If the patient is experiencing normal adjustment reactions, explain to the family what types of behaviors and emotions may be seen. Further educate the family on what symptoms to be concerned about, such as suicidal ideation, prolonged periods of grief resulting in poor compliance with medical regimens, or a dramatic decrease in daily functioning. Since the family may have the most information about the patient's normal mode of functioning, they are a good source of information about the patient. Conversely, because of their closeness to the patient, the family may not be able to objectively view the patient and observe problematic symptoms of depression. Therefore, it is important to educate them on depression and types of symptoms that may be observed. Provide the family with resources where they can go for assistance, like their primary physician, or you, as their therapist. The following statements can serve as a loose guide in talking to the family about depression:

> It is not unusual for people suffering from this type of illness to go through a period of adjustment as they try to cope with all of the changes. Some of the symptoms you may observe are periods of crying, changes in appetite and sleep patterns, expressions of hopelessness, low motivation and no interest in activities you previously enjoyed, and even changes in mood including angry outbursts sometimes directed at you. These reactions are normal and it will be important for you to be as supportive as you can during this period. If you see your loved one struggling and experiencing difficulty with daily functioning for more than a few weeks, it will be important to get help. Depression, left untreated, can result in prolonged emotional suffering and lead to more poor health. You can try discussing your concerns with your loved one and encourage him or her to get help. Remember that when someone is depressed, they are sometimes not able to see past their depression and may need the family's help on where or how to get help.

The family should also receive education about their loved one's medical illness. Support groups typically provide an avenue for education as do home care programs and home visits by home care nurses. The family should be encouraged to ask questions of the medical staff regarding any aspect of care. The handout on page 163 can be helpful for the family in initially guiding them to ask questions.

Preparing Questions for the Medical Staff

It is often helpful to have a list of questions prepared for the doctors when they speak to you about the patient's status. It is not unusual to be so distraught or numb that it becomes difficult to focus on what the doctor is saying or asking. If your partner or family member is too ill, you may be asked to make important medical decisions regarding treatment. Write down what the doctor says so that you can refer to it at later date. Here are some sample questions you may want to prepare beforehand:

- Will you explain what has happened? Can you draw a diagram to illustrate what has happened?
- What risks and immediate concerns are there for my family member?
- What types of treatments are being given?
- What are the advantages and disadvantages of each treatment? How do you plan to go about treating my family member?
- What are the risks of further complications?
- Where can I get reference materials so that I may begin to educate myself about the illness?

Don't be afraid to ask questions as you and your loved one progress with recovery. There will be countless questions that will occur to you as time goes on. The presence of another family member or friend can be of great support to you at this time. Other members of the treatment team such as nurses, social workers, and psychologists can also be helpful to you. They are available to give you more information and direct you to the appropriate resources.

Chapter 10

Suicide

Suicide is a self-inflicted, intentional death. It has been called the "permanent solution to a temporary problem." With estimates of over 30,000 completed suicides annually (National Center for Health Statistics 1991), it has become the eighth leading cause of death among all ages. Physical disease has been identified as an independent risk factor for patients who commit suicide (Kontaxakis et al. 1988). Among all suicide victims, physical illness is present in 25 to 75 percent (Roy 1989), although many had unrecognized psychiatric and neurological illness (Davidson and Ritson 1993). These illnesses typically include depression, substance-related disorders, chronic or terminal illness, hopelessness, agitated delirium, and pain. Subsequently, the evaluation of depression and associated suicidal thoughts and behaviors need to be aggressively explored, particularly among the medically ill.

The medically ill patient is often faced with numerous adjustment and loss issues related to their medical illness that can trigger depression and related suicidal thoughts. These changes may include loss or disfigurement of body parts, loss in ability to work, loss or changes in social networks due to the illness. In addition, the underlying medical condition can lead to suicidal thoughts and plans. Kishi and his colleagues (1996) investigated suicidal plans of patients immediately post-stroke and at three, six, twelve, and twenty-four month follow-ups. They found that 6.6 percent of patients developed suicidal plans during the hospital treatment (acute-onset suicidal plans) and 11.3 percent developed suicidal plans at follow-up (delayed-onset suicidal plans). The development of both types of suicidal plans was strongly associated with major depression. However, acute-onset suicidal patients had more anterior lesion locations, while delayed-onset suicidal patients had more posterior lesion strokes. Delayed-onset suicidal plans were associated with greater physical impairments and poorer social support during the acute post-stroke period. The authors concluded that the suicidal plans during the acute onset phase may be related to biological mechanisms, while delayed-onset plans may be related to psychological mechanisms. Therefore, clinicians may need to closely monitor patients during the acute post-stroke period. It is important to recognize that even patients who may not have many of the traditional psychological risk factors may be at significant risk simply related to the biological mechanisms of the illness. If this is the case, you may need to take safety precautions by utilizing suicide watches while in the hospital, limiting access to lethal items, and educating family and friends about potential risks during the acute phase of treatment. Following the acute phase, social support and level of physical impairment will need to be assessed and treatment strategies implemented to reduce the risk of suicide months after a stroke when the patient may begin to realize the reality of his or her deficits.

In summary, research findings highlight the importance of not only understanding traditional psychological risk factors for suicide, but also the biological triggers related to the medical illness itself. By understanding both the biological and psychological effects of the illness on the medical patient, you can better assess suicide risk factors and implement strategies to reduce them.

A frequent myth is that only patients with chronic or terminal illnesses are at risk for suicide. However, the mediating factor for many illnesses is major depression. The medical illness by itself typically does not pose a risk for suicide in the absence of depression. Henriksson and colleagues (1995) investigated psychological autopsy data on all suicides in Finland over a period of a year. Depressive symptoms were found to be equally common among cancer suicides and other suicides. Further, alcohol dependence and personality disorders were more frequent among non-cancer suicides, while major depression and substance abuse were more common among victims with cancer in remission than in terminal stages. This is consistent with clinical literature on depression and suicide which notes that when patients experience a respite from their pain, either by having resolved the decision to end their life or by temporary relief of physical pain, it is at this point that the risk for suicide is heightened, as now the patient has the energy to carry through on the plan.

Decisions to terminate life-sustaining efforts or refuse life-saving procedures can be considered suicidal actions when major depression is present. Therefore, recognition and treatment of depression among the medically ill, whether caused by biological or psychological mechanisms, is imperative to reduce the risk for suicide and to improve competent decision making regarding termination of life-sustaining procedures. In other words, patients who suffer from major depression may not be competent to make a decision to terminate care until depression and related symptoms of hopelessness, fatigue, and suicidal ideation have been eliminated as factors in the decision-making process.

Risk Factors for Suicide

As a clinician, it is not possible to be able to predict and prevent all cases of suicide. However, identification and improvement of risk factors among the medically ill can reduce suicidal behaviors such as noncompliance, intentional misuse of medications, and refusal of life-sustaining procedures. Patients are most vulnerable to thoughts of suicide when certain stressful situations are experienced, so these situations need to be identified when working with medically ill patients in order to establish a treatment plan that will reduce or eliminate these vulnerability factors. The greater the number of vulnerability factors the higher the risk for suicide. The following factors are particularly common and noteworthy for this population:

- poor social support or perceived feelings of isolation
- ascribing positive meaning to death
- cognitive impairment
- presence of a personality disorder
- increased age
- chronic pain
- chronic fatigue
- feelings of helplessness
- conflict within the family
- limited problem-solving skills
- ambivalence about living

Poor Social Support or Perceived Feelings of Loneliness

Although emotional support is an important component in the treatment of depression in the medically ill, it is *critical* when dealing with the *suicidal* medically ill patient. When medical patients feel overwhelmed by their disease and ambivalent about living in their current condition and do not have someone that can help direct and support them, they are at risk to act impulsively: this may include direct aggressive acts harming themselves or may involve intentional noncompliance with their medical care resulting in death.

Depression among the medically ill often breeds isolation, particularly when the patient feels hopeless about the future and adopts the belief that they do not want to burden others. It is at this time that the person is at greatest risk for suicide. Therefore, strategies to minimize isolation and improve support are critical in reducing suicide potential. Patients are not always willing to admit to having poor support, so questions to evaluate their level of emotional support may need to be broad. The following questions can be used to guide your inquiry into the patient's type and level of social support as it relates to suicide potential:

- Do you feel alone even when in the presence of others?
- Do you have somebody you can confide in when you feel that life isn't worth living?
- Do you refuse emotional support from friends and family members because you feel like a burden?
- Do you think that your family would be less burdened if you were dead?

Supportive Therapeutic Relationship

When suicide risk is high, you may need to take an active role in facilitating social contact for the patient. This contact may be accomplished by increasing the frequency of the therapy sessions as well as decreasing the duration. Physically ill, depressed, suicidal patients often need frequent contact to monitor risk and to improve feelings of support: however, their endurance for long periods of verbal contact may be limited. Therefore, limiting the duration of the therapy will not inadvertently increase the feeling of being overwhelmed.

When working with suicidal patients it is important for you to monitor your own personal feelings and beliefs about the patient, if support is to be maintained. The danger of suicide is magnified when a personality-disordered patient with limited social support and internal resources is deprived of the connection with the therapist (Maltsberger and Buie 1990). The suicidal patient's perception of isolation and loneliness can be magnified when they experience rejection by the therapist. This is a trap that is easy for the clinician to fall into. Chronically suicidal patients may evoke feelings of anger and frustration in the clinician who may feel relief when a patient drops out of treatment. However, the patient may experience this as another failure that in turn evokes feelings of hopelessness and doom. Therefore, when working with a chronically suicidal patient it is important for you to monitor your reactions and to seek out consultation from other clinicians when needed.

Suicidal contracts can be used as a tool to enhance the therapeutic relationship. These contracts involve the communication of the clinician's wish for the patient to live and arranges strategies for the patient to manage self-destructive urges, such as to contact the therapist before acting on an impulse. They are often written in concrete language, spelling out how, when, and under what circumstances to call the clinician (Jamison 1988), and then both parties sign it. Although suicidal contracts have no empirical data, they can often be useful as a type of supportive psychotherapy by reinforcing the collaborative therapeutic relationship (Davidson and Ritson 1993).

Social Support of Family

Improving social contact within the family may require some education about depression, suicide, and related behaviors. Specifically, many family members can become frustrated, indifferent, and angry at the frequent threats of suicide. Helping the family appreciate that the repetitive threats are a symptom of pain and despair is necessary to prevent them from withdrawing their support. When patients feel that others have withdrawn support and emotionally abandoned them, the risk for suicide increases.

Ascribing Positive Meaning to Death

Depressed patients who view death as an opportunity for happiness in a different life are more at risk to act on suicidal ideation. When hope for a better future is gone and feelings of despair and depression is all-pervasive, many patients begin to view death as a true respite from emotional suffering. They may talk about wanting to "be with" a deceased loved one or have the opportunity for rebirth. This kind of thinking places the patient at greater risk to act on suicidal thoughts.

Treatment strategies need to focus on differentiating for the patient the "escape from depression fantasy" from the reality of the current situation. To that end, it is often helpful to have the patient talk about what the deceased relative would want for them. This is a strategy that may help keep the patient grounded in reality and not in the fantasy of death. Further, presenting to the patient the concept that this desire to be dead is the depression talking and that after the depression is treated if he or she still feels that death is the solution then that option can be revisited. This allows the patient to maintain some control and plants the seed that they may view life and death issues differently when the depression is gone.

Cognitive Impairment

Patients who are depressed *and* suffer from a cognitive deficit (for instance, dementia or head injuries) have a higher risk for suicide. Making the differential diagnosis between depression and dementia is covered in the section on disorders with depressed mood as a feature. Demented patients who are depressed may be more impulsive and lack judgment necessary to prevent suicidal acts. Further, among head-injured patients, death by suicide was found to be significantly higher than among other medically ill patients, with 41 percent of the suicides taking place during a depressive psychosis (Marcantonio et al. 1994). Moreover, neurological impairment among epileptics has been implicated as a contributing factor to the high rate of suicide, four to five times that of the general population (Barraclough 1981). Delirium increases the risk for self-injury (Marcantonio et al. 1994), which can be secondary to delusional episodes, poor judgement, and psychotic thinking coupled with emotional lability. Patients with delirium tremens are at high risk for suicide, particularly during the first twenty-four hours if adequate sedation is not given (Hirschfeld and Davidson 1988). Therefore, a thorough mental status exam and history needs to be conducted when depression is found among cognitively impaired patients to monitor deterioration, as this is a significant risk factor for suicide.

The Presence of a Personality Disorder

Pfohl and colleagues (1984) found that rates of non-serious suicide attempts were 11 percent for depressed patients, 39 percent for depressed patients with a personality disorder, and 40 percent for subjects with broadly defined borderline personality disorders. Serious suicide attempts among these same groups were found to be 5 percent and 20 percent respectively. When dealing with depression of patients with personality disorders, treatment strategies will need to be tailored to include more attention to feelings of emptiness, chronic dysphoria, loneliness, and boredom (Cary 1972). Gunderson (1977) reported that the key features of depression among borderline patients include an inner sense of deprivation, badness, and conscious rage from early life. Medical illness can serve as a trigger for feelings of deprivation and punishment for bad behavior. The clinician working with medically ill patients who suffer from depression and borderline personality disorders should be sensitive to these themes and triggers.

Increased Age

The risk of suicide increase with advanced age to approximately four times that of the general population. Multiple losses including physical limitations, cognitive decline, death of friends and family members, reduction in autonomy and poor overall quality of life are among the many factors that contribute to depression and suicide in this population. Indirect acts of suicide such as "accidental" drug overdoses, neglect of physical care, starvation, noncompliance with medical treatment and alcohol abuse, are often common among seniors (Georgotas et al. 1988).

In addition, the increased risk for cognitive deficits among this population makes overt gestures of suicide high. Subsequently, a thorough evaluation focusing on the possession of weapons or stockpiling of medications should be conducted. Treatment may need to involve an occupational therapist to conduct an in-home evaluation for safety risks. These evaluations typically involve asking the patient to demonstrate how to use the stove, washing machine, take medication, and prepare meals. The occupational therapist also evaluates the patient's level of insight and judgment regarding safety issues such as the ability to call 911, to recognize spoiled food, and to safely climb stairs, or get in and out of a tub. When indicated, Adult Protective Services may need to be contacted. This is an organization that investigates potential senior abuses including physical or verbal abuse, neglect, and allegations of fraud (the cognitively impaired senior is particularly vulnerable to mail order scams and theft from family, friends, and organizations). Adult Protective Services will also facilitate the appointment of a guardian to oversee the senior's care if needed.

Chronic Pain

Chronic pain can limit the patient's ability to cope. Pain is a common complaint among medically ill patients. The risk for suicide increases substantially when pain and major depression are combined. This risk factor is to be differentiated from patient's who are in pain and desire termination of treatment to end their pain and suffering. Psychological treatment strategies for pain management for the depressed patient are explored in more detail in chapter 8. Patients who are depressed and suicidal are often looking for an escape from the pain and the limitations of their life due to the pain. With better pain management, the patient is better able to cope. This in turn reduces the risk for suicide.

Chronic Fatigue

Poor energy is a risk factor for suicide. Feeling chronically tired with low energy reduces one's ability to cope. A patient who felt fatigued once confessed that simply being around others who wanted to help was exhausting. Given that fatigue is a common complaint of medically ill patients and of those with depression, the additive effects are particularly problematic and significantly increase the risk for suicide. Treating fatigue is addressed in chapter 7.

Feelings of Hopelessness

As we discussed in the assessment section, feelings of hopelessness are a better predictor of suicide than depressed mood (Beck et al. 1990). It is important for you to monitor sustained periods of hopelessness, particularly when coupled with debilitating and terminal illnesses (Conwell et al. 1990). Instilling hope is a challenge, particularly for the clinician who works with the medically ill. Treatment strategies should focus on providing the patient with alternative options or techniques for coping. Often patients feel hopeless and suicidal because they see no other way to make their lives better. They feel trapped without resources. Empowering them with alternatives gives direction and focus for their lives. In turn, this ultimately increases feelings of control and minimizes the experience of hopelessness.

Conflict within the Family

The need for family members to assume more assistance or care for the chronically ill may artificially force families to interact and subsequently can rekindle old conflicts. You will need to identify potential family conflicts that could increase risk for suicidal behavior. Suicide attempts among the medically ill can be an attempt by the patient to resolve conflict related to feeling like a burden. Medically ill patients often report feeling like an emotional, physical, and financial drain on their family and thereby view suicide as a resolution. Other depressed and angry patients may use suicide as a way of punishing the family for old emotional wounds and injuries. Therapeutic resolution of these conflicts is important not only to reduce the risk factor but also to enlist support from family members in strategies of safety: these include having the family remove weapons and lethal medications, while monitoring increased agitation and impulsive behavior. Please refer to the family section in chapter 9 for a more detailed discussion.

Limited Problem-Solving Skills

In the face of complex and overwhelming stress related to their illness, patients with limited problem-solving skills may view suicide as the only option. A component of treatment is to teach the patient how to be flexible in his or her thinking; techniques should include learning how to examine alternative strategies prior to impulsively responding. Address possible deterrents to suicide with the patient. If partner and family are a deterrent, keep the patient focused in the present on the effect that suicide would have on partner and family.

Ambivalence about Living

Medically ill patients who are depressed can feel ambivalent about life, torn between conflicting feelings of wanting to live and wanting to die. This conflict often results in depression and related feelings of demoralization. Demoralization has been defined in many different ways in the clinical literature, but the most useful clinical definition is subjective distress with feelings of personal incompetence to exert any control over the stressful event. In this case the stressor can be the illness itself or related losses.

Demoralization appears to be a normal response to losses associated with medical illness. It is often precipitated by chronic, disfiguring, progressive, and painful illnesses. Patients are more likely to become demoralized when their illness is inconsistent with their prior self-image or level of functioning, with the result that they feel incompetent or incapable of effectively dealing with the illness: examples include an athletic person becoming paralyzed, an artist or surgeon developing tremors in the hands, a dancer losing a leg, or an independent person becoming dependent on a dialysis machine for survival.

The medically ill, demoralized patient is at risk for developing a major depression with suicidal thoughts when their prior belief about quality of life is incongruent with the reality of the current medical condition. Behaviorally, ambivalence and passive suicidal ideation can manifest itself through noncompliant acts: the patient does not follow medical recommendations.

What drives noncompliant behavior? Several factors seem to be related to noncompliant behavior.

- Patients may have cognitive deficits that prevent them from fully understanding and acting on doctor's recommendations.
- The patient may feel out of control, demoralized, and searching for a way to regain feelings of control by refusing to follow "what he or she has been instructed to do," opting rather to take control and do it their own way.
- Depression may interfere with the patient's desire and ability to comply; when a patient suffers from major depression the all-pervasive theme of "Why bother?" and "There is no hope" can interfere with competent decision-making abilities regarding compliance.
- Patients may feel ambivalent about living. They may not wish to live with their current quality of life but may not be prepared to make a conscious choice to end their life. It is this group of patients that is often the most challenging for the clinicians.

Behavioral manifestations of ambivalence for living or passive suicidal wishes may include the following:

- Poor self-care
- Poor management of medications
- Dietary indiscretions
- "Accidental" drug overdoses

- Engaging in high-risk behavior (smoking, drinking, abusing substances)
- Skipping medical appointments

Therapeutic efforts for addressing ambivalence about living and the related passive suicidal wishes need to focus on resolving the conflicting wish to live and to die. Since the ambivalent conflict may not be fully in the patient's conscious awareness, a direct discussion about death will illuminate the conflict and help the patient see how their behavior and mood may be related to this ambivalence. Further, patients can feel trapped, with suicide as the only option, when they believe that their future is completely out of their control. You need to focus, therefore, on empowering the patient to take control over redefining what constitutes a good quality of life. The concept "reintegration to normal living" has been proposed as a proxy for quality of life (Wood and Williams 1987). Reintegration means having the ability to do what one wants to do and has to do, but does not mean being free of disease or symptoms. The goal is to teach patients how to live fully *with* the disease.

The following therapeutic techniques are designed to both bring death issues to a conscious level and to empower the patient to effectively make choices regarding their quality of life.

Treating Ambivalence

Death does not have to equal failure of either the person or the clinician. Often medical patients are afraid to discuss the desire to terminate treatment or refuse a procedure. Many are afraid that they will be viewed as weak, lacking that "fighting spirit." They are also afraid that by discussing their thoughts about termination of care with the clinician that they will make them feel "inadequate" for not being able to "cure" the patient. In addition, on units where the patient may have been treated for extended periods of time (for instance, spinal cord injury units, dialysis units, oncology wards), close attachments to the staff may have developed. Patients may feel that they are letting the staff down and subsequently causing them pain. In an attempt to avoid this, many will avoid *direct* communication of their desires and will opt for the *indirect* expression through noncompliance and high-risk behavior. Patients who struggle with these issues invariably feel out of control, depressed, demoralized, and continually struggle with their desire to live.

Treatment strategies that focus on resolution of the issue of ambivalence as it relates to protecting others and the facilitation of direct expressions of needs will ultimately increase feelings of control. In turn, compliance will improve and decisions regarding care may directly be expressed. When unconscious acts of noncompliance are replaced by conscious choices, patients feel empowered to let go of uncertainty and anxiety and thereby actively participate in the death or life process. For example, a patient with end-stage renal disease who is on hemodialysis may feel ambivalent about living life on a machine versus dying. This ambivalence may be translated into not showing up for certain dialysis treatments, not following the diet, or taking medication. The patient may be passively hoping that they will die by engaging in these behaviors and therefore would not have to make a conscious choice to discontinue treatment. By bringing issues of death out into the open, the patient begins to feel more empowered and is forced to make conscious choices about his or her quality of life. Oftentimes this type of open discussion about death will free the patient to talk about his or her fears, feelings of inadequacy, and anger and depression about their current quality of life. This sets the stage for treatment to begin on resolving these issues that may contribute to depression. Once depression is adequately treated, competent decisions can then be made about termination of care or other medical treatment issues.

Many patients remain stuck in denial and therefore struggle with internal fears and the external demands of the illness. Facing the limitations of the illness while redefining quality of life is important if the patient is to maintain control, improve their mood, and make competent decisions about *living* or *not living* with the illness. Consider that a patient with end-stage renal disease who is staying alive by a hemodialysis machine may decide that his quality of life is poor for him and therefore wishes to discontinue treatment. Is this suicide? Rodin and associates (1981) argue that we may not call this suicide but the motivation is the same. Others would argue that the patient who is competent, not suffering from depression, dementia, or psychosis, should be allowed to make decisions regarding quality of life. Encouraging the patient to make the illness real by openly discussing it is the first step to resolving the ambivalence about living with the illness. Explore how the illness and related treatment options fit with what the patient values and deems important in life.

Finally, providing the patient with an opportunity to directly explore their options is valuable. Decisions related to discontinuing medical treatment or refusing further treatment is often a very painful struggle for patients and their families. The pain of this dilemma is often magnified when patients feel they need to keep the struggle internal. Many are afraid that openly discussing their feelings would cause too much discomfort for others, including their clinicians. Subsequently, patients can become more discouraged and isolated when a clinician is unable or unwilling to discuss thoughts of death (McKegney et al. 1971).

The direct expression of choices—including death—can free the patient from feelings of isolation and depression. Once the patient is free of depression and competent decision making can occur, you may need to explore various options with the patient. Options may include helping them redefine the quality of their lives with the limitations of the illness or assisting with making choices to end current treatments or refusing further treatment. The latter options are easier for patients to weigh when they have successfully evaluated what does or does not fit with their view of themselves and their world, and when they feel in control of their situation.

Chapter 11

Pharmacological Treatment

The efficacy of antidepressant therapy has been well-established in hundreds of double-blind placebo-controlled trials (Klein et al. 1980). However, Greenberg and Fisher (1989) have begun to challenge the credibility of these findings. They point out that studies that use a placebo pill that mimics the side effects of the active medication have rarely found evidence of a medication effect. This argument suggests that in studies using placebo pills that do not mimic the side effects of the active drug, both the patient and clinical judges can detect which is the active drug, and this introduces bias into the study.

This argument remains controversial and has implications for clinical practice: even if antidepressants are effective with major depression, it is not clear to what extent they are useful with other types of depression. For example, the recent National Institute of Mental Health Treatment of Depression Collaborative Research Project failed to find any advantage for active medications over pill-placebo among less severely depressed patients (Elkin et al. 1989).

This is not to argue that less severe forms of depression do not improve with antidepressant therapy, rather they tend to do as well as those treated with a placebo or non-pharmacological therapies. Given that there are potential risks involved with medications, particularly among the medically ill, it is important to accurately diagnosis the depression and its severity before starting or referring a patient for antidepressant therapy. For example, it has become a frequent practice for primary care practitioners to liberally offer antidepressant medications for feelings of sadness, discouragement, and tearfulness. However, these feelings are often common among the medically ill and do not necessarily require medication.

When considering using or recommending antidepressant medications for a medically ill patient, a careful risk-benefit assessment should be conducted. Potential risks associated with antidepressant therapies that should be considered in this population include:

- Potential complication in the medical condition
- Metabolic abnormalities associated with certain medical conditions increases the chances of drug toxicity (because of the medical condition, the body may not be able to effectively use and remove the drug effectively; therefore large quantities can build up)
- Interaction effects of the antidepressant with other medical medications being given
- Elderly medical patients are at greater risk for developing adverse central nervous system effects (confusion, decreased memory, hallucinations)

Potential benefits of antidepressant therapies have been demonstrated when treating major depression, chronic dysthymia, unresolved grief reactions, bipolar disorders, substance abuse disorders, eating disorders, and comorbid anxiety disorders such as panic, obsessive-compulsive disorder, and post-traumatic stress disorders. Antidepressants have also been used in the management of chronic pain, sleep disorders and incontinence.

The decision of when to think about using an antidepressant medication is clinically complicated and often based on the unique symptoms and level of function of the patient. Keep in mind that the combination of psychotherapy and medications is often quite useful and has been found to be advantageous for many patients. Therefore the following suggestions are offered as a guideline for when it is appropriate to consider an antidepressant medication either alone or in combination with psychotherapy:

- Severe mood disturbance with suicidal ideation or intentions
- The symptoms of depression (fatigue, apathy, and hopelessness) prevent the patient from being able to actively participate in therapy
- The ability of the patient to comply with the medical regimen or to adequately take care of themselves at home is impaired due to the depression
- The patient is suffering from physical or vegetative symptoms of depression (poor sleep, decreased appetite, fatigue, and poor sex drive), which interfere with recovery
- The depressive symptoms appear unresponsive to psychotherapy alone

Prescribing Antidepressants

The use of antidepressants in the medically ill can be a complex issue for several reasons. First, patients are often reluctant to consider antidepressants because of the stigma attached to taking medication for psychological or emotional problems. It is common to hear responses such as "I should be able to cope with this," or "I don't want to take *that* kind of medication." An individual who already has issues with how much change and dependence is present due to their medical condition may have difficulty with feeling as though they need a pill to help them cope. Others may have fears of becoming addicted or believe that medications will be a magic cure, becoming disappointed when they must face the real challenges of their medical illness. Taking a pill that "affects how the brain works" and fears that medication will change their personality can be potentially disturbing to patients.

Further, many patients do not want to add another medication to what may be an already long list of medications they take for their illness. This fear can be very real, particularly due to interaction effects of drugs. The risk of adverse reactions is increased for patients with medical illness. While the use of medication can have a powerful effect on some symptoms of depression, the presence of unintended side effects can cause as much distress as the initial symptoms. This becomes a significant problem for patients who are already reluctant to take medications. Thus the patient's compliance and the effectiveness of an antidepressant is greatly reduced due to premature discontinuation before the medication can reach a therapeutic blood level. Often patients do not reach therapeutic levels of an antidepressant and, subsequently, suffer from troublesome side effects, while their depression remains inadequately treated.

The following points should be kept in mind when addressing the use of antidepressants with medically ill patients.

Evaluate Patient's Condition

A thorough evaluation of a patient's condition is necessary. An accurate diagnosis is essential before starting pharmacological treatment. As described in earlier sections of this book, the evaluation process will include chart review for all medical conditions, history and lab studies, consultation with the admitting or primary physician, and a complete diagnostic interview with the patient. If there is a therapeutic relationship with the patient already, then making a note of depressive symptoms that hinder recovery from other medical conditions is warranted.

Address Fears and Concerns

You may need to address any fears and concerns that the patient may have regarding the use of antidepressant medication. Educate the patient about the potential value of medication and which symptoms will be targeted. It is often helpful to explain to patients that certain symptoms that they have been experiencing, such as vegetative symptoms not necessarily related to their physical illness, can impede their compliance with taking proper care of themselves. This can be empowering to the patient.

How Antidepressants Work

Explain to the patient how an antidepressant works in terms of the connection between neurotransmitters and depression. Take into account the patient's level of understanding and perceptions about antidepressants. Some patients have heard a lot about antidepressants or read about them or may even have prior experience with the use of them. Because of the increasing popularity and acceptance of drugs such as Prozac, the media has devoted more attention to both the positive and negative stories about antidepressants. Therefore, the patient may have some preconceived ideas about these drugs, like which ones are "bad" or "good." It is our experience that when educated about how an antidepressant works, most patients are willing to consider a trial.

Make Medications a Routine

You may need to recommend that medication be taken on a regular basis. Keep the regimen simple, like "take at bedtime" or "first thing in the morning." Patients often will think of antidepressants as something to take when they are having a bad day. Explain to them the importance of maintaining a consistent dosage and how therapeutic blood levels are reached.

Use Minimum Dosages

Keep in mind when you are recommending medications that with the medically ill it is advisable to begin with the lowest doses, possibly even sub-therapeutic levels, and then increase the dosage over time. For example, if the recommended starting dosage for an antidepressant is 50 mg, you may suggest starting at 25 mg and then increase as tolerated. Frequently, many of the antidepressant medications have not been studied in the medically ill and therefore there may be no good guidelines for starting dosages. Therefore, a good rule of thumb is to start slowly and monitor side effects. Remember that side effects can be problematic enough that patients will often discontinue use of an antidepressant prematurely or take the medication inconsistently. It is not uncommon to hear a patient say, "I didn't like how I felt taking that, so I skipped a few days."

Treat Each Patient as Unique

Treat each patient as unique, taking into consideration their medical illness, other medications, and response to antidepressants. What works for one patient may not hold true for another.

Challenges to Choosing Medications

It is critical to realize that the patient you are treating for depression also has other medical conditions. Moreover, although most antidepressant medications are equally effective with certain patients, their use in patients with medical comorbidity presents some severe challenges. New drugs are being offered at a rate of almost two per year. These drugs are being touted to the clinician as "better" drugs to treat depression. As there are increasing number of antidepressants with slight differences, the ability to readily differentiate these agents, and hence choose the best drug for the patient, becomes clinically difficult. Unfortunately, few if any controlled head-to-head studies are undertaken to compare agents, and even fewer are undertaken to look at these agents effect on the chronically ill.

Basic Information about Drug Actions and Interactions

The main target of antidepressant medications is the brain, with the effects focused on the neurotransmitters. The exact mechanism of these effects and their connections to behavioral and emotional changes is still unknown. Hypotheses about the etiology of certain psychiatric disorders such as major depression have come from the response of these disorders to psychopharmacological agents. The actions of these medications are extremely complex, involving neurotransmitters in different brain pathways. Often, patients will hear or read these terms and become overwhelmed with the details and terminology. If needed, answering their questions in lay terms can reduce anxiety. The following is a description of basic concepts and terms used when discussing pharmacological treatment; these are the elements of **pharmacokinetics**.

- **Absorption**—A medication can be administered orally where it is absorbed through the stomach or under the tongue (sublingual area), administered directly into the bloodstream (intravenous), or by injection into the muscle or under the skin (intramuscular or subcutaneous). Absorption rates vary according to how a drug is administered. Absorption rates from taking pill, capsule, or liquid appear to be similar. When the stomach is empty, gastric absorption increases due to the increase in available area or surface space in the stomach.

- **Distribution**—Most antidepressant drugs are absorbed into fatty tissue, including the brain. In patients who have a chronic medical illness or are elderly, albumin (water-soluble proteins found in milk and egg whites) decreases. It is the albumin that tells us about the patient's nutritional status. As albumin decreases, the amount of antidepressant medication floating or unbound increases.

- **Metabolism**—As a drug enters the gastrointestinal system, it is passed through the liver before it enters into systemic circulation throughout the body, thereby being metabolized before the rest of the body is exposed to the drug. This effect is significant because it helps explain that when a drug is administered intramuscularly, it is more potent than oral administrations. Many drugs are metabolized through a common pathway in the liver In the liver, and to some extent in the kidney, the enzyme, P450, helps to break down drugs. Many medications that the elderly and medically ill are on compete for this enzyme. However, the enzyme can only work on one medication and the other has the potential to build to toxic levels. This is because more of the drug is left in the system without being broken down and excreted.

- **Elimination**—A drug and its metabolite (end product after the drug is broken down in the body) are excreted through the kidneys as well as through bile and feces. Small amounts are also excreted through sweat, saliva, or tears. The half-life of a drug is the amount of time needed to excrete half of the drug from the body. This is usually stated as how long it takes to remove half of the drug from the blood. Frequency of drug administration is established by the length of its half-life. That is, based on how long it takes for a drug to be removed from the body will guide decisions of how often to give the medication, such as once a day or four times a day. Renal disease and aging slow down the common route of renal elimination and therefore may alter the half-life of medications.

Choices of Antidepressants

As described in an earlier chapter, the biological theory maintains that depression is associated with decreased levels of central nervous system neurotransmitters norepinephrine, dopamine, and serotonin. Antidepressants are thought to work by blocking the reuptake of these neurotransmitters, therefore leaving them in the receptor sites for a longer period. The exact mechanism of these actions are still being researched.

There are five major classes of antidepressant medications. These include selective serotonin reuptake inhibitors, tricyclic antidepressants, dual mechanism antidepressants, and monoamine oxidase inhibitors. No one antidepressant has been shown to be more effective than another. However, there are factors associated with the patient (medical illness, age, other medications) and the side-effect profiles of each medication that would favor one drug over another. It is essential to realize that each class of antidepressant therapy works in different ways and therefore produces different side effects. You need to understand the mechanisms by which the major group of antidepressant agents work and also to see if one group of drugs maybe be better for use with chronically ill.

Selective Serotonin Reuptake Inhibitor (SSRI)

The selective serotonin reuptake inhibitors is a relatively new class of antidepressants, which increases the neurotransmitter, serotonin. These include fluoxetine (Prozac), sertraline (Zoloft), and paroxetine (Paxil). The mechanism of these agents is presumed to be linked to their inhibition of the central nervous system neuronal uptake of serotonin. While not definitive, it is thought that this is one of the mechanisms by which depression is regulated, and by blocking the uptake of serotonin it increases serotonin locally leading to beneficial mood effects. Studies have shown that this class of drugs has little effect on cholinergic, benozodiazepine, and histamine receptors. By not binding to these receptors the sedative, hypotensive, and cardiovascular effects are minimized with these agents. This typically makes them safer for medically ill patients. It has been recommended that SSRIs be considered as the first choice of an antidepressant for the medically ill. Therefore, as a class of antidepressants, the SSRIs appear to provide further options for the treatment of depression particularly among medically ill and elderly patients.

Although the SSRIs are generally referred to as a pharmacologically homogeneous group, differences in their effect on neurotransmitter receptors and pharmacokinetic profiles do exist. These differences are important when choosing a certain SSRI for treating the elderly patient as receptor densities change with age and disease. It has been shown that elderly patients treated with fluoxetine develop higher plasma levels than younger patients when treated with the same dose. Both sertraline and paroxetine have no significant metabolites and have elimination half-lives of twenty-four hours. In contrast, the major metabolite of fluoxetine, norfluoxetine has a half-life of 8-12 days. This is an important clinical feature especially in cases of drug interactions or intolerable side effects. Further, fluoxetine and sertraline have minimal anticholinergic side effects. The SSRIs are also significantly less lethal than other antidepressants when taken in overdose. They may be preferred in patients with risk for suicide.

When discontinuing an SSRI it should be done with a slow taper to prevent withdrawal symptoms (vivid dreams, nightmares, tremors, dizziness, nausea, disorientation). This gradual taper is particularly important with the SSRIs with shorter elimination half-lives such as sertraline.

Tricyclic Antidepressant (TCA)

Historically, the tricyclic antidepressants have been the most widely used drugs for the treatment of depression. However, due to the differences in side-effect profiles, the SSRIs are becoming more popular. The most commonly used TCAs include amitriptyline, desipramine, doxepin, imipramine, and nortriptyline. In use since the 1940s, the precise mechanism by which they alleviate depression is not well understood. These drugs affect the actions of brain neurotransmitters, blocking the uptake of serotonin and norepinephrine in their respective nerve terminals, thereby increasing their immediate concentration. Most of these drugs produce some form of sedation, which may be of benefit as these patients frequently suffer from sleep loss. However, these agents decrease REM or dream sleep. These drugs alleviate mood in approximately two to three weeks of daily administration.

The side effects of TCAs are most pronounced in the autonomic nervous system. Blurred vision, dry mouth, urine retention is often reported in patients. In addition, a decrease in blood pressure with reflex tachycardia (increase in heart rate) is also seen after a short period of administration. There can be an increase of cardiac arrhythmia in patients with underlying myocardial or heart disease and their appearance should lead to immediate discontinuation of the drug. Overdose of the drug can lead to confusion, dilation of pupils, and a worsening of cardiovascular stability (hypotension or fatal arrhythmia). This needs to be treated in a medical intensive-care setting.

Dual Mechanism Antidepressant

Other antidepressants include nefazodone (Serzone), trazodone (Desyrel), venlafaxine (Effexor), and bupropion (Wellbutrin). One new agent that is different from the SSRI classification is nefazodone.

Nefazodone hydrochloride is a newer antidepressant agent that is primarily metabolized in the intestine and the liver by the P450IIIA4 isozyme—this is the enzyme that helps to break the drug down in the body. Its half-life is approximately 2-4 hours. This antidepressant agent has been found to have less side effects than TCAs and equivalent to that of sertraline, although head-to-head studies have never been performed. Although similar to trazadone, it is much less likely to induce hypotension and priapism (erectile dysfunction), two common side effects of antidepressant therapy that are especially true in the diabetic and hypertensive patient. The major clinical advantages of this agent is that it has been proposed to have less disturbance on sleep and sexual dysfunction, two disorders often found with medically ill patients.

Trazodone is not considered a first line agent for treating depression. It is often used as a hypnotic to induce sleep. It can be recommended alone for treatment of sleep disturbances or in combination with an SSRI. Although trazodone does not cause anticholinergic side effects like the TCAs, it can cause orthstastic hypotension (dropping of the blood pressure when standing up) and cause significant sedation. Many patients complain of feeling "hung over" from the drug. Further, trazodone can enhance the effects of alcohol and barbiturates and therefore should be used with caution among patients who tend to abuse these substances.

Venlafaxine is similar to the TCAs in that it inhibits both norepinephrine and 5HT uptake. The most common side effects include nausea, somnolence, insomnia, dizziness, ejaculatory problems, headache, nervousness, dry mouth, anxiety, and sweating. A particular problem associated with venlafaxine treatment is that of increasing blood pressure. Therefore, it is recommended that it be considered as a second line choice for treating depression particularly among the medically ill.

Bupropion, unlike the TCAs, does not have any anticholinergic side effects, cardiovascular effects, or sexual dysfunction. It is considered a good choice for the elderly as it has a low toxicity profile, suggesting that it does not build up in the body as readily. It is, however, contraindicated with patients who have a known seizure disorder or patients with bulimia or anorexia due to the increased risk for seizure.

Monoamine Oxidase Inhibitor (MAOI)

The MAOIs are not recommended as a first-line antidepressant choice but have remained an important option for atypical depression or those that have been unresponsive to other medications. Unlike many of the other antidepressants discussed above, it is not recommended that primary care providers prescribe MAOIs unless they have extensive experience with the drugs. It is preferable to refer to a psychiatrist when considering using MAOIs.

The reason for the precautions with these drugs is due to their severe adverse side effects and potentially severe drug-drug and food-drug interactions. Patients who are prescribed MAOIs must follow a strict diet to prevent food-drug interactions. These restrictions include eliminating aged cheeses, wine, non-fresh fish, and yeast extracts. Fatal hypertensive (high blood pressure) crisis has occurred when the MAOIs have been used with foods such as those listed above which contain tryptophan or tyramine. These food restrictions can be particularly problematic for patients, such as diabetics or those suffering from renal failure, who are already on restricted diets and now must further limit their choices.

Drugs that must be avoided when using MAOIs include over-the-counter medications such as Actifed, Contact, Vicks NyQuil, Alka-Seltzer Plus, Sine-Off, Tylenol, and Robitussin, to name just a few. In addition, there are numerous prescription medications that can cause drug-drug interactions. These include L-dopa, meperidine, fluoxetine, buspirone, theophylline, calcium channel blockers, anticoagulants, hypoglycemic agents, and carbamazepine. Interaction effects range among fatal reactions, hypertension, confusion, fever, and tremors. Caffeine, cocaine, and amphetamines can also cause drug-drug interactions leading to moderate and severe hypertension. For a more complete list of interactions refer to Alan Stoudemire and colleagues' chapter "Psychopharmacology in the Medical Patient" found in their book *Psychiatric Care of the Medical Patient* (1993).

Chapter 12

The Consultation Process

This chapter will address the evaluation and treatment of a medical patient, either in a hospital setting or in an outpatient setting. It is important to note that when any patient comes to you complaining of depression, you will want to do a thorough evaluation of the patient, using many of the steps discussed in this chapter. This is important because, as we have discussed throughout this book, depression is complicated and can be caused by medical illness or can preexist and be exacerbated by a concurrent medical illness. In order to treat the patient adequately, it is essential that the initial evaluation seek all potential sources of the depressive symptoms.

Patients may come to you in a variety of ways. In a hospital setting, the medical patient may be referred to a mental health clinician for evaluation and treatment of depressive symptoms and other problems such as poor compliance with medical regimen. This is often referred to as requesting a "consultation." That is, the primary treating physician or nursing staff will request a consultation for assistance in managing the patient's care. The medical patient may also be referred to the clinician on an outpatient basis, when the patient is not requiring inpatient care, but still exhibits signs of depression that may interfere with their functioning. Finally, if you are a clinician practicing in an outpatient office setting, any patient may come to you for treatment of their depressive symptoms. As mentioned earlier, good treatment will include a thorough evaluation of any contributing factors that might arise from any medical illness.

We will first address the consultation process in an inpatient medical-surgical hospital setting. We will discuss all of the steps involved in doing a hospital consult, from first receiving the referral to final recommendations. Hospital consultation is typically done by specially trained mental health professionals such as psychiatrists, psychologists, and sometimes, social workers with master's degree training. The mental health clinician should work closely with the health care staff and therefore be comfortable in a medical setting.

The Hospital Consult

As we mentioned earlier, the word depression means different things to different people; it is therefore important to approach the evaluation process by first discussing depression with the staff members who are asking you to evaluate the patient. This first step begins with clarifying the referral question with the staff in order to understand the emotions and behaviors that have been observed by others. Historical information must then be gathered from the medical chart and, if possible, from sources such as family and friends. Finally, the assessment of the patient should include a thorough interview and any psychological tests if needed.

Step One: Clarify the Referral

The referral may be verbal or written. The referral may describe a patient's situation—"Can you please see Mr. Smith, he seems to be having difficulty adjusting?"—it may describe the patient's mood or presentation—"Please evaluate the patient, who is tearful and withdrawn" or the question may suggest a potential disorder—"Evaluate patient with anxiety disorder." At times there may simply be a comment on behavior such as "Patient is noncompliant." A clarification will set a framework for your further assessment. It is helpful to delineate what behaviors, emotions, and cognitive presentation have led to the referral. Consider that an angry, hostile, agitated, and delirious patient may have provoked the staff into labeling him or her as crazy and subsequently they are really looking for confirmation and management of the behavior from you. Or behavior may be labeled as noncompliant by the staff when in fact the behavior may reflect a belief system that is different from theirs, or the manifestation of depression or cognitive deficits. Understanding what has led to the consult and what the expectations are in advance will be helpful to the evaluation process.

Typical referral questions include the following:

- evaluation of suicidality
- evaluation of depression
- differential between depression and dementia
- alcohol withdrawal
- competency evaluations
- noncompliant behavior
- psychotic or bizarre behavior
- differential of delirium and dementia
- evaluation of anxiety and panic disorders

Below are a few thoughts to guide you in clarifying the referral question from the staff:

- Inquire about onset of symptoms or clinical presentation. This will give you information as to how long the problem has been going on and how the depression looks. For instance, "Did the depressive symptoms appear immediately following a surgery or an acute event such as heart attack or did the patient appear depressed before a procedure?" You will begin to get a picture of the patient and some initial idea as to whether the potential medical problem has triggered the depression or whether there is another explanation, such as delirium due to an infection, which looks like depression but requires aggressive treatment by the medical staff.
- Establish what the agenda is for the referral question by asking if the behavior and/or emotional state of the patient is interfering with care or recovery. Try to determine if the patient is noncompliant with treatment or difficult to manage because of his or her behavior. This will give you an idea of how severe the depressive symptoms may be and the potential severity of the impact of poor compliance with medical regimens.
- Has the patient's behavior triggered a positive or negative response in the referring agent? This can be inferred by directly communicating with the individual. You want to know whether the agent is looking for a resolution of staff conflicts as opposed to improving treatment for the patient. A patient who is difficult to care for often triggers conflict in the staff. These patients can include those with personality disorders, patients who are noncompliant, severely depressed patients who may not be an active participant in their care, or agitated delirious patients.
- Was the patient told that a mental health specialist was consulted? Health care providers frequently avoid telling the patients for fear that they will upset or anger the patient and they may not wish to deal with the results. It is important, however, for you to have this knowledge prior to entering the room. If nothing else, it may protect you from being hit with a full bed pan, insulted, or being set up for the patient not to be cooperative with the evaluation.

Step Two: Obtain History

The importance of gathering adequate history cannot be overstated. The history is often invaluable in making a differential diagnosis. History should be collected from old charts and records, from the current chart, from family and friends, and other relevant sources. If possible, this information should be obtained prior to evaluating the patient, as this will help guide your assessment process. The following checklists can be used to help organize historical information.

- **Medical History:**
    - ☐ What was the patient's mood and behavior with other types of illnesses?

- Based on past record of medical history, is the patient prone to becoming delirious?
- When was the patient first diagnosed with the condition?
- What medication is the patient using now or in the recent past?

- **Psychiatric/Psychological History:**
  - Does the patient have a history of a psychiatric disorder?
  - Was he or she ever treated for the same?
  - Is there any known family history?
- **Substance Abuse History:**
  - Is there a past or current abuse of substances including alcohol, narcotics, or illicit drugs?
  - Does the person smoke cigarettes? Has the person been treated in the past?
  - Is there any ongoing follow-up with a support program (e.g., Alcoholics Anonymous, Narcotics Anonymous) or a counselor?
  - Does the person have a sponsor?
- **Vocational History:**
  - What is the vocational history of the patient?
  - How long has he or she remained in a job?
  - What is his or her level of education?
  - Is there any military experience?
- **Social History:**
  - Does the person live alone or with others?
  - What is the level of support from family and friends?
  - Does the patient have a living will, durable power of attorney?
  - What does the person do for fun or pleasure?
  - Have they been incarcerated?
  - What are typical or premorbid coping strategies?

Chart Review

A thorough chart review can provide a wealth of information about the patient. Keep in mind that the goal is to pull information together from a variety of places to develop a solid clinical picture that will provide an answer to the referral question and set the stage for management and treatment. Although medical charts are often organized differently in different facilities, all charts will have the following information. Below is a format for reviewing the medical charts.

1. Begin review of the chart with the doctor's orders. This section will give you information regarding the current condition, scheduled procedures, consult requests, and information regarding medication schedule. When reviewing this section, it is important to note dates and times for the orders. This information will be helpful when examining the connections between the onset of depressive symptoms and the recent addition of medications, discontinuing of medications, or undergoing medical procedures.
2. The progress notes and nursing notes sections will provide a chronological sequence of findings, interpretations, and recommendations. It is in each of these sections where information regarding possible changes in mental status may be noted as well as behavior in the evening versus the daytime hours. For example, in some cases depressive symptoms are worse in the morning hours while dementia and delirium tend to worsen during evening and night (this has been referred to as "sundowning"). When reviewing this section it is important to note the date and possible time of the observations. This information can then be cross-referenced with other information such as changes in medications, or visits from friends and family (downturns can be caused by illicit drugs being brought into the hospital or distressing visits that may provoke anger or depressed affect).
3. Typically medical charts will have a separate section for consults that have been completed by other specialists. Although in the progress note section the specialists will often include a general summary of their findings, the full consult can be found in the consult section.
4. Examine the vital sign section (temperature, pulse, respiration, blood pressure) to learn of acute changes that coincide with other clinical information. For example, a rise in temperature, a change in mental status, and changes in mood could reflect possible delirium secondary to infection. Episodic rises in blood pressure has been associated with cognitive changes and mood disturbances (*Archives of Internal Medicine*, 1997).

Step Three: Assess the Patient

Psychological evaluations in the medical setting can present unique challenges. A person who recognizes that they are depressed may actively seek out psychological treatment and in doing so is operating from their own volition. In contrast, medical patients are typically in the mind-set of being physically ill, and are actively tuned into the function and dysfunction of their bodies. For example, most of their energy and thought may be expended on whether or not they have had a bowel movement or their pain and fear associated with an impending procedure, rather than their depressed mood. As a result, when a psychological evaluation is suggested, patients can often become defensive and angry at the notion of being viewed as "crazy." They can also have realistic fears that if a psychologist is involved in their care then perhaps the medical staff will not take their physical needs seriously and will write their symptoms off as being "in their head." When working with medically ill patients it is therefore important to establish a collaborative working alliance to minimize the stigma often associated with seeing a "shrink." Patients need to be reassured that they are not "crazy" but rather that the depression that they are experiencing is quite common among medical patients.

Establishing Rapport

When approaching medical patients about psychological issues it is important to first establish rapport. Given that they may not readily be inviting you in the front door to treat their emotional disorders, it is important to find common ground from which to begin the evaluation. We often refer to this strategy as coming at the patients through the side door. Typically, a medically ill patient will be operating from a mind-set that focuses on the physical illness. Initial contact should involve discussions of physical symptoms, hospital experience, comfort level, and the patient's understanding of the medical treatment plan. This type of discussion allows the psychologist an opportunity to join the patient in establishing a collaborative alliance in assessment and treatment of the emotional disorder. In addition, valuable clinical information can be obtained by actively listening to the patient's subjective presentation of their medical illness. The therapist should be attempting to answer several questions that will be valuable in the differential diagnosis and treatment plan:

- What is the idiosyncratic meaning of the illness for the patient?
- Is there evidence of cognitive deficits?
- Does the patient spontaneously offer information about emotional distress?
- What is the history of the current presentation? This may be offered directly or may need to be inferred from information about past medical experiences, prior coping strategies, and past emotional distress.

An **adaptive and flexible approach** is essential when working with medical patients in a hospital setting. Given that the predictability and comforts of the office are absent, creativity and sensitivity are needed when attempting to establish some sense of privacy and confidentiality. Assessment and treatment strategies may need to be cut short or tailored to meet the needs of patients who are in pain, easily fatigued, or frequently requiring medical attention throughout the session. Patient's with end-stage renal disease, for example, are typically fatigued or light-headed immediately after dialysis and confused or distracted immediately before treatment. Attention to the physical limitations of your patient without eliminating psychological care is the goal.

Fear and distrust of psychological interventions can exist as patients can be unsure of what they are experiencing. A patient who is delirious, for example, may become quite agitated and frightened by the cognitive limitations that they recognize and the potential hallucinations that frequently can occur. These fears, in part, are born out of being labeled as "crazy," particularly since they themselves feel crazy. A depressed patient may deny the symptoms for fear of being viewed as weak. It is important to **normalize** psychological symptoms. This can be accomplished by educating patients about the frequency of these symptoms among similar patients.

Minimizing the notion that the patient's situation is strange or abnormal increases compliance with the treatment plan.

Humor can be a useful therapeutic tool. Rosenheim describes humor as the "capacity for maintaining a sense of proportion as to one's importance in the life situations in which one finds oneself" (Rosenheim 1974). Using humor with medically ill patients is not to suggest that their situation is funny, but rather that humor, when used in a sensitive manner, can be therapeutic. Humor can serve a facilitative role in establishing rapport and it can be used as a diagnostic tool to gauge level of distress and range of affect. In addition, as a strategy it can help patients distance themselves from difficult material about their current pain and suffering. This distancing serves to allow the patient a respite from the current distress while concurrently mobilizing their resources for future coping needs. The time that humor buys can also be used to assist the patient, paradoxically, thinking about their illness in a different way. On an emotional level, humor can bring enjoyment to life and dramatically intrude on gloom and inertia, which is often associated with depression in the medically ill.

Ideally, rapport will be established and cooperation with the clinical assessment will occur. However, even with the best techniques, some patients, due to their personality styles, underlying psychiatric illness, and level of their current medical or psychological condition, may be limited in the amount of cooperation and rapport that can be established. Therefore, throughout the evaluation process much effort should be given to all aspects of the patient's behavior and expression of emotion. Is the patient irritable and minimally cooperative with verbal questions? Does he or she frequently fall asleep during the evaluation and when aroused not recall what the last question was or even that you had entered the room? This presentation may be consistent with a delirious patient, but if you asked questions and left the room without trying to connect, you may have assessed the patient as irritable and uncooperative and ascribed these behaviors to any number of alternative diagnoses, such as a personality disorder or depression, due to the irritable mood and flat affect.

Mental Status Exam

Studies have reported 24 percent (Anthony et al. 1982) to 37 percent (Jacobs et al. 1977) of general medical patients have some form of cognitive impairment; but this fact it is frequently not recognized by health care providers. Specifically, one study found that 37 percent of the ward physicians, 55 percent of nurses, and 46 percent of medical students did not identify cognitive dysfunction in their general medical patients (Knights and Folstein 1977). Given that cognitive dysfunction can confound the diagnosis of affective disorders, it is imperative that the clinician evaluate cognitive function as a routine component to the assessment process.

There are a number of screening examinations used bedside to identify cognitive dysfunction. Two of the most commonly used are the Mini-Mental Status Examination (Folstein et al. 1975) and the Neurobehavioral Cognitive Status Exam or NCSE (Kiernan et al. 1987). The Mini-Mental Status Exam is the most popular and widely used screening exam. It takes approximately five minutes to administer and has been found to be valid and reliable for use with medical patients (Anthony et al. 1982; Nelson et al. 1986).

The NCSE is a newer exam used to assess cognitive dysfunction. It takes approximately twenty minutes to administer and has been found to have fewer false negative results than its predecessors (Kiernan et al. 1987).

Evaluation of Depression

When evaluating depression among the medically ill, it is important to help them understand how depression can be experienced. Many people believe that depression is only about feeling sad and that if they are not sad then they can't be depressed. You need to help patients understand that they can feel irritable, anxious, or just plain disinterested with many parts of their life while suffering from depression. The questionnaire (on pages 193–194) can be used to help explain depression and to differentiate which are the most distressing symptoms for the patient.

What Does Depression Feel Like to You?

Depressed people often report feeling that activities, events, and people in their lives that used to make them happy no longer do. As a result, many depressed people feel that life is not worth living anymore; some attempt to take their own lives while others simply stop taking care of themselves. Many medical patients who are depressed admit to feeling that following their diet, taking their medication, and keeping up with their medical appointments is not as important to them as it used to be. They appear to adopt an attitude of "Why bother?" or "What is the point?" Patients who are depressed can also experience difficulty with memory, which frequently interferes with their ability to follow the medical plans their doctor has set for them.

The first step to treating depression is to better identify what *kind* of depression you are experiencing so that you can develop more adaptive strategies to manage it. Symptoms of depression can vary, depending on the individual, and can change forms at different times. Read through each of the different ways that people experience symptoms of depression and try to identify which "style" is most consistent with your depressive symptoms. Place a check mark next to all those symptoms that apply to you during times of depression:

Physically Ill Style

- ❑ Tend to have stomachache
- ❑ Tend to have quite a few headaches
- ❑ No energy
- ❑ Multiple body aches and pains
- ❑ Normal bodily pain seems worse
- ❑ Poor concentration
- ❑ Poor memory
- ❑ Poor Appetite
- ❑ Nausea

Anxious Style

- ❑ Feel like you can't sit still
- ❑ Feel like you are "jumping out of your skin"
- ❑ Feel like you are moving at a rapid rate inside but not interested in doing anything
- ❑ Worry a lot
- ❑ Irritability
- ❑ Can't sit still
- ❑ Trouble concentrating on a book or television program

Isolated Style

- ❑ Want to sleep a lot
- ❑ Not interested in interacting with others
- ❑ Isolating yourself
- ❑ Don't feel like talking
- ❑ Tire easily
- ❑ Don't want to go anyplace
- ❑ Call in sick to work frequently
- ❑ Feel irritated when loved ones inquire about how you are feeling

Dependent Style

- ❑ Feel insecure
- ❑ Dependent
- ❑ Want others around all the time
- ❑ Feel frightened most of the time
- ❑ Cry easily
- ❑ Have a chronic knot in your stomach

The purpose in using the above instrument is to help patients identify with one or more of these styles of depression. Many patients do not recognize, and hence often do not report, feelings of depression to their physicians. Many struggle with whether or not the symptoms are related to depression or to their medical condition. With the identification of symptom clusters and the labeling of them as possible depression, the patient is better equiped to recognize early warning signals for their depression and to realize that depression can exacerbate the medical condition.

The following questions can serve as a guide for differentiating specific aspects of the depression. You can preface the questions by telling the patient that you want to more clearly understand their depression and how it is affecting their lives. The criterion numbers refer to the organization of symptoms in the DSM-IV.

Questions for Criterion A1 (Depressed Mood)

1. Do you feel sad or down throughout most of the day?
2. On the days when you physically feel better, do you notice that your mood improves?
3. Do you wake up in the morning feeling depressed?
4. When you have visitors or an opportunity to talk to family or friends, does your mood improve?
5. Does your mood change with different times of the day?

Questions for Criterion A2 (Anhedonia)

1. If you were feeling physically better, what activities would you want to be able to resume?
2. Do you think about returning to these activities? For example, do you hope for the day when you will be able to play golf again or have friends over for dinner?
3. Do you enjoy being around friends and family members?
4. When you are around others do you notice your mood improving even if only for a brief period of time?
5. Are there times when you feel that there is no point in even getting cleaned up and dressed?
6. Even when your appetite is good and you feel physically able, do you find that you are simply not interested in eating?
7. Are there times when you simply do not want to be around anyone? Is this a new behavior for you?
8. Do you find that activities (i.e., reading, visiting with friends, listening to music, sexual activity) that you used to enjoy no longer give you pleasure?

Questions for Criterion A3 (Appetite Disturbances)

1. Do you feel hungry but simply do not feel like eating?
2. Does eating or cooking feel like a struggle?
3. Do you make attempts to force yourself to eat when you are not hungry?

Questions for Criterion A4 (Insomnia or Hypersomnia)

1. Do your sleep patterns get worse when you are physically ill?
2. Do you notice an improvement in your sleep when you feel better?
3. Do you find yourself thinking about many different worries when you lie down to sleep?
4. Do you have trouble falling asleep, because your mind is dwelling on the problems of the day?

Questions for Criterion A6 (Fatigue)

1. Did you begin to feel depressed at the same time that your energy felt low?
2. What tasks are you able to engage in?
3. How long before you get too tired to complete a task?
4. Does your poor energy make you feel disinterested in pleasurable activities?
5. When you physically feel well does your energy return?

Questions for Criterion A7 (Hopelessness)

1. Do you feel that your future is hopeless?
2. Do you feel like a failure?
3. Can you find any hope or positive meaning in your life?
4. Do you feel that your illness is a punishment?
5. Do you feel that there is nothing that you can do to improve your life?
6. Do you feel that you are of no value to anyone?

Psychological Tests for Mood Disorders

Self-report measures alone are not enough to diagnose mood disorders among the medically ill. They can be a useful adjunct for screening, however, if used properly and if the limitations are well understood by the clinician. If a screening instrument is to be successfully used in the medical setting, you need to consider the "hit" rate—the proportion of cases that will be correctly identified by the instrument—and the optimal cut off score. Results can then be compared to diagnostic criteria from the DSM-IV.

A review of definitions regarding psychometric properties may be useful at this time. The *sensitivity* of a test refers to the proportion of individuals who are depressed and who score positively on the test. In like fashion, *specificity* refers to the proportion of individuals who are not depressed and who score negatively on the test. The *positive and negative predictive value* of the test is the proportion of patients who score positively on the test and who are depressed and those with a negative score on the test who are not depressed, respectively. It is important to realize that predictive value is influenced by the prevalence of depression in the group being studied. Therefore, when interpreting studies and the efficacy of the instrument, one must consider prevalence rates for the specific population.

Beck Depression Inventory (BDI)—The BDI has been used in over 1,000 research studies. There are twenty-one depressive symptoms such as sadness, guilt, mood, weight loss, and suicidal ideation. The patient must rate the level of severity for each symptom on a four-point scale. The BDI typically takes about 5-10 minutes to complete. A particular strength of this instrument includes the development of probable cut-off scores for probable nondepression (0-9), mild-to-moderate depression (10-18), moderate-to-severe depression (19-29) and severe depression (30-73). In addition, there is a short version (Beck and Beck 1972) with only thirteen items. Both versions have proven to be valid for medically ill and older adults. A potential concern with the BDI in its use among the medically ill is the need to separate out the somatic items (appetite, sleep, and sexual concerns) which could confound the results. The cognitive items that focus on thoughts and behaviors related to depression appear to be better indicators of depression among the medically ill.

Geriatric Depression Scale (GDS)—The GDS appears to have an advantage over other instruments in that it was specifically developed for older adults (Yesavage et al. 1983). It is a 30-item questionnaire with questions phrased in a simple yes-no format. It takes only 8-10 minutes to administer and the content is focused on mood and mood-related symptoms, while excluding somatic items that may confound the results for the physically ill elderly. The GDS has been shown to be a reliable indicator of depression in elderly inpatients, outpatients, and nursing home patients (Parmelee et al. 1989). A score of 11 or greater is indicative of a probable depression. Caution should be used when using this instrument with cognitively impaired patients.

Evaluation of Risk Factors for Suicide

Patients are most vulnerable to thoughts of suicide when certain stressful situations are experienced. These factors need to be identified when working with medically ill patients in order to establish a treatment plan that will reduce or eliminate these vulnerability factors: the greater the number of vulnerability factors, the higher the risk for suicide. The following factors are particularly common and noteworthy for this population:

- **Poor social support or perceived feelings of loneliness.** It is important to assess the level of emotional support that the individual can receive from others. Inquire about feelings of isolation and loneliness even when in the presence of others. Does the individual have somebody that they can confide in or have they closed themselves off from emotional contacts.

- **Chronic pain can limit the individuals ability to cope.** Pain is a common complaint among medically ill patients.
- **Feeling chronically tired with low energy reduces one's ability to cope.** Poor energy is a risk factor for suicide.
- **Conflict within the family.** The need for family members to assume more assistance or care for the chronically ill may artificially force families to interact and subsequently can rekindle old conflicts. Identify potential conflicts that could increase risk for suicidal behavior either as a genuine attempt for resolution or as anger and punishment of the family.
- **Limited problem-solving skills which may not be adequate to deal with the complexity of chronic illness.** In the face of complex and overwhelming stress related to their illness, individuals with limited problem-solving skills may view suicide as the only option.

The following questions can be helpful in assessing a patient's risk of suicide:

Meaning of Suicide and Death

- What did the patient expect life would be with the current medical illness?
- How different is the reality?
- What would it mean to be dead?
- What would happen to significant others after the patient's death?
- Does the patient ascribe positive meaning to death? Is death the opportunity for rebirth, peace, rejoining of family members?

Evaluation of Hopelessness and Despair

- Does the patient see hope that the depression will get better?
- Can the patient envision feeling content with life despite medical illness?
- Does the patient see only long-term suffering in the future?
- Does the patient feel that the current situation is intolerable?

Assessment of Adaptive Coping Capabilities

- Is there a history of maladaptive coping strategies, such as alcohol and substance abuse?
- How has the patient managed other serious stressors in the past?
- Is the patient capable of flexible thinking? Will he or she be able to examine alternative solutions and strategies?

Deterrents to Suicide

- Can the patient engage in direct communication with physician about possible termination of treatment?
- Are there religious beliefs that would prevent overt acts of suicide?

- Are there dependent children or other family members who would serve as a deterrent to suicide?

Evaluation of a Patient in an Outpatient Setting

The process of evaluating a patient in the outpatient setting is very similar to the one discussed for the hospital setting. The clinician may be asked to see a patient once he or she is discharged from the hospital for the same concerns the medical staff had when the patient was an inpatient. The medical staff is often still heavily involved in a patient's care after discharge from the hospital, providing ongoing care on an outpatient basis. Health care as it is practiced currently has reduced the length of an inpatient stay and has moved to providing more outpatient care. Consultation with the medical staff will require written and oral communication with the primary physician or the primary nurse. Medical information is gathered in the same way as discussed earlier by requesting the medical chart for review or speaking with the physician about potential concerns. Feedback and recommendations are given in a written note back to the physician or primary nurse and placed in the chart.

If a patient comes to your office complaining of depressive symptoms, you may gather medical information by means of a thorough interview of the patient. With the patient's consent, you may contact the patient's physician and request further medical information. Most patients are readily agreeable to having coordinated care between their health care providers. Most physicians are also extremely cooperative with providing helpful information and receiving any potential recommendations for their patient's care. Should any medical concerns be present, the patient should be educated to communicate closely with physicians and you may facilitate this process by maintaining communication with the physician yourself.

Appendix

Case Example

The following is a sample case that integrates all of the information described in the evaluation process as well as in the treatment sections of this book. The case can be used as an example of how a consultation is done. We have also provided a description of the therapy interventions that follow up on the initial evaluation of this case. The actual phrasing of the consult request and the subsequent evaluation of the patient is written below in italics. Commentary on various aspects to be attended to by the clinician is written in regular text.

Initial Evaluation

Referral Question:

Please evaluate this 60-year-old African American male with end-stage renal disease, hypertension (high blood pressure), and borderline personality disorder. Please evaluate and treat passive-aggressive behaviors related to medical regimen.

In reviewing the chart, borderline personality disorder appeared in the problem list section of the medical chart. Clarification of the referral question revealed that the attending physician was extremely frustrated with the ongoing "noncompliant" behavior of the patient. He was receiving hemodialysis three times a week and was showing up late for treatments and had documented 5-6 kilo weight gains between treatments—the normal range is 1-2 kilos—over a six-week period of time. The nursing staff complained to the physician that the patient was "trying to manipulate them" by coming late for treatment, which frequently required them to stay later. They labeled this as passive-aggressive behavior.

Interview of the Patient

Patient was seen in the office following dialysis treatment. He was cooperative with the interview and alert and oriented in all three spheres. Thinking was clear and coherent, with the ability for abstract reasoning. Serial seven subtraction was accurate but slow and deliberate.

He admitted to depressed mood and feeling unmotivated and uninterested in many activities. He stated that he had much difficulty getting up in the morning and was frequently late for his 7 A.M. dialysis appointments. He complained of poor appetite and difficulty initiating and maintaining sleep. He notes that these difficulties began with the onset of dialysis but have worsened over the last several weeks. Although he admits to feeling that life on the machine was not what he had expected and that life may not be worth living in this way, he denied active plans for suicide. Patient does have adequate insight into his behavior and his fears regarding living with dialysis. He states that he does not want to actively participate in his own death (e.g., consciously choosing to stop dialysis) but at times feels that if his noncompliance passively contributes to his death then that would be easier.

Review of History

Medical History: *The patient has been receiving hemodialysis at the medical center since 2/94. His prescription for dialysis is three times a week for 4 hours. His renal history began in 1976 when he developed hypertension. He was followed in the renal clinic on an annual basis and was given medication for his blood pressure. At that time, he was also abusing drugs such as heroin (IV), cocaine, LSD, marijuana, and alcohol. As a result of legal problems related to his drug use and drug trafficking, he was unable to come to the hospital for his yearly appointments and subsequently was getting his blood pressure medications on the "black market."*

In 1986, he was badly beaten with a bat by gang members. He sustained injuries to his kidneys and had his front teeth knocked out. In 1994, he was diagnosed with end-stage renal disease and began dialysis. His course of dialysis treatment was fraught with numerous complications, including injury to his access site used for dialysis and problems with his blood pressure. When his access sites would not work he would have to be dialyzed through his femoral artery, which caused him pain and heightened anxiety during his dialysis treatments.

Significant medical history includes end-stage renal disease secondary to hypertension, peptic ulcer disease, anemia, hepatitis C, and methicillin resistant Staphylococcus aureus bacterium (MRSA).

Review of the lab results in the chart revealed anemia with a hematocrit (HCT) of less than 30, which could contribute to feeling low energy. Further examination of lab results showed that his calcium was elevated at 14 meq/L (normal levels ranged from 8.5-10.5). This condition, called hypercalcemia, is the third most common electrolyte abnormality that can produce profound mental status changes including depression, apathy, paranoia, slowing in mentation, agitation, and aggression.

Social History: *Patient is the oldest of three brothers born to his mother and father. He also has two older half-brothers and a younger half-sister born to his father and his first wife. Larry has two daughters age 35 and 33 and a son age 10, all of whom were born to different women. Larry has never been married. At this time, he is estranged from his children secondary to his history of substance abuse. His two brothers died from renal cell carcinoma, his half-sister died after a renal transplant procedure, and his father died from lung cancer. Currently, Larry resides with his mother. He receives social security disability secondary to his medical condition. He reports spending much of his time watching television alone. Past interests included reading, walking, and writing. Admits to a decline in interest for these activities. Patient reported limited social support. Relationship with family is strained secondary to his years of substance abuse and related behaviors. Family blames him for causing his medical condition and therefore have not been supportive. The majority of his friends are still actively abusing substances and therefore he has intentionally remained estranged from them to maintain his sobriety.*

Substance Abuse History: *Patient admitted to significant past abuse of alcohol, marijuana, cocaine, heroin, and LSD. Reports no substance use since 1990 after treatment at another facility. Several serum drug screens randomly performed at the hospital have been negative and there have been no physical, emotional, or behavioral indicators of current use. He is HIV negative (tested on 2/94).*

Psychological History: *Patient reports biological mother diagnosed with major depression and treated with antidepressants in the past. He denies past psychological history or treatment for himself but believes that he may have used illicit drugs in the past to "treat" depression. Admits that while abusing substances his mood was quite labile. Currently, admits to feeling "down," disinterested in life, hopeless regarding his future, restless, and scared. He claims that his energy and motivation for doing anything is very poor. Patient admits to ambivalent feelings regarding continuation on dialysis.*

Impression: *Patient with a major depressive disorder. Patient presents with a depressed mood, anhedonia, amotivational, poor energy, and ambivalence regarding living. Behaviorally, this is translated into dietary indiscretions, disinterest in dialysis treatment, and worsening mood in early morning hours, which interferes with early dialysis treatment. His energy level and motivation remain consistently low despite periods of time when he feels physically good. Patient provides a history of the above symptoms for the past 6-8 weeks. Review of labs reveals a pernicious anemia and hypercalcemia that can also be contributing to his depressive presentation.*

Although the patient is anemic and hypercalcemic, both of which can contribute to depressed mood, apathetic presentation, and a decrease in concentration and energy, the onset of his symptoms predated his current metabolic condition and his family history of major depression makes a primary mental disorder a more likely diagnosis. The anemia and the hypercalcemia are likely worsening his symptoms of depression.

Although Larry is not reporting active suicidal ideation or intention, he does appear to be quite ambivalent regarding living with dialysis and the option of death. This ambivalence appears to manifest itself in his frequently not showing for appointments, cutting treatment short, and ignoring dietary indiscretions. This behavior seems to be related more to his struggle with life and death issues as opposed to a passive approach to express his anger with the staff. Further, the diagnosis of borderline personality disorder is suspect given that he originally was given this diagnosis in 1976 at which time he was still actively abusing substances.

Upon completion of the initial evaluation, it is expected that you will provide some initial recommendations or the initiation of a treatment plan. Recommendations should include immediate, short-term suggestions for changes in the milieu, initiation of medications, and further medical workup as needed. Further, a potential long-term care plan can be discussed, including psychotherapy (either individual or group) or involvement in a support group. An example of these type of recommendations for the above case are as follows:

Recommendations

- *Since the anemia and the hypercalcemia noted in the patient's chart may be contributing heavily to the patient's already existing problem with depression, suggest medical workup to determine source and treatment of these problems.*
- *Suggest changing Larry's schedule for dialysis to an afternoon time as opposed to the early morning slot. Patients with major depression often have great difficulty getting up in the morning. An afternoon time may make it easier for Larry to get himself into the hospital and would minimize the scheduling conflicts which occur when he does not show up.*
- *May consider a trial of an antidepressant.*

Although it is difficult to tease out what is related to primary depression versus the medical condition in causing this patient's vegetative symptoms, antidepressant therapy has been shown to be effective in the medically ill who have vegetative symptoms as part of the clinical presentation.

- *Suggest regular sessions with the dietician to reinforce dietary compliance. A strategy that will help him see the direct correlation between his noncompliance, the electrolyte imbalances, and the subsequent physical and emotional symptoms may be most effective.*

Motivation to make lifestyle changes (such as quitting smoking or changing one's diet) is greatest when the person recognizes a direct relationship between immediate symptoms and their behavior; for instance, feeling tired and experiencing cramping while on the machine is related to fluid overload and dietary indiscretions.

- *Patient recognizes his ambivalence regarding living on the machine. He also recognizes that his behavior of not showing up or cutting his time short is*

> *related to his fear and feeling of hopelessness, which has left him with an attitude of "why try." These issues will be addressed in psychotherapy.*

The staff had become quite angry with this patient and intentionally or unintentionally had begun to label him as the "problem patient." A goal at this point should be to change the "label" of the patient in an attempt to elicit support and encouragement from the staff.

Outpatient Psychotherapy

Now follows a summary of the treatment that was provided for this case:

Initial Sessions

Larry agreed to begin outpatient psychotherapy to address his depression and related ambivalence regarding living with dialysis. His first appointment was approximately one week after the initial evaluation. During that period of time he was started on Zoloft 25 mg and his dialysis schedule had been changed to late morning.

Establishing Rapport (Week 1)

Larry presented to our initial session somewhat agitated and resistant to the idea that therapy would be helpful. Although he was readily able to admit that he felt depressed, he wasn't sure that he really *wanted* to feel better. My goal for the first session was to establish a rapport that would facilitate a collaborative and supportive relationship. I felt that this was particularly important with this patient as his relationships in the past had been with people who were angry and accusatory (such as his family, who blamed him for his illness) or with people who used him for their own needs (his substance abusing friends). Throughout the first session we discussed his reluctance to talk to a "shrink" and the impact this may have on his medical care. He was already very much aware of the negative view that many of the medical staff felt toward him and he feared that now he may be written off as a "nut case." We openly discussed what information would and would not be included in his medical chart and what information would remain in a private file in my office. Specifically, we decided that information regarding his depressive symptoms, his struggle with deciding about whether or not to continue on dialysis, medication responsiveness and side effects, active substance abuse, and any overt suicidal ideation or intentions would be documented in his medical chart. He also agreed that those concerns that together we felt needed to be shared with the general staff as a way of improving communication—and ultimately his treatment—would also be included in his medical chart. It was agreed that sensitive and/or personal information would remain in a file in my office.

As Larry's anxiety slowly began to decrease with subsequent sessions, his sense of humor became apparent and we used it as a therapeutic tool at times. I used humor with Larry throughout our sessions to facilitate and maintain rapport and as a diagnostic tool to gauge his level of distress, his affective range, and as a way for him to occasionally distance himself from physical and emotional pain when appropriate. This distance would allow brief respite periods during which he could mobilize other adaptive strategies for coping.

With rapport having been established, Larry was able to identify his own symptoms of depression, which included low energy, difficulty sleeping, feelings of hopelessness, irritability, loss of interest in pleasurable activities, thoughts of death, difficulty concentrating, poor memory, poor appetite, difficulty laughing or smiling, and self-hatred. We went through his list of symptoms and identified those that are unique to depression and those that can be shared symptoms with ESRD. We also discussed how depression can exacerbate feelings of pain and discomfort associated with his medical condition and dialysis treatments.

The Meaning of His Illness (Weeks 2-4)

The next goal was to look at the idiosyncratic meaning of his illness. Larry was able to articulate his belief that his family was right that he caused and *deserved* his illness. He felt that he was a weak person, who used substances all of his life to hide from his feelings and problems and as a result deserved to suffer. He was quick to add, however, that as a "weak and passive" person he hoped that he might "just have a heart attack" while on the dialysis machine and therefore would not have to take active responsibility in ending his own life. It was with this admission that he began to cry and admitted that life was not worth living. We processed "worth living" and discovered that it was not that life was not worth living on the machine but was not worth living even before he got sick.

Suicide Assessment for End-Stage Renal Disease Patients

Dialysis is often not presented to patients as *a treatment option*, but rather as the next logical step when their kidneys fail. Subsequently, patients may begin dialysis without having had an opportunity to examine their beliefs and feelings about what *this* treatment option would mean. During an initial honeymoon period, patients describe physically feeling better as the symptoms of uremia are improved. It is at this point that many patients report a reduction in fear and anxiety as they now are familiar with the dialytic therapy. When they begin to settle into their life on dialysis, however, the reality of the limitations and associated stressors can frequently lead to feelings of despair, disappointment, and depression. Patients frequently struggle with the internal conflict of life on the machine versus death. If the conflict remains unresolved, ambivalent feelings and behaviors may surface. These frequently consist of a semi-conscious approach-avoidance style with respect to compliance with the medical regimen, and an overall feeling of "why bother?" But consciously making the decision to terminate treatment and end their lives is difficult for many patients due to fear of staff and family reactions and their slow decline once they are off the machine. For many, the decision to end their lives may not occur in an overt gesture but rather in covert noncompliance. Therefore, evaluation of suicidal ideation and intent for the ESRD patient presents unique assessment and treatment challenges.

You can review the chapter on Suicide and the questions discussed earlier in this chapter.

Larry's history of abusing substances as a way of coping, his current poor social support, poor energy, ongoing conflict in his family of origin, his limited problem-solving skills, and his depression coupled with the demands and stresses related to dialysis, made him a high risk for suicide. I discussed with Larry my concerns and the possibility of an inpatient psychiatric treatment. He refused and felt that he would "not do anything stupid." He quickly laughed and added, "Remember, I'm weak." I discussed my concerns with the nephrology and psychiatry staff on the acute psychiatry unit. Psychiatry was "uncomfortable" having a dialysis patient on the unit unless it was "absolutely necessary." Larry contracted to see me briefly after every dialysis treatment (three times a week) and to maintain himself on dialysis until the depression was adequately treated, at which time he could exercise his right to discontinue treatment. The goal was to empower him and give him some control. He denied he had any weapons at home. Furthermore, he stated that he currently felt comfortable talking about death as an option by discontinuing dialysis. This direct expression of his options and choices empowered him and made the likelihood of an impulsive gesture less likely.

Throughout the following weeks, treatment goals focused on improving his mood and related ambivalence about living on dialysis. Although the major depression was improving, it became clear that Larry was still feeling demoralized by his illness. He viewed his chronic illness as a symbolic representation of being weak, less masculine, and out of control. This was inconsistent with his premorbid view of himself. Subsequently, he would attempt to "gain control" by manipulating his diet and dialysis schedule. We began to redefine what would constitute "good quality of life" for him and how he could accomplish it while recognizing the limitations of his disease. Specifically, we focused on bringing the option of death by discontinuation of dialysis out in the open. We explored how his noncompliant behavior was frequently an unconscious expression of his ambivalence and lack of control. We worked on replacing this behavior with a more direct and conscious discussion about the death process and I encouraged him to discuss options of comfort care with the nephrologist. Following that discussion, Larry reported feeling more in control and less anxious. He began to reengage in the dialysis process and his "life with dialysis." The open discussion of death and the option to discontinue treatment gave him a sense of control which significantly improved his mood and motivation for compliance.

Issues in Ongoing Therapy

Improving Social Support

With the alienation from his family due to his years of substance abuse and his need to avoid old friends who were still actively abusing substances, Larry had a very limited social network. Research has clearly shown that medically ill patients with good social support tend to experience less depression and have better survival rates when compared to patients with poor social support (Frasure-Smith 1983; Barefoot 1997). The first step in improving Larry's support network was to enlist him as a collaborator in the process. I began by outlining for him the physical and emotional benefits associated with a good social network:

- Improvement in his physical health
- Improvement in his emotional contentment
- Improvement in coping
- Increased energy and motivation when feel supported by others
- Opportunity to obtain information about medical condition and the experience of others with the same disease
- Decreased feelings of loneliness and isolation when connected to others

Once Larry agreed that this was an important component to his well-being, we began to evaluate what type of support he would feel comfortable with. He identified the need for an intimate relationship, resolution of conflict with his brother, and connection with other dialysis patients. We began by working on improving assertiveness and social skills. Larry practiced by directly and specifically asking other patients about their experiences on the machine and about services available in the community. He began to develop a group of friends that were dialyzed at similar times and would pass the dialysis time by engaging them in conversations. This was at times difficult for him, as past "friendship" usually centered around drugs and alcohol.

Our next goal was to improve his relationship with his brother. Larry asked that I contact the brother for the first session. His brother George was reluctant but agreeable to the meeting. Although the initial session was uncomfortable for both, as they had not seen each other in over ten years, subsequent sessions became easier. Issues that were addressed included resolution over George's "discomfort" with Larry's illness. What Larry had perceived as anger and blame for *causing* his illness turned out to be George's distress over *facing* Larry's illness. This illness triggered feelings of unresolved grief that George carried for his other two brothers who had died of renal cell carcinoma. This was never shared with Larry prior to these sessions. George admitted to not knowing how to be supportive of Larry. Studies have shown that support efforts that are intended to be helpful are often perceived by the patient to be unhelpful (Davidowitz and Myrick 1984); in part, they seem to fail when the support person feels compelled to do or say the right thing and ends up using empty platitudes such as "things will get better."

In the sessions, Larry was encouraged to outline for George what he needed from him. Specifically, Larry identified a need to talk to George when he feels overwhelmed, an occasional ride to dialysis when he doesn't feel well, and more involvement from George in his medical care (attending meetings with physicians, observing the dialysis procedure). Larry shared with his brother his desire to return to work in some limited capacity. Although George expressed concerns about Larry's health and the potential for Larry to "push himself too far," he offered Larry a job in his insurance business on a part-time basis. Over the next several months Larry's mood, energy, confidence, and self-esteem continued to improve. Larry reported feeling physically better and expressed great optimism for his future. He began to focus on his future and life after transplant.

Improving Coping Style

My goal was to assess Larry's style of coping in an attempt to tailor coping techniques to his style and meet the demands of the multiple stressful events throughout the pre-, peri- and postoperative phases. Larry described himself as someone who seeks out information, usually in great detail, about events and circumstances. He reports that during his last several medical procedures (endoscopy, colonoscopy, and his multiple surgeries for his grafts) he examines the instruments in the room, asks many questions regarding how things will feel and subsequently feels very anxious and often feels as if he will vomit. Larry and I worked on identifying situations in the past and future where distracting himself may be a better strategy and when actively gathering information may be most useful. The goal was to teach Larry to be flexible in his coping styles and utilize different techniques with different stressful events. We identified medical procedures that were pending in the near future for him, including another surgery to create a new access in his arm for dialysis, the dialysis procedure itself, and a repeat endoscopy to examine his stomach. We identified cues and triggers in the environment that make him feel anxious (smells in the room, site of the instruments, sound of the machine) and began practicing some distraction techniques to improve his coping abilities and decrease the physiological symptoms of anxiety.

Larry began to practice using deep breathing exercises, imagery, reading when on the dialysis machine, and avoiding eye contact with surgical objects in the room. Further, we identified medical situations that require Larry to remain vigilant about seeking information and monitoring his physical symptoms and sensations; he needed detailed information about side effects of drugs, symptoms of severe anemia, pain near his access. We role-played future situations related to a potential kidney transplant, including actively seeking information about his medications and diet and distracting himself during medical examinations and preoperative procedures. After practicing these techniques for several weeks while on dialysis and in the examination room, Larry reported feeling more confident in his ability to cope effectively with the expected and unexpected concerns related to the transplant procedure.

References

Abboud, C. F. 1986. Laboratory diagnosis of hypopituitarism. *Mayo Clinical Proceedings* 61:35-42.

Abrams, H. S, G. L. Moore, and F. B. Westervelt, Jr. 1971. Suicidal behavior in chronic dialysis patients. *American Journal of Psychiatry* 127:1199.

Adams, P. W., V. Wynn, D. P. Rose, M. Seed, et al. 1973. Effects of pyridoxine hydrochloride (vitamin B6) upon depression associated with oral contraception. *Lancet* 1:897-904.

Akiskal, H. S. 1983. Dysthymic disorder: Psychopathology of proposed chronic depression subtypes. *American Journal of Psychiatry* 140:11-20.

Alighieri, Dante. 1995. *The Inferno of Dante*. Translated by Robert Pinsky. Farrar Straus & Giroux Publishers.

Anda, R., D. Williamson, D. Jones, et al. 1993. Depressed affect, hopelessness, and the risk of ischemic heart disease in a cohort of US adults. *Epidemiology* 4:285-294.

Anthony, J. C., L. LePesche, U. Niaz, et al. 1982. Limits of the "Mini Mental State" as a screening test for dementia and delirium among hospital patients. *Psychological Medicine* 12:397-408.

Archives of Internal Medicine. 1997. Joint National Commission IV. 157:2413-2420.

Aspinwall, L. G., and S. E. Taylor. 1992. Modeling cognitive adaptation: A longitudinal investigation of the impact of individual differences and coping on the college adjustment performance. *Journal of Personality and Social Psychology* 63(6):989-1003.

Atkinson, A. B. 1991. The treatment of Cushing's syndrome. *Clinical Endocrinology* 34:507-521.

Atkinson, J. H., T. L. Patterson, J. L. Chandler, et al. 1994. Predicting depression in HIV disorders. In *New Research Program and Abstracts*. American Psychiatric Association 150th Annual Meeting, Philadelphia, Pa.

Babior, B. M. 1990. The megaloblastic anemias. In *Hematology*. 4th ed. Edited by W. J. Williams. New York: McGraw-Hill.

Baldewicz, T., K. Goodkin, D. Feaster, N. T. Blaney, M. Kumar, et al. 1998. Plasma pyridoxine deficiency is related to increased psychological distress in recently bereaved homosexual men. *Psychosomatic Medicine* 60(3):297-308.

Bandura, A. 1977. Self-efficacy: Toward a unifying theory of behavior change. *Psychological Review* 84:191-215.

Barefoot, J., and Schroll, M 1996. Symptoms of depression, acute myocardial infarction and total mortality in a community sample. *Circulation* 93:1976-1980.

Barefoot, J. C. 1997. Depression and coronary artery disease. *Cardiologia* 42:1245-1250.

Barraclough B. 1981. Suicide and epilepsy. In *Epilepsy and Psychiatry,* edited by E. H. Reynolds and M. R. Trimble. Edinburgh and London: Churchill Livingstone.

Barraclough, B., J. Bunch, B. Nelson, et al. 1974. A hundred cases of suicide: Clinical aspects. *British Journal of Psychiatry* 125:35-373.

Beck, A. T., 1963. Thinking and depression: 1. Idiosyncratic content and cognitive distortions. *Archives of General Psychiatry* 9:324-333.

———. 1976. *Cognitive Therapy and Emotional Disorders.* New York: International Universities Press.

Beck, A. T., and R. W. Beck. 1972. Screening depressed patients in family practice: A rapid technic. *Postgraduate Medicine* 52:81-85.

Beck, A. T., A. J. Rush, B. F. Shaw, et al. 1979. *Cognitive Therapy of Depression*. New York: Guilford Press.

Beck, A. T., R. A. Steer, and M. G. Garbin. 1988. Psychometric properties of the Beck Depression Inventory: Twenty-five years of evaluation. *Clinical Psychology Review* 8:77-100.

Beck, A. T., G. Brown, R. J. Berchick, B. L. Stewart, and R. A. Steer. 1990. Relationship between hopelessness and ultimate suicide: A replication with psychiatric outpatients. *American Journal of Psychiatry* 147:190-95.

Beck, W. S. 1991. Diagnosis of megaloblastic anemias. In *Annual Review of Medicine,* edited by W. P. Creger. Stanford, Calif.: Annual Reviews.

———. 1991. Neuropsychiatric consequences of cobalamin deficiency. *Advances in Internal Medicine* 36:33-37.

Beers, M. H., and L. J. Passman. 1990. Antihypertensive medications and depression. *Drugs* 40:792-799.

Berkman, L. F. 1995. The role of social relations in health promotion. *Psychosomatic Medicine* 57:245-254.

Bilezkian, J. P. 1989. Etiologies and therapy of hypercalcemia. *Endocrinology Metabolism Clinics North America* 18:389-412.

Bilezkian, J. P. 1992. Management of acute hypercalcemia. *New England Journal of Medicine* 326:1196-2001.

Black, D. W., G. Winokur, and A. Nasrallah. 1987. Treatment and outcome in secondary depression: A naturalistic study of 1087 patients. *Journal of Clinical Psychiatry* 48:438-441.

Blacker, C., and A. Clare. 1987. Depressive disorders in primary care. *British Journal of Psychiatry* 150:737-751.

Blau, E., and B. A. Ober. 1988. The effect of depression on verbal memory in older adults. *Journal of Clinical and Experimental Neuropsychology* 10:81.

Bloom, J. R. 1982. Social support, accommodation to stress and adjustment to breast cancer. *Social Science and Medicine* 16:1329-1338.

Boland, R. J. 1993. Requests to evaluate "depression" in the general hospital. Proceedings of the 49th Annual Meeting of the Academy of Psychosomatic Medicine, New Orleans, La.

Borch, K. 1986. Epidemiologic, clinicopathologic and economic aspects of gastroscopic screening of patients with pernicious anemia. *Scandinavian Journal of Gastroenterology* 21:21-34.

Breitbart, W. 1987. Suicide in cancer patients. *Oncology* 1:49-53.

Bukberg, J., P. Penman, and J. C. Holland. 1984. Depression in hospitalized cancer patients. *Psychosomatic Medicine* 46:199-212.

Burke, M. L., M. A. Hainsworth, G. G. Eakes, and C. L. Lindgren. 1992. Current knowledge and research on chronic sorrow: A foundation for inquiry. *Death Studies* 16:231-245.

Burton, H. J., S. A. Kline, R. M. Lindsay, et al. 1984. The relationship of depression to survival in chronic renal failure. *Psychosomatic Medicine* 48:261-254.

Caine, E. D., and I. Shoulson. 1983. Psychiatric syndromes in Huntington's disease. *American Journal of Psychiatry* 140:728-733.

Callahan, C. M., S. L. Hui, N. A. Nienaber, and B. S. Musick. 1994. Longitudinal study of depression and health services use among elderly primary care patients. *Journal of the American Geriatrics Society* 42(8):833-838.

Carney R. M., R. D. Wetzel, J. Hagberg, and A. P. Goldberg. 1986. The relationship between depression and aerobic capacity in hemodialysis patients. *Psychosomatic Medicine* 48:143-147.

Carney, R. M., M. W. Rich, A. Tevelde, J. Saine, et al. 1987. Major depressive disorder in coronary artery disease. *American Journal of Clinical Psychiatry* 45:14-18.

Carney, M. W. 1990. Vitamin deficiency and mental symptoms. *British Journal of Psychiatry* 156:878-882.

Carver, C. S. 1993. How coping mediates the effect of optimism on distress: A study of women with early stage breast cancer. *Journal of Personality and Social Psychology* 65(2)375-390.

Cary, G. L. 1972. The borderline condition: A structural dynamic viewpoint. *Psychoanalytic Review* 49:33-54.

Cassileth, B. R., and T. A. Egan. 1979. Modification of medical student perceptions of the cancer experience. *Journal of Medical Education* 54(10):797-802.

Cassem, N. H. 1995. Depressive disorders in the medically ill: An overview. *Psychosomatics* 36(2)S2-S9.

Catalano, E., and K. Hardin. 1996. *The Chronic Pain Control Workbook*. Oakland, Calif.: New Harbinger Publications.

Cavanough, S. A. 1983. The prevalence of emotional and cognitive dysfunction in a general medical population, using the MMSE, GHQ, and BDI. *General Hospital Psychiatry* 5:15-24.

———. 1991. Depression in the medically ill. *In Handbook of Studies on General Hospital Psychiatry*, edited by F. K. Judd, G. D. Burrows, and D. R. Lipsitt. Amsterdam, The Netherlands: Elsevier Science Publishers.

———. 1995. Depression in the medically ill: Critical issues in diagnostic assessment. *Psychosomatics* 36(1):48-59.

Cavanough, S. A., D. Clark, R. Gibbons. 1995. Diagnosing depression in the hospitalized medically ill. *Psychosomatics* 24:809-815.

Chanarin, I. 1987. *The Megaloblastic Anemias.* 3d ed. Oxford: Blackwell.

Coleman, R. M., H. P. Roffwarg, S. J. Kennedy, et al. 1982. Sleep-wake disorders based on polysomnographic diagnosis. A national cooperative study. *Journal of the American Medical Association* 247(7):997-1003.

Cohen, F. 1984. Coping. In *Behavioral Health: A Handbook of Health Enhancement and Disease Prevention*, edited by J. D. Matarazzo. New York: Wiley.

Cohen, S., and T. A. Wills. 1985. Stress, social support, and the buffering hypothesis. *Psychological Bulletin* 98(2):310-357.

Conwell, Y., M. Rotenberg, and E. D. Caine. 1990. Completed suicide at age 50 and over. *Journal of American Geriatric Society* 38(6):640-644.

Corkin, S. 1982. Some relationships between global amnesias and memory impairments in Alzheimer's disease. In *Alzheimer's Disease: A Report of Progress in Research,* edited by S. Corkin, K. L. Davis, J. H. Growden, E. Usdin, and R. I. Wurtman. New York: Raven Press.

Cousins, N. 1990. The laughter connection. *East/West,* February, 58.

Craik, F. I., and J. M. McDowd. 1987. Age differences in recall and recognition. *Journal of Experimental Psychology*: Learning, Memory, and Cognition, 13:474-479.

Craven, J. L., G. M. Rodin, L. Johnson, et al. The diagnosis of major depression in renal dialysis patients. *Psychosomatic Medicine* 49:482-492.

Cummings, J. L. 1989. Dementia and depression: An evolving enigma. *Journal of Neuropsychiatry and Clinical Neurosciences* 1:236-242.

———. 1992. Depression in Parkinson's disease: A review. *Journal of Psychiatry* 149:443-454.

Cunningham, L. 1994. Depression in the medically ill: Choosing an antidepressant. *Journal of Clinical Psychiatry* 55:9(suppl A)90-97.

Dackis, C. A., and M. S. Gold,. 1992. Psychiatric hospitals for treatment of dual diagnosis. In *Substance Abuse: A Comprehensive Textbook.* 2d ed. Edited by J. H. Lowinson, P. Ruiz, R. B. Millman, et al. Baltimore, Md: Williams and Williams.

Dackis, C. A., A. L. Pottash, M. S. Gold, et al. 1986. Evaluating depression in alcoholics. *Psychiatric Research* 17:105-109.

Davidowitz, M., and R. D. Myrick. 1984. Responding to the bereaved: An analysis of "helping" statements. *Research Record* 1:35-42.

Davidson, K. M., and E. B. Ritson. 1993. The relationship between alcohol dependence and depression. *Alcohol* 28:147-155.

Davis, B. H. 1987. Disability and grief. *Social Casework* 68:352-357.

Depression Guideline Panel: Depression in Primary Care: Treatment of Major Depression. Clinical Practice Guideline. Vol. 2, no. 5, Rockville, Md., U.S. Department of Health and Human Services, Public Health Service, Agency for Health Care Policy and Research, April 1993 (AHCPR Publ. no. 93-0551).

DeFronzo, R. A. 1992. Clinical disorders of hyperkalemia. In *The Kidney: Physiology and Pathophysiology.* 3d ed. Edited by D. W. Seldin and G. Giebisch. New York: Raven.

Derogatis L. R., and M. Lopez. 1983. *Psychosocial Adjustment to Illness Scale (PAIS) and (PAIS-R): Scoring Procedures and Administration Manual.* Baltimore: Clinical Psychometric Research.

Derogatis, L. R., and T. N. Wise. 1989. *Anxiety and Depressive Disorders in the Medical Patient.* Washington D.C.: American Psychiatric Press.

Devins, G. M., Y. M. Binek, D. J. Hollomby, P. Barre, and R. D. Guttman. 1981. Helplessness and depression in end-stage renal disease. *Journal of Nervous and Mental Disorders* 90:531-545.

Devita, M. V., and M. F. Michelis. 1993. Perturbations in sodium balance: Hyponatremia. *Clinical Laboratory Medicine* 13:135-151.

Diagnostic and Statistical Manual of Mental Disorders. 4th ed. (DSM-IV.) 1994. Washington, D.C.: American Psychiatric Association.

Dunkle-Schetter, C., L. G. Feinstein, S. E. Taylor, and R. L. Falke. 1992. Patterns of coping with cancer. *Health Psychology* 11:79-87.

D'Zurilla, T. J. 1986. *Problem-Solving Therapy: A Social Competence Approach to Clinical Intervention.* New York: Springer.

Eastwood, M. R., S. L. Rifat, H. Nobbs, et al. 1989. Mood disorder following cerebrovascular accident. *British Journal of Psychiatry* 154:195-200.

Eaton, W. W., M. Mengel, L. Mengel, et al. 1992. Psychosocial and psychopathological influences on management and control of insulin-dependent diabetics. *International Journal of Psychiatry and Medicine* 22:105-117.

Ebrahim, S., D. Barer, and F. Nouri. 1987. Affective illness after stroke. *British Journal of Psychiatry* 151:52-56.

Eisenberg, M. G. 1984. Spinal cord injuries. In *Helping Patients and Their Families Cope with Medical Problems,* edited by H. B. Roback. San Francisco: Jossey-Bass.

Elkin, I., M.T. Shea, J. T. Watkins, S. D. Imber, et al. 1989. NIMH Treatment of Depression Collaboration Research Program: I. General effectiveness of treatments. *Archives of General Psychiatry* 46:971-982.

Elliot, T., and S. W. Harkins. 1991. Psychosocial concomitants of persistent pain among persons with spinal cord injuries. *Neurology Rehabilitation* 14:9-18.

Erikson, E. 1963. *Childhood and Society.* 2d ed. New York: Norton.

Fava, G. A., N. Sonino, and M. A. Morphy. 1987. Major depression associated endocrine disease. *Psychiatric Developments* 4:321-348.

Fawcett, J., W. A. Scheftner, L. Fogg, et al. 1990. Time-related predictors of suicide in major affective disorder. *American Journal of Psychiatry* 147:1189-1194.

Fawcett, J. 1990. Targeting treatment in patients with mixed symptoms of anxiety and depression. *Journal of Clinical Psychiatry* 51(suppl):40-43.

Feifel, H., S. Strack, and V. T. Nagy. 1987. Degree of life-threat and differential use of coping modes. *Journal of Psychosomatic Research* 31:91-99.

Filteau, M., Y. D. Lapierre, D. Bakish, A. Blanchard. 1993. Reduction in suicidal ideation with SSRIs: A review of 459 depressed patients. *Journal of Psychiatry and Neuroscience* 18(3):114-119.

Folstein, M. F., S. E. Folstein, and P. R. McHugh. 1975. Mini Mental State: A practical method for grading the cognitive state of patients for the clinician. *Journal of Psychiatric Research* 12:189-198.

Folstein, S. E., M. H. Abbott, G. A. Chase, et al. 1983. The association of affective disorder with Huntington's disease in a case series and in families. *Psychological Medicine* 134:537-542.

Ford, C. B., and P. Castelnuovo-Tedesco. 1977. Hemodialysis and renal transplantation: Psychopathological reactions and their management. In *Psychosomatic Medicine: Its Clinical Applications,* edited by E. D. Wittkower and H. Warnes. New York: Harper and Row.

Frasure-Smith, N., F. Lesperance, and M. Talajic. 1993. Depression following myocardial infarction: Impact on six month survival. *Journal of American Medical Association* 270:1819-1825.

Freud, S. 1917. Mourning and melancholia. In *Collected Works of Sigmund Freud,* Vol. 4. 1950. London: Hogarth Press and the Institute of Psychoanalysis. Also, 1917/1953. In *The Standard Edition of the Complete Psychological Works of Sigmund Freud,* Vol.14. London: Hogarth Press.

Friedberg, F. 1995. *Coping with Chronic Fatigue Syndrome.* Oakland, Calif.: New Harbinger Publications.

Fry, H. 1997. Humor and its healing effects. *APA Monitor* 27(9).

Gallagher, D. 1986. Assessment of depression by interview methods and psychiatric rating scales. In *Handbook for Clinical Memory Assessment of Older Adults,* edited by L.W. Poon. Washington D.C.: American Psychological Association.

Ganzini, L., J. R. Walsh, and S. M. Millar. 1993. Drug-induced depression in the aged. *Drugs and Aging* 3:147-158.

Gawin, F. H., and H. D. Kleber. 1984. Cocaine abuse treatment: Open pilot trial with desipramine and lithium carbonate. *Archives of General Psychiatry* 41:903-909.

Georgotas, A., R. E. McCue, T. B. Cooper, et al. 1988. How effective and safe is continuation therapy in elderly depressed patients? *Archives of General Psychiatry* 45(10)929-932.

Gerber, P., J. Barrett, E. Manheimer, R. Whiting, and R. Smith. 1989. Recognition of depression by internists in primary care: A comparison of internist and "gold standard" psychiatric assessments. *Journal of General Internal Medicine* 4:7-13.

Goldman, M. B., D. J. Luchins, G. L. Robertson. 1988. Mechanisms of altered water metabolism in psychotic patients with polydipsia and hyponatremia. *New England Journal of Medicine* 318:397-404.

Goodnick, P. J. 1993. Recognizing and treating depression in outpatients with diabetes. *Clinical Diabetes*. Nov/Dec.

Greene, S. M. 1989.The relationship between depression and hopelessness: Implications for current theories of depression. *British Journal of Psychiatry* 154:650-659.

Greenberg, P. E., L. E. Stiglin, S. N. Finkelstein, et al. 1993. The economic burden of depression in 1990. *Journal of Clinical Psychiatry* 54:405-418.

Greenberg, R. P., and S. Fisher. 1989. Examining antidepressant effectiveness: Findings, ambiguities, and some vexing puzzles. In *The Limits of Biological Treatments for Psychological Distress,* edited by S. Fisher and R. Greenberg. Hillsdale, N.J.: Erlbaum.

Gregory, R. J., D. C. Jimerson, B. E. Walton, et al. 1992. Pharmacotherapy of depression in the medically ill: Directions for future research. *General Hospital Psychiatry* 14(1):36-42.

Grimsley, S. R., and M. W. Jann. 1992. Paroxetine, sertraline and fluovoxamine: New selective serotonin reuptake inhibitors. *Clinical Pharmacy* 11:930-957.

Gunderson, J. G. 1977. Characteristics of borderlines. In *Borderline Personality Disorders,* edited by P. Hartocollis. New York: International Universities Press.

Hall, R. C., and J. R. Joffe. 1972. Aberrant response to diazepam: A new syndrome. *American Journal of Psychiatry* 129:114-118.

Hall, R. C., M. K. Popkin, S. K. Stickney, et al. 1979. Presentation of steroid psychoses. *Journal of Nervous and Mental Disorders* 167:229-236.

Hall, R. C., S. K. Stickney, and E. R. Gardner. 1980. Behavioral toxicity of non-psychiatric drugs. In *Psychiatric Presentations of Medical Illness: Somatopsychic Disorders,* edited by R. C. Hall. New York: Spectrum Publications.

Hall, R. C., and M. G. Wise. 1995. The clinical and financial burden of mood disorders: Cost and outcome. *Psychosomatics* 36(2)S11-S19.

Hamburger, J. I. 1987. The autonomously functioning thyroid: Goestch's disease. *Endocrine Review* 8:439.

Hanson, S., S. P. Buckelew, J. Hewett, and G. O'Neal. 1993. The relationship between coping and adjustment after spinal cord injury: A five year follow-up study. *Rehabilitation Psychology* 38:41-52.

Hansten, P. D., and J. R. Horn. 1994. *Drug Interactions & Updates Quarterly*. Vancouver, Wash: Applied Therapeutics (quarterly updates).

Hasher, L., and R. T. Zacks. 1979. Automatic and effortful processes in memory. *Journal of Experimental Psychology*: General 108:356-388.

Hauri, P. 1985. Primary sleep disorders and insomnia. In *Clinical Aspects of Sleep and Sleep Disturbance,* edited by T. L. Riley. Boston: Butterworth.

Heitzmann, C. A., and R. M. Kaplan. 1988. Assessment of methods for measuring social support. *Health Psychology* 7(1):75-109.

Helz, J. W., and B. Templeton. 1990. Evidence for the role of psychosocial factors in diabetes mellitus: A review. *American Journal of Psychiatry* 147:1275-1282.

Henriksson, M. M., E. T. Isometsa, P. S. Hietanaen, H. M. Aro, and J. K. Lonnqvist. 1995. Mental disorders of cancer suicides. *Journal of Affective Disorders* 36(1-2):11-20.

Herbert, V. 1988. Don't ignore low serum cobalamin (vitamin B_{12}) levels. *Archives of Internal Medicine* 148:1705-1709.

Herman, J. 1992. *Trauma and Recovery: The Aftermath of Violence—from Domestic Abuse to Political Terror*. New York: Basic Books.

Heston, L. L. 1992. *Mending Minds: A Guide to the New Psychiatry of Depression, Anxiety and Other Serious Mental Disorders*. New York: Freeman and Co. Publishers

Hintz, S., J. Kuck, and J. J. Peterkin. 1990. Depression in the context of human immunodeficiency virus infection: Implications for treatment. *Journal of Clinical Psychiatry* 51:497-501.

Hirschfield, R. M., and L. Davidson. 1988. Risk factors for suicide. In *American Psychiatric Press Review of Psychiatry*, edited by A. J. Frances and R. E. Hales. Washington D.C.: American Psychiatric Press.

Hoge, D. R. 1996. Religion in America: The demographics of belief and affiliation. In *Religion and the Clinical Practice of Psychology*, edited by E. P. Shafranske. Washington D.C.: American Psychological Association.

Holland, J. C., A. H. Korzun, S. Tross, et al. 1986. Comparative psychological disturbance in patients with pancreatic and gastric cancer. *American Journal of Psychiatry* 143:982-986.

Holmes, T. H., and R. H. Rahe. 1967. The social readjustment rating scale. *Journal of Psychosomatic Research* 11:213-218.

House, J. S. 1981. *Work Stress and Social Support*. Reading, Mass.: Addison-Wesley.

Holland, J. C., A. H. Korzun, S. Tross, et al. 1986. Comparative psychological disturbance in patients with pancreatic and gastric cancer. *American Journal of Psychiatry* 143:982-986.

Hsing, A. W. 1993. Pernicious anemia and subsequent cancer. *Cancer* 71:745-51

Israel, M. 1986. Depression in dialysis patients: A review of psychological factors. *Canadian Journal of Psychiatry* 31:445-451.

Jacobs, J. 1991. Family therapy with families with chronically ill members. In *Reweaving the Family Tapestry* 9th ed. Edited by F. Herz-Brown. New York: W. W. Norton.

Jacobs, J. W., M. R. Bernhard, A. Delgado, et al. Screening for organic mental syndromes in the medically ill. *Annals of Internal Medicine*. 86:40-46.

Jacobson, A. M., S. T. Hauser, P. Lavori, et al. 1990. Adherence among children and adolescents with insulin-dependent diabetes mellitus over a four year longitudinal follow-up: The influence of patient coping and adjustment. *Journal of Pediatric Psychology* 15:511-526.

Jacobson, E. 1974. *Progressive Relaxation*. Midway reprint. Chicago: University of Chicago Press.

Jamison, K. R. 1988. Suicide prevention in depressed women. *Journal of Clinical Psychiatry* 49(suppl):42-45.

Joffe, R. T., G. P. Lippert, T. A. Gray, et al. 1987. Mood disorder and multiple sclerosis. *Archives of Neurology* 44:376-378.

Kamel, K. S., and R. A. Bear. 1993. Treatment of hyponatremia: A quantitative analysis. *American Journal of Kidney Disease* 21:439-451.

Kapadia, C. R., and R. M. Donaldson. 1985. Disorders of cobalmin (vitamin B_{12}) absorption and transport. *Annual Review of Medicine* 36:93-99.

Kathol, R. G., A. Mulgi, J. Williams, et al. 1990. Diagnosis of major depression in cancer patients according to four sets of criteria. *American Journal of Psychiatry* 147:1021-1024.

Katon, W., P. P. Vitaliano, K. Anderson, et al. 1987. Panic Disorder: residual symptoms after the acute attacks abate. *Comprehensive Psychiatry* 28:151-158.

Kazniak, A. W., and G. D. Christenson. 1994. Differential diagnosis of dementia and depression. In *Neuropsychological Assessment of Dementia and Depression in Older Adults: A Clinician's Guide*, edited by M. Storandt and G. R. VandenBos. Washington, D.C.: American Psychological Association.

Kennedy, S. H., J. L. Craven, and G. M. Rodin. 1989. Major depression in renal dialysis patients: An open trial of antidepressant therapy. *Journal of Clinical Psychiatry*. 50:60-63.

Kershner, P., and R. Wang-Cheng. 1989. Psychiatric side effects of steroid therapy. *Psychosomatics* 30:135-139.

Kiernan, R. J., J. Mueller, J. W. Langston, et al. 1987. The Neurobehavioral status examination: A brief but differentiated approach to cognitive assessment. *Annals of Internal Medicine*. 107:481-485.

Kishi, Y., R. G. Robinson, and J. T. Kosier. 1996. Suicidal plans in patients with stroke: Comparison between acute-onset and delayed-onset suicidal plans. *International Psychogeriatrics* 8(4):623-634

Kimmel, P. L., K. Weihs, and R. A. Peterson. 1993. Survival in hemodialysis patients: The role of depression. *Journal of American Society of Nephrology* 4(1):12-27.

Klein, D. F., R. Gittelman, F. Quikin, and A. Rifkin. 1980. *Diagnosis and Drug Treatment of Psychiatric Disorders: Adults and Children*. 2d ed. Baltimore: Williams and Wilkins.

Kleinman, A. 1988. *The Illness Narratives: Suffering, Healing and the Human Condition*. New York: Basic Books.

Knochel, J. P. 1982. Neuromuscular manifestations of electrolyte disorders. *American Journal of Medicine* 72:521-536.

———. 1984. Hypokalemia. *Advanced Internal Medicine* 30:317-329.

Kocsis, J. H., J. L. Croughan, M. M. Katz, T. P. Butler, et al. 1990. Response to treatment with antidepressants of patients with severe or moderate nonpsychotic depression and of patients with psychotic depression. *American Journal of Psychiatry* 147:621-624.

Koenig, H. G., H. J. Cohen, D. G. Blazer, C. Pieper, et al. 1992. Religious coping and depression among elderly, hospitalized medically ill men. *American Journal of Psychiatry* 149:1693-1700.

Kontaxakis, V. P., G. N. Christodoulou, V. G. Mavreas, et al. 1988. Attempted suicide in psychiatric outpatients with concurrent physical illness. *Psychotherapy Psychosomatics* 50:201-206.

Koranyi, E. K. 1979. Morbidity and rate of undiagnosed physical illnesses in a psychiatric clinic population. *Archives of General Psychiatry* 36:414-419.

Knights, E. B., and M. F. Folstein. 1977. Unsuspected emotional and cognitive disturbances in medical patients. *Annals of Internal Medicine* 87:723-724.

Kraepelin, E. 1913. *Lectures on Clinical Psychiatry*, Vol. 3. 8th ed. Leipzig: J. H. Barth.

Kral, V. A., and O. B. Emery. 1989. Long-term follow-up of depressive pseuodementia of the aged. *Canadian Journal of Psychiatry* 34:445-446.

Kupfer, D. J. 1991. Long-term treatment of depression. *Journal of Clinical Psychiatry* 52(suppl 5):29-35.

Langer, R. 1987. Post traumatic stress disorder in former POW. In *Post Traumatic Stress Disorders: A Handbook for Clinicians*, edited by Tom Williams. Cincinnati: Disabled American Veterans.

Lazarus, R. S. 1993. Coping theory and research: Past present and future. *Psychosomatic Medicine* 55:234-247.

Lazarus, R. S., and S. Folkman. 1984. *Stress, Appraisal and Coping*. New York: Springer.

Lazarus, R. S. and J. B. Cohen. 1977. Environmental stress. In *Human Behavior and Environment,* Vol. 2. Edited by I. Altman and J. E. Wohlwill. New York: Plenum.

Lefebvre, P., and J. C. Norbert. 1972. Psychological and psychopathological reactions in relation to chronic hemodialysis. *Canadian Psychiatric Association Journal* 17:SS9-SS13.

Lehman, D. R., J. H. Ellard, and C. B. Wortman. 1986. Social support for the bereaved: Recipients' and providers' perspective on what is helpful. *Journal of Consulting and Clinical Psychology* 54(4):438-446.

Lerman, C., M. Daly, A. Masny, and A. Balshem. 1994. Attitudes about genetic testing for breast-ovarian cancer susceptibility. *Journal of Clinical Oncology* 12(4):843-850.

Lerman, C., and K. Glanz. 1997. Stress, coping and health behavior. In *Health Behavior and Health Education: Theory, Research and Practice.* 2d ed. Edited by K. Glanz, F. M. Lewis, and B. K. Rimer. San Francisco: Jossey-Bass.

Lerman, C., and M. Schwartz. 1993. Adherence and psychological adjustment among women at high risk for breast cancer. *Breast Cancer Research and Treatment* 28:145-155.

Lesperance, F., N. Frasure-Smith, and M. Talajic. 1996. Major depression before and after myocardial infarction: Its nature and consequences. *Psychosomatic Medicine* 58(2)99-110.

Lewis, D. A., and R. E. Smith. 1983. Steroid-induced psychiatric syndromes: A report of 14 cases and a review of the literature. *Journal of Affective Disorders* 5:319-322.

Lipsey, J. R., R. G. Robinson, G. D. Pearlson, et al. 1984. Nortriptyline treatment of post-stroke depression: A double blind study. *Lancet* 1:297-300.

Lishman, W. A. 1987. *Organic Psychiatry: The Psychological Consequences of Cerebral Disorder.* 2d ed. Osney Mead, Oxford: Blackwell Scientific Publications.

Litman R. E. 1989. Long-term treatment of chronically suicidal patients. *Bulletin Menninger Clinic* 53:215-228.

Livneh, H., and R. F. Antonak. 1997. *Psychosocial Adaptation to Chronic Illness and Disability.* Gaithersburg, Md.: Aspen Publishers.

Lustman, P. J., L. S. Griffith, R. E. Clouse, et al. 1986. Psychiatric illness in diabetes mellitus: Relationship to symptoms and glucose control. *Journal of Nervous and Mental Disorders* 174:736-742.

Lynch, J. 1977. *The Broken Heart: The Medical Consequences of Loneliness.* New York: Basic Books.

Maddison, D. C., and W. L. Walker. 1967. Factors affecting the outcome of conjugal bereavement. *British Journal of Psychiatry* 113:1057-1067.

Mallette, L. E. 1992. The hypercalcemias. *Seminar in Nephrology* 12:1590-1599.

Maltsberger, J. T., and D. Buie. 1990. Common errors in the management of suicidal patients. In *Suicide: Understanding and Responding,* edited by D. Jacobs and H. N. Brown. Madison, Ct.: International Universities Press.

Marcantonio, E. R., G. Juarex, L. Goldman, et al. 1994. The relationship of postoperative delirium with psychoactive medications. *JAMA* 272(19):1518-1522.

Marcus, M. D., and R. R. Wing. 1990. Eating disorders and diabetes: Diagnosis and management. *Diabetes Spectrum* 3:361-400.

Maricle, R. A. 1993. Psychiatric disorders in Huntington's disease. In *Medical-Psychiatric Practice.* Vol. 2. Edited by A. Stoudemire and B. S. Fogel. Washington, D.C.: American Psychiatric Press.

Martin, J. B., and J. F. Gusella. 1986. Huntington's disease. *New England Journal of Medicine* 315:1267-1276.

Marzuk, P. M., H. Tierney, K. Tardiff, et al. 1988. Increased risk of suicide in persons with AIDS. *Journal of American Medical Association* 259:1333-1337.

Massie, M. J., and J. C. Holland. 1990. Depression and the cancer patient. *Journal of Clinical Psychiatry* 51(suppl 7)12-17.

Matas, M., D. Staley, and W. Griffin. 1992. A profile of the noncompliant patient: A thirty-month review of outpatient psychiatry referrals. *General Hospital Psychiatry.* 14:124-130.

Matsakis, A. 1994. *Post-Traumatic Stress Disorder: A Complete Treatment Guide.* Oakland, Calif.: New Harbinger Publications.

Mayeux, R., Y. Stern, J. B. Williams, et al. 1986. Clinical and biochemical features of depression in Parkinson's disease. *American Journal of Psychiatry* 143:756-759.

Mayeux, R. 1990. Depression in the patient with Parkinson's disease. *Journal of Clinical Psychiatry* 52:20-23.

McDougal, I. R. 1991. Graves' disease concept. *Medical Clinic North America* 75:79-123,

McKegney, F. P., and P. Lange. 1971. The decision to no longer live on chronic hemodialysis. *American Journal of Psychiatry* 128(3):267-274.

Meltzer, H. Y., G. A. Gudelsky, and J. Koenig. 1987. Antipsychotics, tricyclic antidepressants and lithium. In *Handbook of Clinical Psychoneuroendocrinology,* edited by C. B. Nemeroff, P. T. Loosen, et al. New York: Guilford Press.

Mendez, M. F., J. L. Cummings, and F. Benson. 1986. Depression in epilepsy: Significance and phenomenology. *Archives of Neurology* 43:766-770.

Minden, S. L., J. Orav, and P. Reich. 1987. Depression in multiple sclerosis. *General Hospital Psychiatry* 9:426-434.

Minden, S. L., and R. B. Schiffer. 1990. Affective disorders in multiple sclerosis. *Archives of Neurology* 47:98-104.

Minuchin, S. 1974. *Families and Family Therapy.* Cambridge Mass.: Harvard University Press.

Morris, P. L., R. G. Robinson, P. Andrzewjewski, et al. 1993. Association of depression with 10-year post-stroke mortality. *American Journal of Psychiatry* 150:124-129.

Moss, M. B., M. S. Albert, N. Butters, and M. Payne. 1986. Differential patterns of memory loss among patients with Alzheimer's disease, Huntington's disease, and alcoholic Korsakoff's syndrome. *Archives of Neurology* 43:239-246.

Mueller, T. I., R. A. Brown, and P. R. Recupero. 1993. Depression and substance abuse. *Rhode Island Medicine* 76:409-413.

Munck, M. 1984. Physiological function of glucocorticoids in stress and their relation to pharmacological actions. *Endocrine Review* 5:25-49.

Myers, J. K., M. M. Weissman, G. L. Tischler, et al. 1984. Six month prevalence of psychiatric disorders in three communities. *Archives of General Psychiatry* 41:959-967.

Narins, R. G. 1982. Diagnostic strategies in disorders of fluid, electrolyte and acid-base homeostasis. *American Journal of Medicine* 72:496-503.

National Center for Health Statistics. 1991. Births, marriages, divorces and deaths for October 1990. Monthly Vital Statistics Report 39 (10). Hyattsville, Md.: U.S. Public Health Service.

Nelson, A., B. S. Fogel, and P. Faust. 1986. Bedside cognitive screening instruments: A critical assessment. *Journal of Nervous and Mental Disorders* 174(2):73-83.

Nezu, A. M. 1986. Efficacy of a social problem-solving therapy approach for unipolar depression. *Journal of Consulting and Clinical Psychology* 54(2):196-202.

Nezu, A. M., and M. G. Perri. 1989. Social problem-solving therapy of unipolar depression: An initial dismantling investigation. *Journal of Consulting and Clinical Psychology* 57(3):408-413.

O'Hara, M. W., J. A. Schlechte, D. A. Lewis, et al. 1991. Prospective study of postpartum blues: Biological and social factors. *Archives of General Psychiatry* 48:801-806.

Orleans, C. T., L. K. George, J. L. Houpt, et al. 1985. How primary care physicians treat psychiatric disorders: A national survey of family practitioners. *American Journal of Psychiatry* 142:52-57.

Ormel, J., T. Oldehinket, E. Brilman, et al. 1993. Outcome of depression and anxiety in primary care. *Archives of General Psychiatry* 59:759-766.

Ornstein, R., and D. Sobel. 1989. *Healthy Pleasures*. Reading, Mass.: Addison-Wesley.

Oxman, T. E., and J. G. Hull. 1997. Social support, depression, and activities of daily living in older heart surgery patients. *Journal of Gerontology* 52B:1-14.

Palinkas, L. A., E. Barrett-Connor, and D. I. Wingard. 1991. Type 2 diabetes and depressive symptoms in older adults: A population-based study. *Diabetes Medicine* 8:532-539.

Parkes, C. M. 1972. Components of the reaction to loss of a limb, spouse or home. *Journal of Psychosomatic Research* 16:343-349.

Parmelee, P. A., M. P. Lawton, and I. R. Katz. 1989. Psychometric properties of the Geriatric Assessment Scale among the institutionalized aged. *Psychological Assessment* 11:331-338.

Pascualy, M., and R. C. Veith. 1989. Depression as an adverse drug reaction. In *Aging and Clinical Practice: Depression and Coexisting Disease*, edited by R. G. Robinson and P. V. Rabins. New York: Igaku-Shoin.

Patten, S. B., and C. J. Lamarre. 1992. Can drug-induced depressions be identified by their clinical features? *Canadian Journal of Psychiatry* 37:213-215.

Paykel, E. S., R. Flemenger, and J. P. Watson. 1982. Psychiatric side effects of antihypertensive drugs other than reserpine. *Journal of Clinical Psychopharmacology* 2:14-39.

Pearlin, L. I., and C. Schooler. 1978. The structure of coping. *Journal of Health and Social Behavior* 19:2-21.

Perez-Stable, E., J. Miranda, R. Munoz, and Y. Ying. 1990. Depression in medical outpatients: Under recognition and misdiagnosis. *Archives of Internal Medicine* 150:1083-1088.

Perkins, D. O., R. A. Stern, R. N. Golden, et al. 1994. Mood disorders in HIV infection: Prevalence and risk factors in a nonepicenter of the AIDS epidemic. *American Journal of Psychiatry* 151:233-236.

Petrie, W. M., R. J. Maffucci, and R. L. Woosley. 1982. Propanolol and depression. *American Journal of Psychiatry* 139:92-93.

Pfhol, B., D. Sangl, and M. Zimmergan. 1984. The implications of DSM-III personality disorders for patients with major depression. *Journal of Affective Disorders* 7:309-318.

Popkin, M. K. 1988. Prevalence of major depression, simple phobia, and other psychiatric disorders in patients with longstanding type-1 diabetes mellitus. *Archives of General Psychiatry* 45:64-68.

Popkin, M. K., and T. B. Mackenzie. 1980. Psychiatric presentations of endocrine dysfunction. In *Psychiatric Presentations of Medical Illness*, edited by R. C. W. Hall. New York: Spectrum Publications.

Popkin, M. K., A. L. Callies, and E. A. Colon. 1987. A framework for the study of medical depression. *Psychosomatics* 28:27-33.

Prinz, P., E. Peskind, and P. Vitaliano. 1990. Changes in the sleep and waking EEG of nondemented and demented elderly subjects. *Journal of American Geriatric Society* 30:86-93.

Rabins, P. V., A. Merchant, and G. Nestadt. 1984. Criteria for diagnosing reversible dementia caused by depression. *British Journal of Psychiatry* 144:488-492.

Rabins, P. V., B. R. Brooks, P. O'Donnell, et al. 1986. Structural brain correlates of emotional disorder in multiple sclerosis. *Brain* 109:585-597.

Rait, D. S., P. B. Jacobsen, M. S. Lederberg, and J. C. Holland. 1988. Characteristics of psychiatric consultations in a pediatric cancer center. *American Journal of Psychiatry* 145(3):363-4.

Rand, E. H. 1991. Choosing an antidepressant to treat depression. *American Family Physician* 43(3):847-54.

Rao, R. H. 1989. Bilateral massive adrenal hemorrhage: Early recognition and treatment. *Annals of Internal Medicine* 11:227-237.

Reding, M., J. Haycox, and J. Blass. 1985. Depression in patients referred to a dementia clinic: A three-year prospective study. *Archives of Neurology* 42:894-896.

Reed, G. M. 1994. Realistic acceptance as a predictor of decreased survival time in gay men with AIDS. *Health Psychology* 13(4):299-307.

Reed, P. G. 1987. Spirituality and well-being in terminally ill hospitalized adults. *Research in Nursing and Health* 10:335-344.

Regenstein, Q. R. 1987. Sleep disorders in the medically ill. In *Principles of Medical Psychiatry*. 1st ed. Edited by A. Stoudemire and B. S. Fogel. Orlando, Fla.: Grune and Stratton.

———. 1992. Sleep disorders in the medically ill. In *Principles of Medical Psychiatry*. 2d ed. Edited by A. Stoudemire and B. S. Fogel. New York: Oxford University Press.

Robertson, G. L. 1983. Thirst and vasopressin function in normal and disordered states of water balance. *Journal of Laboratory Clinical Medicine* 101:351-359.

Robertson, M. M., and M. R. Trimble. 1983. Depressive illness in patients with epilepsy: A review. *Epilepsia* 24:190-196.

Robins, L., R. A. Numoz, S. Marin, et al. 1972. Primary and secondary affective disorders. In *Disorders of Mood,* edited by J. Zubin and F. A. Freyhan. Baltimore: John Hopkins Press.

Robinson, R. G., L. B. Starr, K. L. Kubos, et al. 1983. A two-year longitudinal study of post-stroke mood disorder: Findings during the initial evaluation. *Stroke* 14:736-741.

Robinson, R. G., and A. W. Forrester. 1984. Neuropsychiatric aspects of cerebrovascular disease. In *Textbook of Neuropsychiatry,* edited by R. E. Hales and S. C. Yudofsky. Washington, D.C.: American Psychiatric Press.

Robinson, R. G., P. Bolduc, and T. R. Price. 1987. A two-year longitudinal study of post-stroke depression: Diagnosis at one and two year follow-up. *Stroke* 18:837-843.

Rockefeller, E., and A. Luks. 1988. Beyond Health. *American Health,* March, 51-55.

Rodin, G., J. Chmara, J. Ennis, S. Fenton, H. Locking, and K. Steinhouse. 1981. Stopping life-sustaining medical treatment: Psychiatric considerations in the termination of renal dialysis. *Canadian Journal of Psychiatry* 26:540-44.

Rodin, G. M., and K. Voshart. 1987. Depressive symptoms and functional impairment in the medically ill. *General Hospital Psychiatry* 9:251-258.

Rodin, G. M., J. Craven, and C. Littlefield. 1991. *Depression in the Medically Ill: An Integrated Approach.* New York: Brunner & Mazel.

Rose, B. D., and H. G. Rennke. 1994. *Renal Pathophysiology: The Essentials*. Baltimore: Williams and Wilkins.

Rose, B. D., and R. M. Black. 1988. *Manual of Clinical Problems in Nephrology* Boston: Little Brown.

Rosenberg, S. J., R. A. Peterson, and J. R. Hayes. 1987. Coping behaviors among depressed and nondepressed medical inpatients. *Journal of Psychosomatic Research* 31:653-658.

Rosenheim, E. 1974. Humor in psychotherapy: An interactive experience. *American Journal of Psychotherapy* 20:313–316.

Rotter, J. B. 1966. Generalized expectancies for internal versus external control of reinforcement. *Psychological Monographs* 80(1):1-28.

Roy, A. 1989. Suicide. In *Comprehensive Textbook of Psychiatry V*, edited by H. I. Kaplan and B. J. Sadock. Baltimore: Williams and Wilkins.

Ruark, J. E., and T. A. Gonda. 1988. Grief and morning. In *Depression and Mania,* edited by A. Georgatas and R. Cancro. London: Elsevier.

Rubini, M. E., and R. Goldman. 1968. Chronic renal disease: Some sociological aspects of dialysis and transplantation. *California Medicine* 108:90-95.

Ruberman, W., E. Weinblatt, and J. D. Goldberg. 1984. Psychosocial influences on mortality after myocardial infarction. *New England Journal of Medicine* 311:552-559.

Rundell, J. R., and M. G. Wise. 1996. *Textbook of Consultation-Liaison Psychiatry.* Washington, D.C.: American Psychiatric Press.

Sabo, E., C. F. Reynolds III, D. J. Kupfer, et al. 1991. Sleep, depression and suicide. *Psychiatry Research* 36:265-277.

Sacks, C. R., R. A. Peterson, and P. Kimmel. 1990. Perception of illness and depression in chronic renal disease. *American Journal of Kidney Disease* 15:31-39.

———. 1994. The relationship between perception of illness, role disruption and kidney dialysis treatments. Paper presented at the meeting of the Society of Behavioral Medicine, Boston.

Salzman, C. 1992. *Treatment of Anxiety.* In *Clinical Geriatric Psychopharmacology,* edited by C. Salzman. Baltimore, Md.: Williams & Wilkins.

Sanders, C. M. 1989. *Grief: The Mourning After.* New York: Wiley.

Saravay, S. M., and M. Lavin. 1991. Psychological co-morbidity and length of stay in the hospital. *American Journal of Psychiatry* 148:324-329.

———. 1994. Psychiatric comorbidity and length of stay in the general medical hospital: A critical review of outcome studies. *Psychosomatics* 35:233-252.

Satel, S. L., L. H. Price, J. M. Palumbo, et al. 1991. Clinical phenomenology and neurobiology of cocaine abstinence: A prospective inpatient study. *American Journal of Psychiatry* 148:1712-1716.

Satir, V. 1972. *People Making.* Palo Alto, Calif.: Science and Behavior Books.

Scheier, M. F., and C. S. Carver. 1989. Dispositional optimism and recovery from coronary artery bypass surgery: The beneficial effects on physical and psychological well-being. *Journal of Personality and Social Psychology* 57:1024-1040.

———. 1992. Effects of optimism on psychological and physical well-being: Theoretical overview and empirical update. *Cognitive Therapy and Research* 16(2):201-228.

Schlaghecke, R. 1992. The effect of long-term glucocorticoid therapy on pituitary response to exogenous corticotropin-releasing hormone. *New England Journal of Medicine* 326:226-32.

Schmale, S. M., A. H., H. P. Iker. 1966. The affect of hopelessness and the development of cancer. *Psychosomatic Medicine* 28:714-721.

Schmale, S. M., and G. L. Engel. 1967. The giving-up given up complex illustrated on film. *Archives of General Psychiatry* 17:135-145.

Schoenfeld, M., R. H. Myers, and L. A. Cupples. 1984. Increased rate of suicide among patients with Huntington's disease. *Journal of Neurology, Neurosurgery and Psychiatry* 47:1283-1287.

Schubert, D. S., I. Gabinet, W. Friedman, et. al. 1979. The identification of psychiatric morbidity by internists and subsequent selection for psychiatric referral. *International Journal of Psychiatry in Medicine* 33(12):1002-1005.

Schulberg, H. C., M. Saul, M. McClelland, M. Ganguli, W. Christy, and R. Frank. 1985. Assessing depression in primary medical and psychiatric practice. *Archives of General Psychiatry* 42:1164-1170.

Schulberg, H. C., and A. J. Rush. 1994. Clinical practice guidelines for managing major depression in primary care practice: Implications for psychologists. *American Psychologist* 49(1):34-40.

Schwab, J. J., M. Bialow, J. M. Brown, et al. 1967. Diagnosing depression in medical inpatients. *Annals of Internal Medicine* 64:695-670.

Schwartz, M. D. 1995. Coping disposition, perceived risk, and psychological distress among women at increased risk for ovarian cancer. *Health Psychology* 14(3):232-235.

Seligman, R. 1974. Depression and learned helplessness. In *The Psychology of Depression: Contemporary Theory and Research,* edited by R. Friedman and M. Katz. Washington, D.C.: Winston.

———. 1991. *Learned Optimism.* New York: Knopf.

Shor-Posner, G., D. Feaster, N. T. Blaney, and H. Rocca. 1994. Impact of vitamin B-sub-6 status on psychological distress in a longitudinal study of HIV-1 infection. *International Journal of Psychiatry in Medicine* 24(3):209-222.

Shulman, R., J. D. Price, and J. Spinelli. 1986. Biopsychosocial aspects of long-term survival on end-stage renal failure. (26)2:210-215.

Shukla, U. A., J. P. Shea, and R. E. Gammans. 1987. Single and multiple dose pharmacokinetics of nefazodone and two metabolites in healthy volunteers. *Clinical Pharmacy Therapy* 41:205.

Shuman, R. 1996. *The Psychology of Chronic Illness.* New York: Basic Books.

Siegelman, E. Y. 1990. *Metaphor and Meaning in Psychotherapy.* New York: Guilford Press.

Simon, G. E., and D. J. Katzelnick. 1997. Depression, use of medical services and cost-offset effects. *Journal of Psychosomatic Research* 42(4)333-344.

Simonton, O. C., and R. Henson. 1992. *The Healing Journey.* New York: Bantam Books.

Sinyor, D., P. Jacques, D. A. Kaloupek, et al. 1986. Post-stroke depression and lesion location: An attempted replication. *Brain* 109:537-546.

Smith, S. 1972. Dominant and non-dominant hemispherectomy. In *Drugs, Development and Cerebral Function,* edited by W. L. Smith. Springfield, Ill.: Thomas.

Smith, B. D., and C. Salzman. 1991. Do benzodiazepines cause depression? *Hospital and Community Psychiatry* 42:1101-1102.

Smith, C. A., K. N. Haynes, R. S. Lazarus, and L. K. Pope. 1993. In search of the hot cognitions: Attributions, appraisals and their relation to emotion. *Journal of Personality and Social Psychology* 65(5):916-929.

Smith, C. A., and R. S. Lazarus. 1993. Appraisal components, core relational themes and the emotions. *Cognition and Emotion* 7(3-4):233-269.

Smith, T. 1993. Good Health: More than Absence of Disease. *Church News*, November 13, 7.

Smith S. 1972. Dominant and non-dominant hemispherectomy. In *Drugs, Development and Cerebral Function*, edited by W. L. Smith. Springfield, Illinois: Thomas.

Sobel, D., and R. Ornstein. 1996. *The Healthy Mind, Healthy Body Handbook.* Los Altos, Calif.: DRx.

Soldatos, C. R., J. D. Kales, M. B. Scharf, et al. 1989. Cigarette smoking associated with sleep difficulty. *Science* 207:551-553.

Starkstein, S. E., R. G. Robinson, M. A. Honig, et al. 1989. Mood changes after right hemisphere lesions. *British Journal of Psychiatry* 155:79-85.

Starkstein, S. E., T. J. Preziosi, P. L. Bolduc, et al. 1990. Depression in Parkinson's disease. *Journal of Nervous and Mental Disorders* 178:27-31.

Steiner, M. 1992. Female-specific mood disorders. *Clinical Obstetrics and Gynecology* 35:599-611.

Steptoe, A., and J. Sullivan. 1986. Monitoring and blunting coping styles in women prior to surgery. *British Journal of Clinical Psychology* 24:143-144.

Storandt, M., and G. R. VandenBos. 1994. *Neuropsychological Assessment of Dementia and Depression in Older Adults: A Clinician's Guide.* Washington D.C.: American Psychological Association.

Stoudemire, A., and B. S. Fogel, eds. 1993. *Psychiatric Care of the Medical Patient.* New York: Oxford University Press.

Stoudemire, A. 1995. Expanding psychopharmacological treatment options for the depressed medical patient. *Psychosomatics.* 36:S19-S26.

Strange, K. 1992. Regulation of solute and water balance and cell volume in the central nervous system. *Journal of American Society of Nephrology* 3:12-19.

Suda, T. 1988. Effects of corticotropin-releasing hormone and dexamathasone on propiomelancortin messenger RNA level in human corticotroph adenoma cells in vitro. *Journal of Clinical Investigation* 82:110-116.

Tassett, J., J. S. Singh, and A. J. Pesce. 1985. Evaluation of amitriptyline pharmacokinetics during peritoneal dialysis. *Therapeutic Drug Monitoring* 7:255-257.

Taylor, S. E., V. S. Helgeson, G. M. Reed, and L. A. Skokan. 1991. Self-generated feelings of control and adjustment to physical illness. *Journal of Social Issues* 47:91-109.

Taylor, S. E. 1992. Optimism, coping, psychological distress and high risk sexual behavior among men at high risk for acquired immunodeficiency syndrome (AIDS). *Journal of Personality and Social Psychology* 63(3):460-473.

Tiller, J. W., and I. Schweitzer. 1992. Benzodiazepines: depression or antidepressants. *Drugs* 44:165-169.

Tix, A. P., and P. A. Frazier. 1998. The use of religious coping during stressful life events: Main effects, moderation and mediation. *Journal of Consulting and Clinical Psychology* 66(2)411-422.

Uchino, B., and L. Cacioppo. 1996. The relationship between social support and physiological processes: A review with emphasis on underlying mechanisms and implications for health. *Psychological Bulletin* 119:488-531.

Verbosky, L. A., K. Franco, and J. P. Zrull. 1993. The relationship between depression and length of stay in general hospital patients. *Journal of Clinical Psychiatry* 54:177-181.

Vitiello, M. R., P. Prinz, J. P. Personaius, et al. 1990. Nighttime hypoxia is increasing in abstaining chronic alcoholic men. *Alcoholism* 14:38-41.

Wallston, B. S., S. W. Alagna, B. M. DeVellis, and R. F. DeVellis. 1983. Social support and physical health. *Health Psychology* 2:367-391.

Wallston, K. A., and B. S. Wallston. 1978. Locus of control and health: A review of the literature. *Health Education Monographs* 6(2):107-117.

Waters, H. M. 1993. High incidence of type II autoantibodies in pernicious anemia. *Journal of Clinical Pathology* 46:45-52.

Weingartner, H. 1986. Automatic and effort-demanding cognitive processes in depression. In *Handbook for Clinical Memory Assessment in Older Adults,* edited by W. Poon. Washington D.C.: American Psychological Association.

Weissman, M. M., and J. K. Myers. 1978. Rates and risks of depressive symptoms in a United States urban community. *Acta Psychiatry Scandinavia* 57:219-231.

Wells, K. B., A. Stewart, R. D. Hays, et al. 1989. The functioning and well-being of depressed patients: Results from the medical outcomes study. *Journal of the American Medical Association* 262:914-919.

Wells, K. B., J. M. Golding, and M. A. Burnam. 1988. Psychiatric disorders in a sample of the general medical population with and without chronic medical conditions. *American Journal of Psychiatry* 145:976-981.

Wells, K. B. 1994. Depression in general medical settings. Implications of three health policy studies for consultation-liaison psychiatry. *Psychosomatics* 35(3):279-296.

Wilkinson, D., D. Q. Borsey, P. Leslie, et al. 1988. Psychiatric morbidity and social problems in patients with insulin dependent diabetes mellitus. *British Journal of Psychiatry* 153:38-43.

Williams, G. H., and R. G. Dluhy. 1989. Diagnostic imaging of the adrenal gland. In *Endocrinology*. 2d ed. Edited by L. G. DeGroot et al. Orlando, Fla.: Grune and Stratton. p 1633-1681.

———. 1996. Diseases of the adrenal cortex. In *Harrison's Principles of Internal Medicine*. New York: Wiley.

———. 1996. Pheochromocytoma. In *Harrison's Principle's of Internal Medicine*. p 1975-1978.

Wilner, P. 1984. Cognitive functioning in depression: A review of theory and research. *Psychosomatic Medicine* 14:807-823.

Wood, S., and J. I. Williams. 1987. Reintegration to normal living as a proxy to quality of life. *Journal of Chronic Disease* 40:491-499.

Worby, C. M., and R. Babineau. 1974. The family interview: Helping patient and family cope with metastatic disease. *Geriatrics* 29(6):83-90.

Wortman, C. B., and D. R. Lehman. 1985. Reactions to victims of life crises: Support attempts that fail. In *Social support: Theory Research and Applications,* edited by I. G. Sarason and B. R. Sarason. Dordrecht, Netherlands: Martinus Nijhoff.

Wulfratt, N. M. 1988. Immunoglobulins of patients with Cushing's syndrome due to pigmented adrenocorticoal micronodular dysplasia stimulate in vitro steroidogenesis. *Journal of Clinical Endocrinology Metabolism* 66:301-312.

Yapko, M. D. 1988. *When Living Hurts: Directives for Treating Depression*. New York: Brunner/Mazel.

Yesavage, J. A., T. L. Brink, T. L. Rose, O. Lum, et al. 1983. Development and validation of a geriatric depression screening scale: A preliminary report. *Journal of Psychiatric Research* 17:37-49.

Young, S. M., S. E. Smith, R. O. Pihl, and F. R. Ervin. 1985. Tryptophan depletion causes a rapid lowering of mood in normal males. *Psychopharmacology* 87(2):173-177.

Zelnik, T. 1987. Depressive effects of drugs. In *Presentations of Depression: Depressive Symptoms in Medical and Other Psychiatric Disorders,* edited by O. G. Cameron. New York: Wiley.

Index

E

F

N

O

P

QRS

T

UVW

XYZ

Lori Stevic-Rust, Ph.D., is a health psychologist in private practice, a staff psychologist at the Louis Stokes Cleveland Veterans Affairs Medical Center, and adjunct professor, Department of Psychiatry at Case Western Reserve University in Cleveland. Dr. Stevic-Rust is also Clinical Director of the Geriatric Assessment Program at Lake Hospital. She is the co-author of *The Stop Smoking Workbook* and *Heart Therapy.*

Anita Maximin, Psy.D., is a health psychologist in private practice, a staff psychologist at the Louis Stokes Cleveland Veterans Affairs Medical Center, and adjunct professor, Department of Psychiatry at Case Western Reserve University. Dr. Maximin is also on staff at St. John West Shore Hospital in Cleveland. She is the co-author of *The Stop Smoking Workbook* and *Heart Therapy.*

Michael B. Ganz, M.D., is associate professor of medicine at Case Western Reserve University School of Medicine and Chief of the Division of Nephrology, Department of Medicine at Veterans Affairs Medical Center.